Soldier to Sojourner: The Journal

A Richly Laid Table with Parrot: Jan Davidsz de Heem

Laddies and Lassies, you are about to embark on a grand adventure, so BYOBB and dig in!

Gordon Schwerzmann

Copyright © 2022

All Rights Reserved

Table of Contents

Introduction or Mea Culpa 1

Korea Introduction 3

    Chapter 1: "Ask Not What the Army Can Do For You, But What You Can Do For the Army" 7

    Chapter 2: A Friend in Need Is a Friend Indeed 11

    Chapter 3: Sinchon 14

    Chapter 4: Love with the Proper Stranger 17

    Chapter 5: Prom Night 19

    Chapter 6: "One Stinks, One Keeps You Up, And One Tastes Sweeter Than Wine" 20

    Chapter 7: Enter the Dragon Lady, the Enigmatic Miss Lee (Part I) 24

    Chapter 8: The Soldier Goes Back to School 27

    Chapter 9: Who's That Knocking? 28

    Chapter 10: The Hermit Meets the Saint 30

    Chapter 11: The Assembly Line 33

    Chapter 12: A Scared New Yorker and a 4-F Hero 35

    Chapter 13: The Four Hundred Pound Gorilla Next Door 42

    Chapter 14: Special Assignments 46

    Chapter 15: A Tale of Two Cities 49

    Chapter 16: The Chaplain 51

    Chapter 17: Korean Rhapsody 53

    Chapter 18: Comfort Women 55

    Chapter 19: School Marm' 58

    Chapter 20: Korean Countryside 66

    Chapter 21: The Martyred 71

    Chapter 22: Dark Night of the Soul 73

    Chapter 23: A Reverie: Homage to Coleridge 78

    Chapter 24: A Modern One-Act Morality Play 80

    Chapter 25: An Ju: She Said 84

    Chapter 26: On Photographing An Ju 88

    Chapter 27: An Ju: He Said 93

    Chapter 28: Admiral Yi: The Man and His Statue 95

    Chapter 29: The Troubles 98

    Chapter 30: The Return of the Dragon Lady the Enigmatic Miss Lee (Part 2) 101

Chapter 31: "Children of the Dust" Amerasians in Korea and Southeast Asia 104
Chapter 32: What Does It All Mean? An Existential Conversation With Myself 109
Chapter 33: Rick Lewis 113
Chapter 34: A Farewell to Arms 115
Chapter 35: Babysan 117

Japan: Home of Samurai, Sony, and Sake 121

Chapter 36: Japan 122
Chapter 37: The Nambans Strike Back 130
Chapter 38: Samurai and the Evolving Concept of Bushido 133
Chapter 39: "The Big Noodle" 137
Chapter 40: General Douglas MacArthur and the Japanese Economic Miracle 141
Chapter 41: Yukio Mishima 144
Chapter 42: Kabuki 147
Chapter 43: "Who'll Stop the Rain?" 149
Chapter 44: Yoshiwara 150
Chapter 45: Storyville 153
Chapter 46: The Floating World 155
Chapter 47: The Japanese Screen: A Metaphor for Religion and Life 160
Chapter 48: The Swiss Who Came Down From the Mountain 164
Chapter 49: Yoko Ono 166
Chapter 50: A Modern Geisha Tale 168

Nationalist China 172

Chapter 51: Taiwan: China in Miniature 173
Chapter 52: Chiang Kai Shek 176
Chapter 53: Taipei National Museum 179
Chapter 54: The Right Way, the Wrong Way, and the Tao Way 183
Chapter 55: A Visit to the Countryside 186
Chapter 56: Motorcycle as Metaphor 189

Hong Kong: "Go Your Own Way" 194

Chapter 57: Hong Kong 195
Chapter 58: Peking Opera 199
Chapter 59: Mao's Little Red Book 203
Chapter 60: Hong Kong II 205
Chapter 61: Baby Slippers, Dragon Eggs, and Ivory Soap 210
Chapter 62: Hong Kong III 215

    Chapter 63: Revolutionary Opera 218
Macau 222
    Chapter 64: Macau 223
    Chapter 65: Hong Kong IV 230
Philippines: Santos and Uncle Sam 232
    Chapter 66: Welcome to Blue Jeans, English and Rock and Roll 233
    Chapter 67: From Soldier To Shopper: The Jeepney 238
    Chapter 68: Jesus Has Still Not Come Home 240
    Chapter 69: Sacred Images 243
    Chapter 70: Reading, Ritin' And Rithmatic 248
    Chapter 71: Old Manilla 251
    Chapter 72: Fort Santiago 254
    Chapter 73: A Little Trip to The Country 257
    Chapter 74: Hokey Pokey 265
    Chapter 75: Last Day In Manilla 268
Burma: A Buddhist Paradise 271
    Chapter 76: Burma 272
    Chapter 77: Flying Tigers 275
    Chapter 78: Pagan 277
    Chapter 79: Rangoon or Bust 280
    Chapter 80: The Crack-Up 282
    Chapter 81: The Continuing Adventures of Flash Gordon 285
Acknowledgments 287
Bibliography & Notes 288
About the Author 320

This is dedicated to:

ARDEN GALLAGHER,

without her love, help, and understanding,

this book would never have been written

Introduction or Mea Culpa

General (Yes, Sir!) Introduction

A note on bibliographies, periodicals, music, YouTube videos, and the kitchen sink or "Now I understand what the hell he is babbling on about."

Sources are an essential tool to get a more complete story, while travel writers like myself usually give a "Cliff Notes" or "Travelling for Dummies" description ("If this is Tuesday, it must be Belgium"). I have tried to whet the appetite of potential seekers and explorers, but I have not gone into the in-depth research or concentrated on the historical or cultural background that the reader needs to connect the dots to make sense of a culture or attitude of a country. For example, the Chinese have been exploited, drugged, raped, and murdered by Western countries and Japan for hundreds of years. Is it really surprising that they closed their borders and built up their country in isolation (ironically, just like the old Chinese empire they fought so hard to replace?) However, I have tried to give a concise background, and my bibliography contains the sources that will help (or, in some cases, confuse) the reader to understand the country more fully, a topic or issue I have written about. More importantly, I talked to ordinary people about their countries and issues that were on their minds.

The books, articles, and videos that I cite in my travelogue were invaluable to me in making sense of my experiences. Hopefully, they will entice the reader to explore these countries firsthand or at least armchair vicariously experience some of the topics, places, and people that I have written so opinionated about.

Music has always been an important part of my life: I am a member of the Woodstock Generation (even though I was serving on active duty in West Germany when the festival took place). I had originally planned to reproduce the lyrics of songs that represented the feelings I experienced when writing the chapters of this book. However, due to copyright infringement, I cannot do this. So, I have listed the title and artist of the particular song in the hopes that the reader will look up these songs on YOUTUBE or any of the commercial music-providing venues and listen to the full song.

As a soldier, the prevailing approach to explaining or teaching any subject is KISS, Keep It Simple Stupid, and this is what I have endeavored to do. The paralleling analogies that I make to American culture and cities, particularly New York City, help me to understand how connected we are, not because we live in the global economy world, but because we are all one people trying to solve our common problems with the same tools, resources, and brainpower (or considering our Congress, lack thereof).

I have strived to avoid being a political or economist polemist, but in the 1970s, we had countries dominated by political philosophies that affected their peoples' social and economic wellbeing. Much of Asia was war-torn, and I could not avoid putting in my own two cents on issues, giving an Army grunt take on what was really happening (The Gospel according to GI Gordon).

If all of this sounds like the fast-talking announcer giving his exclusions and disclaimers at the end of the wonderful product he is selling (which means it is not such a wonderful product), you are right. But this is my Asia, how I saw it in words and photographs (my written travelogue has a companion book of my photographs, which is available on the same site you are seeing this (this is an unpaid photographic book endorsement, and I approved this message). I hope you enjoy this book, but if you don't and hate it with a passion, I'll leave you with the infamous words of an anonymous Army grunt: "Fuck 'em if they can't take a joke."

Korea Introduction

Korea: Land of the Morning Calm

"Hello Muddah, Hello Faddah

Here I am at Camp Grenada"

"A Letter from Camp Grenada" by Allan Sherman

I arrived in Korea in early November 1970. I was a first lieutenant in the U. S. Army, having served for two years, the last eighteen months of which I served in West Germany. My tour in Korea would be thirteen months, and this was my first duty assignment in Asia.

I come from a lower-middle-class family in suburban New Jersey and was the first member of my family to attend college. To help defray college costs, I joined ROTC, which paid my tuition for the last two years if I would serve 18 months of active duty in the Army. I am a product of an all-men's liberal arts college called Lafayette College in Easton, Pa. I see myself as being liberal, believing the Vietnam War was a senseless waste of men and money. In my senior year of college, I even participated in a closely monitored candlelight protest against the war. I know somewhere in the bowels of the Pentagon, there is a glossy 8 X 10 photograph of me, singing an anti-war song. My choices were limited: either serve or go to Canada (and since I didn't have flannel underwear, the latter was out).

When I started my service, the Army needed warm bodies for Vietnam and offered me eighteen months anywhere the Army had a presence if I would give them an extra year of service. A lot of my ROTC fellow officers chose Hawaii, but with my father coming from the German section of Switzerland, I chose West Germany. My duties there involved logistics, moving ammunition and war equipment overseas, and depleting our war stocks in Europe to send them to Vietnam.

It was a great choice. I fell in love with the small medieval towns, with their fretwork (dark beams set in a bed of white plaster on the front of houses) and majestic churches. I loved the variety of local unique tasting beers and, even more, the variety of local unique tasting frauleins. It was especially fun drinking with the older Germans, all of whom had never fought the Americans in World War II. They always fought the Russians. I imagined to myself their counterparts, the East Germans, drinking with their Soviet Army comrades, telling them they never fought the Russians, only the Americans. This assignment was great because I got to see something of the world before I got my ass shot up in the jungles.

As luck would have it, when my tour in West Germany was over, I was given orders to report to Korea (it wasn't luck, just the fact that we were winding down in Vietnam and Korea just happened to be the next hot spot). The Korean war never officially ended, the North Koreans were always provoking the South, and the U. S forces (we had 60,000 U. S. troops) were there to defend South Korea. The North Koreans made headlines in 1968 when they captured our Navy gunboat, The Pueblo, and imprisoned its crew for violating their territorial waters. They also dug tunnels to the South and sent spies and saboteurs to undermine the South Korean government. We lose a few American soldiers every year, killed by North Koreans in the DMZ (border of North and South Korea). Furthermore, there is a nationwide curfew of midnight to contain this situation. This was the scenario that I was trepidly stepping into: "Despair all ye who enter herein," to quote Dante's "Inferno".

"You better watch out, North Korea, and stop misbehaving. There's a new Marshal in town!"

(Author at the age of five)

The stirring music of the symphonic poem "Les Preludes" by Franz Liszt plays loudly in the background.

Episode 3: "The Land of the Rock Creatures"

Flash Gordon: Doctor Zharkov, we must stop Emperor Ming from using his death ray machine to destroy the Earth. Wait, the rocks are moving, changing into human form. They are attacking- I can't hold them off- we'll be crushed to death!

The Announcer: Will Flash and his companions escape from the rock creatures?

Well, good news, kids! You don't have to wait until next week to watch at your local theater for the answer. You can find out right now: just keep reading!

"The Continuing Adventures of Flash Gordon" (filmed in South Korea before a live studio audience, no laughter or booing allowed unless the director holds a sign requesting applause or disagreement).

Korean Family 1910

This is going to be a tough audience to wow!

Chapter 1: "Ask Not What the Army Can Do For You, But What You Can Do For the Army"

"YOU'RE IN THE ARMY NOW, YOU'LL NEVER GET RICH, YOU SON OF A BITCH, YOU'RE IN THE ARMY NOW" - Army Bootcamp Marching song

My assignment was ASCOM Depot, a huge sprawling installation with the standard barracks, mess hall, and recreation area. We also had a general hospital, a recycle-yard, a non-denominational church, and a prison. There were eight gates that connected us to the Korean countryside of rice fields; it fronted a dirty cinderblock and rusted sheet-metal village called Bup Yong (the Ville). We had around a hundred and fifty officers and 1000 enlisted men, and nine hundred local Korean workers. The Korean workers maintained all our heavy-duty road equipment, did various infra-structure jobs such as paving, plumbing, and electrical work, and generally kept the place running.

ASCOM Quonset Barracks: The Army version of Levittown

I lived in a large, corrugated sheet metal up-turned ark called a Quonset hut. The EMs (Enlisted soldiers) also lived in Quonset huts but had a dormitory-style living, rows of beds with a personal footlocker at the base of the bed, and one huge bathroom. The officers and high-ranking sergeants had individual rooms that were partitioned off on either side of the hut, complete with a small bathroom and, thank you, God, for a space-heater that kept me warm through the cold Korean winter and served as a stove to have my lunchtime ramen, cooked on top.

I made my room quite cozy, with a record player, bookcase, and minibar. I covered my walls with Korean and American posters, original hand-painted comic book artwork, and some of my blown-up photographs of Korea. After a few months, I even bought a small black and white TV to watch Armed Forces Network Programs and Korean-language soap operas, and variety shows. The nice thing about this room was that you could also bring Korean girlfriends here. Although they were supposed to leave by the midnight curfew, nobody enforced that rule.

Duties

"Young soldier, in order to get ahead, you need to clean the head first": "Fatherly" advice from the Top Sergeant to a new recruit.

Lou Reed's "Walk on the Wild Side"

This song gives a whole different etymology for the word head

"What I did in the War" was as follows: I arrived in Korea expecting to go right into the trenches. We were the expendable buffer between North and South Korea, and we were in a state of preparedness for renewed invasion from the belligerent North. But like previous experiences in the Army, it was "hurry up and wait." ASCOM Depot didn't have a job for me, and after two weeks of daily donning a freshly starched set of fatigues (all dressed up with nowhere to go) and picking my nose, the command saw my true potential (a really low bar to excel at!). I would escort a USO show for a month, introducing the group and arranging bus schedules and performance venues, and generally keeping the band sober and drug-free for their performances. I learned how the USO worked, and they were great, bringing a slice of American Pie to lonely soldiers in boondock installations.

I was escorting a Christian Country Rock group from Nashville: The Gene Cotton Band. They were great musicians, very professional and businesslike, keeping on schedule and effortlessly working with the limited technical staff at these bases for electrical and lighting hookups for their shows. They had the right mix of country humor, familiar standby songs, and heartfelt delivery. It also didn't hurt that they had a wholesomely beautiful blond as their lead singer.

The GI audience loved them and kept screaming for encores, which they obliged, thankfully. I wasn't familiar with this kind of music, but for an hour and a half, they brought God, mom, and apple pie to a homesick audience, and who wouldn't like this.

I got to see a hell of a lot of Korea, driving through snow-covered rice fields, endless blocks of drab concrete houses, dozens of muddy-lined little villages, and every out-of-the-way Army post throughout the Republic. We traveled in a Greyhound-like tour bus during the day, arriving at a forlorn little base, setting up, performing, and breaking down the equipment. Then we drove for a few hours to a small but clean hotel for the night.

Gene Cotton also managed the group, getting this gig as a chance to secure funding for an ambitious concert tour in the American South that he had planned this coming spring. He was also a Nashville veteran, adept at working the ins and outs of the music business for over ten years.

I did my "Here's Johnny" before every concert and worked with base commanders to handle any crowd rowdiness.

The USO picked performance groups that ran the gamut from honkey-tonk Rock and Roll to Soul music. Once, we shared a hotel with a black R&B Soul group just starting their tour. I got to talk to the lead singer of this group and asked him how he liked performing here. With a straight face, he told me, "This is a very hip country. Where else would you have a capital city named "Soul."

After the USO gig ended, I went back, and they gave me another job commensurate with their expectations of me (they lowered the bar even further!). I would be the director of the Army Recycle Yard (in other words, junkyard). I had a staff of about twenty-five GIs and 800 hundred Korean workers, who sorted, stored, and repaired everything that was overstocked, damaged, obsolete, or generally not wanted by the US Army. This sounded like a cushy "Mr. Roberts" assignment ("Well, I'll water the palm, and then I'm done for the day"), but unfortunately, it was one of the most dangerous jobs in South Korea. The last director, a captain, his first sergeant, and five enlisted men were convicted of black marketeering, and a few were jailed right here in ASCOM Depot. The South Koreans were still recovering from the war, and they could use most of the equipment, tools, and electronics that we were throwing away. One of our GIs was even caught trying to drive a large earthmover out of the junkyard to sell to a Korean construction company.

Then the Korean workers got really slick: they took what they wanted, tractors, backhoes, and electronic equipment, and gave it to their business cronies for twenty-nine days, with the proviso that it comes back to the depot in time for the monthly inventory. This went un-policed because the Army was always doing road and communications work outside of the depot daily. If I needed an earthmover for a project, it would be brought back the next day with no one the wiser that it had been used by a Korean apartment-building contractor for the last month. We tried to get a handle on this business, but with hundreds of pieces of equipment going out daily, it was a losing battle. On the positive side, they did maintain the equipment, which would have deteriorated and been useless if left sitting unused around our depot.

I managed to keep my hands clean, and as long as the assignments I gave the workers were accomplished, I turned a blind eye to their "arrangements". I concentrated on my soldiers and tried to counsel my men from getting into situations where the only way to pay back Korean loan sharks was to steal our equipment and sell it on the Black Market. I warned them of the consequences: jail time and how a third of the previous soldiers were in jail because of this. I kept an open door policy to encourage them to talk about their problems with me. However, everyone looked away when an EM would buy at the PX American whiskey, cigarettes, and electronics for hundreds of US dollars each payday (twice or three times more than they made in a typical month) to sell on spec to the local economy. The standing joke was the day after payday, the shelves of the PX would be bare of radios, record players, and black-and-white TVs. The only items left were dozens of color TVs. Why? Because the South Koreans didn't have the color bandwidths in place to watch color TV, only the Armed Forces Television Network had the color capability. My duties took me over all of Korea, checking equipment readiness and assessing damaged equipment to be sent to ASCOM Depot to be repaired or disposed of.

Chapter 2: A Friend in Need Is a Friend Indeed

The officers were a great group of men that you either met through your work or living quarters, while others you met for drinks at the bar at the Officer's Club. Like my fraternity at college, I developed my own cliche of close friends, but we all knew each other and worked together with the same goals.

I developed a lasting friendship with two married officers that brought their wives over for the thirteen-month tour. Sam Jackson was a "good old boy", a Texas bourbon-drinking lawyer whose slow Southern drawl belied a razor-sharp mind. I often went to dinner at their apartment located off base, and we had some good conversations about the Army and the Vietnam War. Like myself, he thought it was a terrible waste of men and money. He was a Staff Lawyer in the Judge Advocate Branch. His job was to prosecute Black Market, drug, and assault cases, that our soldiers committed in Korea. The constant onslaught of having to defend the dregs of society, whether at home or here, may have jaded his perspective but never clouded his judgment.

My other friends, Brad Morris and his wife, Arlene, were also from the South, Alabama, but they were representatives of the "New South": very progressive views on civil rights, education, and politics, and of course, they were very vocal against the Vietnam War.

However, my best friend in Korea was another bachelor captain, Rick Lewis, from Indiana. We worked together, got drunk together, and went clubbing together. He was tall and lanky and always up for a good time. He was also a prodigious drinker, and I told him, "You can drink everyone under the table, and I can screw everyone under the table. We make a good team: "The Hardy Boys take on Korea".

We had about ten officers at a party at Brad and Arlene's apartment, and after an hour of Trivial Pursuit (Brad and Arlene trounced all of us with their encyclopedic knowledge and quick responses.), we started talking about the Vietnam War, Lieutenant Calley, and the problem of guilt. Three of the officers had been to Vietnam, lost buddies, and had very strong opinions on this subject.

Marty, a Vietnam veteran from Pennsylvania, believed that "We shouldn't punish Lt. Calley - it was the "higher-up" command that was responsible for sending him on that pointless mission. Even the whole American Military system taught us that it was OK to kill the Viet Cong, whether they are 10 or 30 years old." Marty had also heard about kids and women carrying grenades and killing GIs in suicide missions, and he fully empathized with Calley.

I opted for the devil's advocate, claiming that Americans are better than this, even though this "idealistic" stand was unrealistic in real-time war. I also realized that the Court Martial judges viewed the facts "coolly", unaffected by the "hot" experience of fear, fatigue, and the anger of prolonged combat, seeing your friends die right next to you. The judges viewed this as a "black and white" judgment – they needed a scapegoat, so it wouldn't affect the commanding officers above. "The questioners had that beautiful detachment and devotion to stern justice of men dealing in death without being in any danger of it." A Farewell to Arms"-Hemingway.

As an officer, it is your primary duty to protect your men. If one child blew up your soldiers, what about the next little kid or the crying woman, not stopping when you yell at them, "STOP!" Do you act first and damn the consequences to protect your platoon? Let's take this one step further: if your men go rogue and kill innocent civilians, you are still responsible, but should not the individual rogue soldiers also be put on trial? The individual soldier must be held responsible for the crimes that he commits, yet, for example, no individual soldier in Lt. Calley's platoon went to trial for murder, even though they did the actual killing of unarmed civilians. As a soldier, you must be able to choose right from wrong in a split second. You must refuse an immoral order. As an officer, you do not put your morality aside in warfare; you must lead by example and punish the soldiers that committed the actual crimes (and hold yourself responsible for not knowing or controlling what actions your soldiers committed).

President Truman

"Now I am become Death, the Destroyer of Worlds". Robert Oppenheimer's quoting of the Bhagavad Gita, in reference to the first detonation of an atom bomb that he and his fellow scientists developed at Los Alamos Laboratory.

We couldn't resolve the Lt. Calley issue because each one of us, myself included, wouldn't know how we would act if we found ourselves in his shoes and the circumstances that would affect our response. I changed the discussion to President Truman's decision to drop the atom bomb on Japan. We had just lost thousands of soldiers, taking one useless island or coral atoll after another, and now we were poised to invade the mainland. Military "experts" estimated we would sacrifice a million American servicemen in taking Japan.

As an amateur military strategist, I thought we really screwed up the Pacific War Theater. By late 1943 we had effectively destroyed the Japanese fleet and their air-strike capacity. They couldn't resupply these islands. Our submarine fleet had sunk most of their cargo and ammunition vessels, nor could they escape by sea or air. If I were the Commander-in-Charge, I would have naval blockaded the islands. In effect, starving them out while we blitzed the major Japanese urban centers like General Doolittle did earlier in the war when he destroyed much of Tokyo in his surprise bombing raid. Bombing the mainland into submission, while Japan's best soldiers were isolated and stuck in their island fortresses. This would have accomplished the ending of the war, but Americans were sick of the war and wanted a quick victory. It fell on the head of the Commander-in-Chief, President Truman, to make a momentous decision: Do we drop the atom bomb, saving American and Japanese lives, since the same "experts" estimated between one and two million Japanese lives would also be lost in the taking of the mainland. "Enola Gay, You Have a Go."

I believe Truman made the right decision, even though he knew he would be killing thousands of unarmed men, women, and children to attain this victory. Everyone agreed with me, but then I threw this in: "What if America had lost the War? President Truman would have been arrested and tried in a Nuremberg-Style Tribunal as a war criminal. He surely would have been convicted of "high crimes" against a defenseless populace, just as the high-ranking Nazis were convicted of killing six million defenseless Jews." There are no easy answers, but history is always written by the victors.

Chapter 3: Sinchon

"Kisses Sweeter Than Wine" - Jimmy Rodgers.

This is what many GIs felt about Korean women.

Korean geisha girls in Training 1910

Sinchon is the red-light district that grew up around ASCOM Depot. The "Ville", as most G.I.s call Sinchon, has an almost 1880's Western cowboy town atmosphere. A facade of cinderblock, wood, rusted sheet metal, and grimy glass restaurants, barber and hair salons, clothing stores, tailor and shoe shops, cheap souvenir and record stores, all with glaring neon and huge blinking electric signs over the shop fronts. Every night after five, the Ville wakes up in a flurry of activity. The loan shark sits with a frozen smile in his bare office- a desk with a chair and an American calendar. He only gets busy after the 15th of the month when most of the GIs are broke. The clothing and souvenir shops are bustling with GIs arguing prices, getting fitted for the latest fashion suits or suede boots, and eating barbeque pork and dog in the storefront restaurants.

The main street is a dirt road, dusty in summer and muddy in winter. As you walk the main street, you are assaulted by the overpowering smells of kimchi, dried fish, spit-cooked dogmeat, and excrement and deafened by the pulsating sounds of American rock and roll coming from every storefront. There are young "slickey boys" in Chinese baggy pants, wearing 'I Love NY' tee shirts and slouching baseball caps, offering black market money changing. There are children everywhere: running, crying, riding bicycles, begging, and shitting in the side alleys.

One of the most surreal sights is, amidst all this, you see an older Korean couple in traditional costume dress: the woman in a beautifully billowing kimono dress and the man in black baggy pants with freshly starched white smock shirt, gray-robed smock, and tied black stove pipe hat. You turn a corner and see a group of blacks dressed in Bonnie and Clyde pinstripe suits of rainbow colors, with "Superfly" felt hats, spouting ostrich plumes, walking arm in arm with Korean girls in the latest mini-skirt and fancy hot pants, strutting hurriedly toward a soul club in silver-speckled platform shoes.

But it is the bars that really make the Ville hum. They have typical American names: "Green Door", "Dreamboat", "Playboy", and the biggest, "Apollo", each having a separate clientele. There are tee-shirt bars (nickname for white GIs, since you can always see white tee shirts under regular shirts), black soul clubs, and even a hillbilly club, where the country lament song, "I Wanna Go Stateside", blares loudly every night.

Most of the girls come from small, poor farm towns, where the families prize sons and see daughters as just another mouth to feed. When a mamasan (lady pimp) comes to a poor farmer, she brings cash to "buy" the unwanted daughters, ostensibly promising to apprentice them to seamstresses or families needing domestic help, but in reality, for her stable of working prostitutes. Others are the second generation in this profession, their mothers having kids by long-gone GIs.

These girls are not your typical stateside, curbside whores that give you a hurried blow job and fuck (no kissing, please) in your car front seat, with the attitude of let's get this over so I can move on to my next John. These girls are your "instant loving" girlfriend. The sweetly innocent girl from your church choir, the unobtainable bitch that put you down in high school, the forbidden fruit desire for your best friend's girl, or any other fantasy – it was yours for the taking.

The Korean girls flirt back and forth from bars like moths around a flame, frantically searching for a Yobo (boyfriend) for the evening. The girls range from 17 to 35, come in all sizes, with Western-style hair styles, milk-white skin, and that sweet, subdued oriental smile so guileless that it fools you every time.

You are the kid with a dollar in the ice cream shop –you can get any one of 31 flavors (as long as she has long black hair, almond-shaped brown eyes, and speaks broken English). And this paradise is cheap: $10.00 for a "quickie", $15 for an overnight. Their customers are mainly 19 or 20-year-olds, and it is their first time away from home. In the beginning, they hate Korea, dreaming of their girlfriends back home or of just hanging out with school buddies. But when they find out that they can get a gorgeous piece of ass dirt cheap and a pack of 20 filter-tipped marijuana cigarettes for under five bucks, they quickly go native. Many find steady girlfriends and virtually live in the local economy.

Chapter 4: Love with the Proper Stranger

"I want to feel real love, with all the church bells ringing and the banjos playing our song": Angie Rossini (Natalie Wood) to Rocky Papasano (Steve McQueen), after rejecting his marriage proposal because he tells her that he will "take his medicine" and "do the right thing" for his pregnant girlfriend. - Love with the Proper Stranger, 1963 film.

Korean boy 1910

I wonder if this Young Korean boy found "Love with the Proper Stranger" in his arranged marriage? The white "horsehair" hat signifies that he is engaged to be married in a pre-arranged marriage.

You buy your "date" a champagne cocktail (kickback to the bar's owner), and you sit with her girlfriends, who are chattering away: pointing to potential clients, bragging about what their yobo (boyfriend) bought them or raving about the latest fashions. There is a large dancefloor with a strobe light ball that glamorizes the dancers, and the music is the latest American pop-rock, either canned or with a live Korean band.

The girls are great dancers, swirling their stuff to attract yobos. You grab your girl and start dancing; she'll follow your every move and never break a sweat while you're drenched after a few fast songs. You sit down, order more champagne, and smoke about a pack of cigarettes-the cigarette smoke haze with the strobe light gives the effect of a surreal fog. The dancers push in and out of this haze like a song that fades/amplifies in and out on a distant radio station.

Finally, at 11:30 P.M, everyone makes for the exit so that they can get a taxi before the midnight curfew. You arrive at her house (the mamasan owns the building and rents rooms to the girls). You pay the amount agreed upon at her house unless you "bought her for the month" (you paid the mamasan upfront for this pleasure).

You finally reach your destination, a small courtyard of a muddy back alley. This is enclosed by cinder block walls topped with jagged shards of glass. You enter through a small door cut out of the corrugated tin. She calls out, "Yobo sayo!" and the door rattles open. You enter her small room, crowded with a queen size bed with a metal canopy, an electric heater, a radio, and a small boudoir (makeup table, topped with a round table mirror, cosmetic box, and chair) and a well-worn wood wardrobe dresser. The floor is covered with a faded wall-to-wall linoleum (the floor is heated by charcoal from the ground below, which gives a warming radiant heat but could lead to carbon monoxide poisoning if there is a crack in the linoleum).

Once you're alone with her, she changes from a hardened whore to a demure girlfriend. She helps you undress, kissing you and tucking you into her bed. Then there is the customary wait time, where she freshens her makeup, douches, and comes to you in a kimono robe. She dims the light, slips out of her robe, and snuggles next to you. She feigns shyness; you must initiate the lovemaking. You start by massaging her breasts and gently stroking her vagina. Slowly she warms up, moving her hand to your penis, working it to hardness, and then helps you by arching her body to accept it. The lovemaking is punctuated with her moans, "ooh baby, you number hana (1)". Afterward she leaves to douche and then returns to fall asleep in your arms, the perfect porcelain doll.

Chapter 5: Prom Night

"Nobody but You" - Dee Clarke

Typically, I went to the clubs a few times a week after my USO gig ended. I didn't have to wait long to find a "Proper Stranger". There was always a dazzling array of beauties to befriend and bed. I picked out a cute, long-haired girl, and we agreed on a price. We split the scene; my breath fogged up the outside window of the club as we waited for a taxi.

We finally got to her house; her room was small: bed, mirrored table on which sat a hot plate cooker, and wardrobe. The bathroom, a hole in the floor with a bucket of water nearby, was in the outside corridor of the house. I tumbled into the bed, she helped undress me, and we were soon entangled in a frenzied swirl of kisses and strokings. Her body was silky smooth, and I kissed every part of it; she responded by gently tugging on my penis and giving me long wet kisses. I moved on top of her, and we started lovemaking, slowly moving in rhythmic synch until I came with a burst of urgency, clutching her hard ass and burying my head in her breasts. We stayed up, drinking rum and cokes and talking about her life and loves.

She said she was still in love with this Chinese American Captain, who had transferred out to a fort in South Carolina last month. She confined in me that she was dating a Specialist Four Sergeant, who was madly in love with her. Her plan was to marry this lovestruck Sergeant, get him to take her to the States, divorce him and find her old love, Captain. What a bitch, I thought, but she was a great lay (a bird in the hand and in the bush too!). I never saw her again after that night and always wondered if she married that naïve Sergeant and then tracked down her elusive Captain in the States (ahh, ain't love grand?).

Chapter 6: "One Stinks, One Keeps You Up, And One Tastes Sweeter Than Wine"

Korean Merchant circa 1900

"If you don't see anything you like, in the back room, I have a snake oil that will cure your rheumatism and some potent ginseng that will put a spark in your love life."

Kimchi

Kimchi is the signature dish of Korean cooking, and you either love it or hate it, but you must experience it. Kimchi can be made with any kind of fermented vegetable: long-leaved Chinese cabbage, long-root, and ponytail radishes are the most popular kinds of kimchi.

To make winter kimchi, you need red chilis, garlic, a fish paste or sauce, ginger, and most importantly, patience. You lace the long-leaved cabbage with salt and add finely cut chilis, garlic, and fish paste, preferably previously fermented anchovies and fresh ginger. You place it in a huge earthenware jar called an "onggi", seal the top and then bury it in your own backyard. After a few months, you dig it up and serve it; the longer it stays in the ground, the stronger it tastes. Each Korean housewife adds her own set of spices to make her kimchi unique.

However, before you try this kimchi, you should take a test to see if you have the fortitude for the experience. My favorite test is to ride a crowded, standing-room-only commuter bus of ordinary Koreans going to work: if you can survive the first 20 minutes of intense garlic breath, sweat, and body odor in a close claustrophobic space without throwing up or fainting, then you're ready for the kimchi experience.

Kimchi should be eaten with rice and lots of OB (Korean) beer. It can be fiery hot and surprisingly tastes better than it smells. It's important to remember that if you go to a restaurant and order kimchi with your girl, both of you must eat the kimchi unless you're looking to end the relationship and never keep kimchi in your room unless you want to find new lodgings.

Kimchi is the perfect way to preserve vegetables when you don't have a refrigerator. It became very popular when Buddhism became the main religion, with its emphasis on eating a vegetarian diet. Kimchi goes back to the earliest days when Chinese officials praised this fermented vegetable over two thousand years ago. Curiously, the main ingredients for present-day kimchi: chilis, long-leaf cabbage, and garlic weren't used until the seventeenth century A.D. The Portuguese introduced chili to Korea in the sixteenth century (it is a New World vegetable); garlic was adopted in the eighteenth century, as well as the long-leaved cabbage, both coming from China. There is kimchi for every season; the summer one is fresh vegetables, not fermented, made with cabbage or radish in a soup, but the best known is the afore-mentioned winter kimchi.

South Korean troops fought bravely alongside US troops in Vietnam. They were excellent soldiers, accepting the heat, monsoon rain, and enemy bullets without complaint. What really bothered them was that they couldn't get their kimchi in the jungle.

Ginseng

Both North and South Korea are world-famous for their ginseng, which is a wild root. This root is touted to boost your immune system, improve memory, cure mild forms of diabetes, and most importantly, as an aphrodisiac for sexual performance (WOW! More Ovaltine Mom!). It has long been cultivated from the wild root, and in its early days, emperors used to post guards on ginseng fields to prevent thievery.

Korean ginseng is the most potent ginseng in the world and is a major source of export income. There are two types of ginseng: white, which is not steamed but dried, and red, which is first steamed and then dried. Both are primarily used in teas and other drinks, and the taste is remarkably bitter. In the United States, it is sold as a vitality product, but in Korea, it's a staple of homeopathic medicine. It is an herbal cure-all and is even used to make a hard liquor called: Insam ju, which is very popular in South Korea.

As for enhancing sexual performance, I've tried it, but I didn't notice any appreciable change. I won't be testifying that I'm a born-again believer after a river baptism; however, I'll keep taking it. I think I'll need a lot more practice with the local bar girls to give an educated opinion - I'll keep you posted.

Persimmons

While I was walking around the Sinchon market, I saw this curious vegetable, which I thought was a yellow tomato. The merchant told me it was a sweet fruit, so I bought a couple and took them back to my quarters. The persimmon felt hard to the touch, but I quartered it, taking the whole quarter into my mouth. At once, I puckered up – my tongue was tingling madly with the astringent taste. This forbidden fruit didn't give me knowledge of good and evil, but it caused me to invoke the higher being. "Goddam! this is killing my tongue; where is my Drambuie?"

Afterward, I was told to let the fruit get soft so that I could break the skin with my finger. Persimmons have the consistency of an oyster in the half shell or crushed plum and the taste of a juicy, over-ripe peach crossed with a Comice pear, which adds that subtle tartness. If this is hard to imagine, just think back to your grammar school days, when the teacher told you to write a twenty-five-word essay on: "What does a banana taste like?"

"Ah…it doesn't taste like chicken", which was the usual response to some new dish.

The runny sweetness, with that pinch of tartness, makes it irresistible. I had a fantasy vision of lying on a divan, dressed in a white toga, while a scantily clad Korean girl would lean over and drip the gelatinous fruit into my open mouth while being serenaded by the whining sounds of Korean erhu (Chinese violin) music. "Wake up, Captain Mitty; you're at work."

Chapter 7: Enter the Dragon Lady, the Enigmatic Miss Lee (Part I)

So won't you, please? Be my little baby. "Be My Baby" - The Ronettes

Miss Lee

It was a cold December night, and the warmest place in the Ville was the Apollo Club. It was right after payday, so the Club was filled with T-shirts and Korean courtesans. I spotted her at a table with her girlfriends, chatting away, oblivious to the strobe rock n' roll dance floor and the gyrating bodies. She possessed a luminous aura with her short, coifed hair, porcelain white skin, conservative white top, and long black skirt. She looked like a 1940s Hollywood femme fatale, a Korean Lauren Bacall with a smokey voice and sultry demeanor. This was a woman in control, who seemed to have years of experience, but seemed never to have lost that appealing girl-next-door freshness. My first thought was, "what's a nice girl like you doing in a gin joint like this?" but I knew this would be lost on her, so I settled for "Hello" and offered to buy her a drink. She looked up, sized me in a glance, rebuffed my advance, and without skipping a beat, returned to her chatting. I was dumbfounded, dejected, and finally annoyed. This was the land where the dollar was king, and you could have any of the maidens for the right price. I sullenly went back to my table and proceeded to get drunk with Rick, licking my wounds while eyeing her through the pale-yellow glass of my beer. Rick and I had a few more drinks, and we returned to the camp before curfew.

I didn't see her for about three weeks, thinking she was a high-maintenance hooker from Seoul, slumming in the provinces before going back to her well-healed army colonel yobo. It was a slow Wednesday night, payday was a week away, and there were a lot of girls but no customers. Again, I spotted her at a table across the dance floor, talking with a girlfriend. Her friend left for the bathroom, and I took my chances, approached her, and again offered to buy her a drink. She looked up at me annoyingly and spoke in clear English, "Why you come to me when you can have short time with any of these girls?"

"I want a real relationship, not just one night," I stammered, lying through my teeth, "I am serious and would make a good yobo."

"You think so," she shot back, her stare penetrating right through me. I was on the defensive, and she was playing all the right chords to make me feel the lecherous GI that only wanted a short time lay. We bantered back and forth for a few moments, and then she said I could take her out to eat. We left and went to a nearby restaurant. She had a good command of English and understood everything when I talked slowly. She told me a little about her life. A mamasan came to her village and bought her from her father. The mamasan then brought her to Seoul to learn the trade. She was ambitious, playing on her radiance to pay off her mamasan, and now she was her own boss. I guessed she was in her early 20s, having hooked for about five years. She said she had a steady yobo last year, but he returned to the States, and she was heartbroken about it. With a straight face, I lied again, telling her I was looking for a steady girl.

After dinner, I convinced her to take me with her back to her room, and we would drink rum and cokes and just talk (and if you believe that, then I've got a bridge in Brooklyn that I can sell you). She grudgingly agreed, and we grabbed a taxi. She lived in a simple, one-story Korean house, surrounded by high, broken glass encrusted cement walls. We entered through a rusted, perforated steel door. Her room was large, with patterned wallpaper, a small table with a radio, and a mirror for her makeup. We talked, drank a few rum and cokes, and then I came on to her. I held her face and kissed her. At first, she feigned resistance but soon returned my kisses, delicately frenching my tongue. My hands gently massaged her breasts, searching for the buttons of her blouse. She stopped me and ran into the bathroom, saying she would be right back. I was sitting on her bed, getting harder and harder in anticipation. Finally, she emerged from her toilet in her pajamas. She turned out the light and proceeded to undress me. She finished undressing me and pushed me under the covers, slipping in beside me. I undid her top and kissed her nipples, rolling my tongue gently over them. She kept gently massaging my penis until I was totally erect. I finally got her pajama pants off, feeling her moist vagina, and I mounted her. She was tight and helped me get the right angle, and the rhythm took possession of us. After I had climaxed, she kissed me and snuggled in my arms. We made love once more that night, interspersed with giddy high school romantic banter and endless cigarettes and rum and cokes. I left at the crack of dawn to be at my job and promised I'd see her that night at the club. As I struggled out into the chilly dawn, I had an epiphany: the sun rose ruby-red over the muddy lanes and run-down houses, bathing them in a golden phosphorescence, and I felt as one with the universe.

We met again and started playing house. After my 9 to 5, I would get to her room; we would eat out, buy fruit and rice wine and go back to her place for lovemaking. Then abruptly, she moved out with no forwarding address. I knew her girlfriends, and they didn't (or wouldn't) know where she went. I assuaged my loneliness with booze and women, plucking women like you would the petals of a daisy: she loves me, she loves me not. Why did I even care? Maybe because somewhere in the back of my mind, she might be the one I wanted to share my life with.

(We'd have a house in the suburbs, two kids, and she would be a soccer mom, driving a minivan). To be continued…

"IT'S GOOD TO BE THE PRINCESS" 1910

Chapter 8: The Soldier Goes Back to School

"Show them what you learned, son – Speak some Algebra for the Ladies" (anonymous joke)

I had been in Korea for about two months – with one month of that touring with my USO Christian rock group - and felt the need to learn more about Asia. So, I signed up for a University of Phoenix course on Far Eastern history and a beginner's course on the Korean language. The classes were over by 8:00 P.M, so I still had time to make it to the clubs afterward (all study and no play makes Gordon a dull boy). I was a history major in college, but my knowledge of Asia was a gaping hole.

Our bible was Fairbank's <u>East Asia: The Great Tradition</u>. China had the greatest civilization in the world, while Europe was mired in the Dark Ages of feudalism, superstition, and blood thirsty, marauding Vikings (my mother's ancestors). I especially liked the Tang dynasty, with its beautiful funerary, multicolored horses, and Buddhist cave art. I believe that this course crystallized my desire to travel around Asia when my army duty ended. This would be my Grand Tour – seeing, feeling, hearing, and smelling the essence of Asia, just like Byron and Shelly toured the ancient civilizations of Italy and Greece. But I would do it with a pen and camera, recording civilizations and ways of life that would soon be gone forever. My Korean course was much more difficult: I had to learn a new alphabet, Hangul, and a new way of pronunciation. My teacher was a young Korean school teacher who was teaching this course to supplement her meager teacher's salary.

Chapter 9: Who's That Knocking?

"Who's that knocking on my door all last night and the night before?" - Genies: "Who's that Knocking at My Door?"

"Does Your Faucet Drip? Call the "Culligan Man" to Fix That Drip, Hey Culligan Man!" Culligan Plumbing Company Radio Commercial.

I had found this beautiful girl in the Apollo Club about a week before payday. My friend Rick and I became the lifesavers of the Korean courtesan community: when the enlisted men blew their wad in the first few weeks after payday, we as officers always had some money left to fuel the local economy. So, the Girl on the Half Shell was ours to pluck. Rick had picked a fiery banshee and I, a demure elf of a girl, to fulfill my desires for a quickee, not an overnight stay. I took this girl to her rented room, not in a mamasan house, but a fleabag hotel in the Ville. This girl was typical of the women that flited from one GI hellhole to the next, always looking for a steady yobo. This one was all for business, getting 2 to 3 GIs a night to build up her savings, so she could get her own place. Anyway, she was eager to get it on, collecting the money and zip stripping me while she quickly undressed herself. She pushed me onto the bed and lunged at me. She pinned me down with fiery wet kisses while I massaged her breasts which were like small hard torpedoes. We swirled together, my penis eager to plunge into her moist vagina. Suddenly there was a loud knock on the door, "Yobo say O!" (Let me in). It was her girlfriendless roommate who wanted to come in for the night.

My girl abruptly yanked me out and ran for the door. "You get dressed; we go to other room." Here I was with an erection that wouldn't fit into my pants; she trying to dress me hurriedly. It was like a scene from those old porn films where the father discovers his daughter in bed with the traveling salesman while she is pushing him out of the window. I was carrying my pants, shirt, and shoes, hobbling to a room down the hall with my penis sticking through my underpants like a long lance in a jousting tournament of medieval knights.

We get into the room, and she calmly says," No problem, we fuckee now." Again, we started the ritualized foreplay, she kissing me while tugging at my penis. I rolled her over and penetrated her, starting the slow rhythmic dance. Suddenly, out of the blue comes another knock on the door, "Yobo Say O, you done? I have number Hanna boy want meet you". The soap opera began anew; she pulled me out and ran to the door, now chattering with this friend. The girl left, and she came back, "So sorry, we fuckee now." She grabbed my penis, stuck it in her hole, and began grinding away. I was totally pissed, but my penis wasn't listening to me; it just wanted to ejaculate all that pent-up sperm. I came quickly. She moaned, "you're the best," and then pulled out and started getting dressed. "You go now. I leave." I cursed, got dressed, and took a taxi back to the base.

The next morning, I tried to piss, and all I could was drip painfully. The bitch had given me gonorrhea! These girls were required to have monthly checkups, but since she came from up north, she didn't get her checkup. So, I got dressed and went to our base health clinic. When I got there, it was "take a number"; there was a long line of us, each having a drip problem. The doctor was used to this daily parade. He had it down to a routine: penicillin shot in the ass, dispensed some pills, and gave us the standard spiel, use a rubber during sex. Of course, we all ignored this warning and returned to duty until the next time.

Chapter 10: The Hermit Meets the Saint

Korean Buddhist Monk around 1910

The history course taught us how traditional and isolated Korea was in the 19th century. Korea was called the Hermit Kingdom because of this isolation. It was only opened to trade and international relations in 1875 by Japanese warships that imposed trading rights for Japanese businesses. This was very ironic since American warships under Admiral Perry had opened isolationist Japan less than twenty-five years before.

Before that, the country was ruled by traditional Confucian-style monarchs and bureaucrats, which mirrored the closed Chinese Society. Korea was a "tributary" nation of China, meaning China had nominal sovereignty over Korea. However, in the seventeenth century A. D., Korean diplomats returned from China with Christian-Chinese books written by the Italian Jesuit Missionary living in China, Mateo Ricci. Ricci impressed the Chinese Emperor with his scientific knowledge but failed to convert the Court to Catholicism. Ricci's Chinese books, however, planted the first seeds of Christianity in Korea.

The Catholic church took a different proselytizing approach in Korea. The missionaries worked with local officials to do grassroots conversions of the common people. These conversions started slowly, but by the 1750s, there were sizable numbers of lower-class Christian converts in Korea. This worried the conservative Emperor, who then outlawed the religion. He started persecuting Christians, culminating in thousands being killed, along with seven French missionaries in 1866. This persecution ended when Korea was finally forced into Japanese and Western treaties.

What was at stake were two conflicting worldviews: the Confucian world, where a man knows his fixed place in society, women have no rights, and children are completely controlled by their parents. The Christian view stated that everyone was equal in the eyes of God; this not only had religious significance but social and political ramifications. The people, being equal, should have a say in their government. Women should be equal to men and should be given opportunities for education and social freedom. One Christian idea that gained widespread acceptance was the right for widows to remarry after their spouse died, which was forbidden under Confucian policies.

This is how Christianity spread in the Roman Empire; women were converted, wanting equality in their social lives, and they then convinced their husbands to adopt the new religion. St. Paul first converted the poorer classes, and their steadfast faith and willingness to be martyrs for their faith eventually converted the ruling classes in imperial Rome. Similarly, in Korea, the Catholic and Protestant missionaries emphasized this equality by establishing schools for men and women. In the eighteenth century, the Catholic church started services in the Korean language. One Scottish Presbyterian missionary, John Ross, translated the bible into Hangul (the Korean written language). This gave the poorer classes access to Christianity, who couldn't read Chinese, the official language of the Court. This was the original intent for the invention of the Hangul script. King Sejong the Great developed the phonetic Hangul in 1446 to increase the literacy of the common classes.

The Catholics and Protestants started 293 schools, including both men's and women's universities and nursing colleges, which attracted the business middle class as well as the lower class. When Japan annexed Korea and tried to assimilate it into the Japanese Empire, it was the religious schools that kept Korean nationalism alive. Spiritual leaders went to jail because they wouldn't bow to the image of the Japanese Emperor. Nationalists saw this as a political, as well as religious, resistance to the Japanization of Korea. Japan wanted to destroy Korean culture, demanding worship at Shinto shrines. Here Christians fought this, also starting religious labor and farm unions to stop the Japanese exploitation of Korean workers.

After WWII ended and Korea achieved independence, it was Christianity that continued to attract the middle class and intellectuals. They saw Christianity as a progressive religious philosophy that bolstered modernization of the country on Western models. This is similar to how the Protestant Reformation spurred the rise of Capitalism in the West. Many Korean politicians also gave tacit approval to Christianity because it served as an ideological bulwark against the Communist ideals of the North. Now Korean churches send missionaries all over the world, and Christianity is increasing so rapidly that it may soon replace Buddhism as the largest religious body in South Korea.

Chapter 11: The Assembly Line

Bobby Bare: "Detroit City". The song wistfully sings of making cars in the daytime and spending his nights making girls in a bar.

The Ford Automobile Assembly Line 1913

One of the most surreal nights I spent in Korea was with this Korean girl, Su Yi, who had just moved to Sinchon.

I thought she was stunning, and we agreed on a price for a short time. We took a taxi to her room in one of the shabby dirt alleys of Sinchon. Her room was like a youth hostel dormitory. There were three beds lined up in a row, separated only by a sheet hung between each bed. Three girls shared this space, and there was already a girl sleeping in the middle bed. This didn't bother Su Yi; she just put her hand to her mouth," Shh!". Needless to say, there was very little foreplay. I undressed while she ran to the bathroom. When she came back, she was wearing a Japanese-style robe, which she unceremoniously dumped on the floor. She was smaller than most Korean women; she had ruby red painted lips, chalk-white skin, crooked teeth, bumps for breasts, and a very luxuriant, silky-black vagina.

She kissed me once and then wiggled under me, saying again, "shh!" She had to help me get it in her, arching upward, grabbing my penis, and shoving it in her dark forest. We started grinding, and she became wet, easing my penetration. She moaned quietly while I was looking over at her sleeping girlfriend (the sheet had been pulled back, revealing her supine girlfriend), sleeping like a rock. While we were pounding away, I heard the loud lovemaking of a GI with his girl in the third bed. I felt like an assembly line worker in a Ford car plant, only here we make girls, not cars. I came quickly, lost in the absurdity of the scene. I briefly imagined that since I finished Su Yi, I must move on to the next girl, sleeping or not, you must keep the production line going. In the third bed, the GI was already snoring, so I could do his girlfriend too.

Chapter 12: A Scared New Yorker and a 4-F Hero

"Song Of Roland" - Medieval French epic poem, Anonymous author.

This poem is eerily prescient of the retreat from Chosin Reservoir. In the French poem, Roland is the rear guard, protecting Charlemagne's retreat from Spain. He is too proud to blow the ivory horn calling for help, and dies a warrior's death, immortalized by the medieval bards.

Through these fields of destruction, you did not desert me. "Brothers in Arms": Dire Straits.

Serving as a soldier in Korea, I was naturally curious to find out what really happened in the Korean war. I was four years old when the war broke out and knew very little about the conflict. It has been rightly called "The Forgotten War", our first "lost" war and one that was quickly lost to memory in prosperous 1950s America.

In high school, I dutifully read "The Red Badge of Courage" and saw all the John Wayne war movies. War is heroic and patriotic, and the ultimate test of character was the popular party line, and I bought it wholeheartedly. When I got to college, I had to reread the novel for Freshman English. This novel was "De Regnier" at my school because the author, Stephen Crane, was our most famous dropout. Lafayette College, a bastion of solid (and stolid) middle-class values, had its 15 minutes of fame when the rebellious Crane was in attendance. It seemed he liked the college baseball team more than his studies and flunked out. (In my time at the college, all the football jocks joined one fraternity Delta Upsilon, DU for short and DUH! for real, since many flunked out their freshmen year). The college, however, rewarded Crane's behavior by naming various buildings on the campus after him ("Furthermore, if I am elected, I promise to do nothing for you").

Stephen Crane 1896

Rereading the book, however, gave me a new insight into it: "Red Badge" is not a "war" novel per se but a study of fear and guilt. The hero is "Everyman" in this allegorical tale, who has faith (idealism and patriotism), endures a battle where he loses that faith (fear and cowardness), and slowly regains a stronger faith (courage). This is not really a transformation in the "Morality Play" sense because he did everything to deceive his fellow soldiers (the bloodied knock on his head by a crazed soldier) to prove he wasn't a coward. In the end, he carries the Regimental flag unarmed in battle, comes through unscathed, and considers himself a "hero". That criticism aside, this is still the greatest "war" novel in American literature, written by a young New York reporter who had never been in a war. This is war from a "grunt's" point of view. You are on the muddy ground, anxiously waiting, deafened by the roar of cannons shooting next to you. The charge is given. You wildly dash with hundreds around you, colliding and stabbing with your bayonet. A whole row of men fall before you; you step over them and continue thrusting. Men are groaning and shouting; there is dark red blood everywhere, and your eyes are stinging with sweat and dirt. You become separated from your platoon (did you run away?). You are in a dense verdant green forest. You come across a soldier with his face blown away. The stench and flies on the corpse confuse you–which direction is your front line? You hear rifle shots nearby, you are frightened – you have just one purpose: to survive at all costs. God is not on your side; nature is indifferent. The corn stalks in the field you entered will keep growing, even though there are hundreds of dead in the neatly planted rows. The Mexican muralist, Diego Rivera, carried this theme even further in his mural, "The Blood of Revolutionary Martyrs Fertilizing the Earth", where a dead buried revolutionary's blood is greedily feasted upon by the thirsty roots of cannibalistic corn stalks.

Diego Rivera "The Blood of Revolutionary Martyrs Fertilizing the Earth"

You are totally alone in your "fear and trembling," and then suddenly, there is the eerie quiet; the battle is over. You look over the killing field and are shell-shocked with guilt. Whether you ran away or stayed steadfast, you see the dead. I knew that soldier. Why did he die and not me?

I knew soldiers that volunteered for Nam two and three times. WHY? Did they get an adrenaline "high" from living on the axis of fear and total "aliveness"? Or did they want to get back to their unit line buddies "to keep their backs safe"? Or had combat changed them? Their life was not back home but, here in the jungle - this is where they belonged.

"Red Badge" captures all these chaotic emotions that the ordinary foot soldier experiences, not the bruised ego of the hero Achilles or the moody posturing of Napoleon in "War and Peace".

There is one surrealistic, even hallucinogenic song that typifies the fear, confusion of battle, and outright insanity that a typical grunt experiences in combat:

"Run Through the Jungle": Creedence Clearwater Revival

Chosin Reservoir

In my readings about the Korean War, one of the decisive battles of the War was the Chosin Reservoir. UN forces, mostly US Marines and Army, were advancing to the Yalu River, the border of Korea and Red China, when a superior one hundred-twenty thousand men Chinese force surrounded the thirty thousand Marines and GIs at Chosin Reservoir. Neither God nor the weather cared for either side. It was snowing and 25 degrees below freezing. Both sides lost thousands of men due to the cold. Then the seventeen-day battle began - the long retreat to the Port of Hung Nam. The army Commander, General Almond, was given the assignment to protect the flanks of the withdrawing Marines. His forces bore a great brunt of the fighting and suffered heavy casualties. The retreating First Marine Division Commander, General Oliver Smith, held off the Chinese as long as he could at the reservoir, losing thousands in the hand-to-hand combat with the Chinese. When his position became untenable, he was ordered to evacuate and stated forcefully, "Retreat Hell! We are not retreating; we are just advancing in a different direction."

There was one soldier that stood out in my mind: Lt. Colonel Don Faith Jr. of the Thirty-first Regiment Combat Team (RCT) of the Seventh Infantry Division.

Don Faith Jr. could have been the poster child of the anti-war "activists", "Suppose they started a war and nobody came." He was the son of an army Brigadier General, but when he tried to enter West Point, he was found to be 4F (medically unfit). When WWII started, he tried to enlist but was again rejected. After an appeal to his Draft Board, he was finally accepted. He graduated from

Officer's Candidate School and served honorably as a Staff Officer and Aide to General Matthew Ridgeway, serving all over the European Theater. After the War, he was transferred to serve in China and Japan. When the Korean War broke out, he was a Lt. Colonel assigned to the Seventh Infantry Division as a Battalion Commander.

His job was to protect the Marine Retreat and get his own men out, all the while keeping a tight, orderly formation while under heavy enemy fire. The Chinese were blocking the only road to the port and rained-down fire from the surrounding hills on the struggling column below. Lt. Colonel Faith took over command after the RCT Commander was killed. With the help of close air tactical support, he personally led a squadron of soldiers, cleared the roadblocks, and ensured that his men would have a way through.

In clearing one enemy roadblock, he was severely wounded by a Chinese grenade and moved to a truck that was carrying out the wounded and dying. The army credo is: "No soldier left behind", and the Thirty-First RCT used their rations and ammunitions trucks to accomplish this mission. Tragically these trucks were easy prey for hilltop Chinese gunners, who strafed his truck, killing him instantly. The other wounded were taken out and carried by other soldiers until they reached the Port. Their steadfastness and heroism are truly epic in the same way that the Greek Xenophon recorded the tactical retreat of the Greek mercenary soldiers stuck thousands of miles from home in hostile Persian territory in his "Anabasis". For his heroic actions, Lt. Colonel Faith was awarded the Congressional Medal of Honor posthumously.*

What was the significance of the Battle at the Chosin Reservoir? Through their heroic delaying action and army decimation of Chinese forces, the marines and army units bought time for the Eighth US army to regroup and consolidate forces south of the 38th Parallel, preventing the Chinese from over-running all of the Korean peninsula. Chosin Reservoir had no inspiring Flag-Raising photo like Iwo Jima to stir the popular imagination. Furthermore, it wasn't a glorious victory but a heart-breaking defeat. Of the twenty-five hundred men of the Thirty-First RCT who started the retreat, only one thousand fifty got through to the port, and of these, only three hundred eighty-five were still combat-ready for action. Lt. Colonel Faith, the Seventh Infantry, and the First Marine Division in their defeat were just as important as the deaths of three hundred Spartans at Thermopylae. Unfortunately, it is hard for the American public to glamorize a lost war, so they conveniently forget it.

There was no "Song of Roland" Troubadour to sing the praises of these doomed heroic soldiers. They were just grunts, the Everyman of Crane, doing a necessary but thankless job, pawns on the chessboard of the Superpowers America and Red China. We are now losing the Vietnam War. Will we just as conveniently forget the colossal waste of men and money, the war-profiteering, the vilification of the ordinary servicemen returning home to jeers instead of parades, and the shattered country we left behind?

As a soldier and as an American, I will remember their sacrifices. "I salute you, my brothers-in-arms."

*Lt. Colonel Faith's body was abandoned on the destroyed truck, and he was officially listed as "Missing In Action." It wasn't until 2013 when an American Graves Registration Company discovered his remains in a vast unmarked GI grave site in the Chosin Reservoir. After 63 years, Lt. Colonel Faith returned to America, and he was given a full burial with Military Honors at Arlington National Cemetery.

Congressional Medal of Honor Recipient LTC Donald Faith, Jr

Chapter 13: The Four Hundred Pound Gorilla Next Door

"Who controls the past controls the future. Who controls the present controls the past." - George Orwell: "1984"

The best thing about taking my East Asia history and culture class was the discussions during and after classes between the students and the professor. One night we discussed North Korea; all of us students were pretty much unaware of what was happening a short twenty-five miles away. There had been saboteurs and North Korean raids. One where thirty North Korean military commandos entered South Korea through a well-constructed tunnel in a failed assassination on the South Korean primer, Park Chung-hee. They attacked the Presidential Palace, and all were killed or captured before they could accomplish this mission.

There were also a few military and prison guard defectors that painted a grim picture of mass starvations, political indoctrination, and intricate networks of political concentration camps in North Korea. The gruesome horror stories that these defectors told were as bad as the Nazi Death Camps in World War II. In the political prisons, the people were thrown into jail without due process, just on the word of an influential Party member or even a jealous neighbor; these unfortunates were given life sentences where they were forced into hard labor, beaten, and starved. What made it particularly inhumane was that everyone in the immediate family of the "traitor", sometimes three generations of an extended family: wife, grandparents, and children were also forced into prison with no hope of parole. Women were raped daily and forced to have abortions when they became pregnant. These defectors told that the guards looked at their prisoners as "sub-humans" and would do anything they wanted to them. If a person was not performing his work with enthusiasm, he was beaten or denied his daily food rations. Rats and worms were eaten eagerly to supplement the daily staple of field corn. At one camp, Yobok, the mortality rate was over 50% because of accidents that occurred due to the malnutrition diet or outright killing of "disobedient" prisoners.

Besides these political prisons, there were also "re-education" prisons, where black marketeers, smugglers, Christians, and family members of defectors were incarcerated. These prisoners were forced to perform the same hard labor, farming or mining with primitive hand tools. At the end of each workday, they were forced to memorize speeches from the North Korean leader Kim il-Sung.

These re-education prisons at least offered a slim hope that the "prisoners" would be rehabilitated and released. There were estimates that ranged from 150,000-to 250,000 Koreans in the political and re-education gulags.

After hearing stories that deserters had told the South Koreans about the indoctrination at the prison camps, I remembered Arthur Koestler's book "Darkness at Noon."

Propaganda Poster of Kim-IL-Sung

An old-line Party bureaucrat Rubashov, has been accused of treason and arrested: now, he tries to understand how this could be? He had always adhered to the Party line. He still believed in the "revolutionary vision", but somehow the Party had lost this idealism.

"The Party denied the free will of the individual - and at the same time, it exacted his willing self-sacrifice. It denied his capacity to choose between two alternatives - and at the same time, it demanded that he should constantly choose the right one. It denied his power to distinguish good and evil - and at the same time spoke pathetically of guilt and treachery." "Darkness at Noon".

Rubashov is a flawed hero, putting the Party above individuals, turning in fellow comrades and even a lover who did not believe that the Party always knows what is correct and necessary for the people.

Now the party had turned against him: he is the reactionary now. He tries to understand this intellectually, is the party the best for the people? An old revolutionary friend, Ivanoff, now his interrogator, tries to convince him that he is wrong: the party is always right. A younger interrogator, Glekin, thinks intellectual persuasion will not work; only torture will bring the required confession of wrongdoing. Rubashov is tortured and finds out his friend, Ivanoff, has been executed for similar crimes. He has nowhere to turn; he cannot support the Party on intellectual or moral grounds. However, rather than see his whole life as a lie, he confesses; that the party must be believed in above any individual rights. He is brainwashed to admit crimes he never committed; the individual will be subservient to the party's will. In the end, he is executed.

In North Korea, the Communist Party has been subsumed by the "personality" cult of Kim il-Sung. If you do not praise Kim il Sung excessively or object to his policy of starving the people to build up the army - you are a traitor and must be reeducated or executed. At first, I thought this only affected the political elites, but defectors told of ordinary citizens being turned in because of jealousy of their neighbors, being a Christian, or hoarding rice for their own families. Everyone was afraid of their neighbors, and no one would speak up. This made me realize why the South Koreans fought so hard in the Korean War. They did not want to live in a regime under constant fear. Everything we take for granted, they had to fight for. It may sound naïve, but even though we were the expendable buffer in any future conflict between the North and South, I was proud to be there to help them in their struggle.

This also led me to reevaluate my views on communism. We were losing the war in Vietnam - soon, that country would be one unified communist state. Would the outcome be as horrifying as North Korea? And what about the rest of Southeast Asia - Laos and Cambodia? President Wilson's ideal that people should be allowed to have "self-determination", their choice of government. The U. N. was established to make this ideal a reality. When North Korea invaded the South, the U. N.

called for a multi-nation response, but even more important was the tenacity of the South Korean army, fighting at a tremendous loss of lives, to ensure that their democracy would be preserved.

When I signed up for the Korean language class, the teacher, Hwa Yi, was a shining representative of the new Korea: smart, educated, and idealistic: proud of her Korean heritage and the hard-won freedom that took the lives of millions of South Koreans to achieve.

UN Memorial Cemetery Pusan

As a soldier, I walked somberly through the field of thousands of white crosses at the U. N. Memorial Cemetery in Pusan. Here were the remains of twenty-three hundred soldiers from twenty-one countries that gave their lives defending South Korea. Each country has a memorial to the fallen soldiers, honoring their commitment to keeping South Korea free. Was the Korean War a "just" cause, or was it a senseless waste of men and money as Vietnam had become? I witnessed the ceremony of the Korean changing-of-the-guards at the Pusan Cemetery and caught sight of a Korean family laying flowers on a gravesite. To me, this symbolized the vigilance, resilience, and hope of the Korean people that these deaths were not in vain.

Chapter 14: Special Assignments

Part of the fun or drudgery of the job were the extra-duty assignments at the depot. Two assignments stand out: one was lifelong wish fulfillment, and the other was a sobering check on the reality of how we interact with people and the consequences of these actions.

This could be me on the way back from Finance when I had three million won! 1905

"MULTI-MILLIONAIRE FOR A DAY OR HOW TO LOSE THREE MILLION IN FIVE HOURS."

Every two weeks, the Korean workers on the base are paid. Unlike the army, which pays by check, the Koreans get cash. So, on a Friday afternoon, I went to the Payroll Office with my first sergeant, and we brought back three heavy duffle bags of cash, approximately three and a half million won. (The exchange rate was one hundred and sixty won for one US dollar.) My sergeant and I sat at a small wooden table with a water-filled sponge (All that money kinda sticks to your fingers, and we can't have that!) and a huge spreadsheet listing all of the Korean workers' names and their salaries. We had about 800 Koreans to be paid, and my first sergeant checked IDs, and I faithfully counted out the required amount due, and I had the person sign for the amount paid. So, what started out as champagne for all ended with the feeling that I was a Texas oilman who sees his last well run dry, and he goes belly-up the same day.

THERE IS NO "GET-OUT-OF-JAIL-FREE" CARD.

The other duty was Prison Warden for the night. ASCOM Depot had the only prison in Korea for US servicemen. Due to the Status of Forces Agreement with the Republic of Korea, any US serviceman who commits a crime, either on base or outside in the Korean countryside, is tried and jailed by the US Military Judge Advocate. This jail was not for overnight drunks but for black marketeering, assaults, and murderers. When I had my duty watch, there were about twenty-five prisoners, with three murderers incarcerated here.

I had never been in jail before, but after countless movies, I half expected to see a wise old con, like Edward G. Robinson, who exerts a quiet control over the prisoners and guards alike. There would be this jailbird comradeship among the prisoners, where Robinson would dole out easy jobs like laundry or medical assistant to the drunk Doctor, to men who paid him in cigarettes and did him favors. And there was always an oddball prisoner, like Burt Lancaster, who ax murdered a whole family, but now gently nursed wounded birds back to life and became the mascot of the guards.

The reality was far worse: there was a pervading feeling of hopelessness and oppressive loneliness. These condemned men were far from home; they had no family members visiting, and no one cared what happened to them. When the "lucky" ones were released, they could look forward to a dishonorable discharge and dead-end jobs for the rest of their lives.

You made your rounds, did your head counts, and reflected on these lost souls. I saw one cellmate, a black enlisted man, sentenced to life for killing his Korean girlfriend. Crimes of violent passion were in the eighth circle in Dante's "Inferno", and these men relived their acts in solitude, eternally remembering they had destroyed their loved ones.

Chapter 15: A Tale of Two Cities

It was the best of times; it was the worst of times, it was the age of wisdom, it was the age of foolishness, it was the epoch of belief, it was the epoch of incredulity, it was the season of light, it was the season of darkness, it was the spring of hope, it was the winter of despair, we had everything before us, we had nothing before us, we were all going direct to heaven, we were all going direct the other way. . . Charles Dickens "A Tale of Two Cities"

"I joined the army because my draft notice number was low, and it would only be a matter of time before they called me up. Besides, there was no job back home, and I hadn't seen my ex-girlfriend or my daughter for two months. I thought I'd be sweating in jungles, shooting at the gooks, or getting drunk back at the camp. Then my orders came down for Korea, Second Division in the north. I lucked out and looked forward to an easy assignment with no one shooting at me. Korea is two worlds: the camp, with its defined rules, bad cafeteria food, and regimented military exercises, to show the North Koreans that we would kick their butts if they crossed the line. The other Korea is like the old West that you see in the movies: wooden storefronts housing tailor shops, dirty restaurants, loan sharks, neon-lit clubs, and the most beautiful girls in the world.

On my first payday, I ordered a double-breasted wool suit with a monogrammed shirt, white mother of pearl cuff links, silk tie, and two-tone leather shoes. And I still had money left over for the clubs. It was just like back home: white gloves and black gloves, and you knew your place. The brothers were friendly. The Soul Music: Marvin Gay, Sly, and James Brown were loud in the club, and the girls were "Oh so fine." It didn't take me long to hook up with a beautiful, long-haired girl, Sue, who even spoke a little English. I gave her mamasan about half a month's pay, and this bought her for the month. I went to her small room, where she cooked me ramen and kimchi. I let the kimchi pass. Instead, I brought over Spam and other canned meats. We drank OB Korean beer and made love twice a night before curfew, which was midnight.

Yet every night she wanted to go dancing at the clubs to meet her friends. This cost me the rest of my paycheck, and by the twentieth of each month, I was broke.

I tried to get to her room by 5:30 each night after duty, but sometimes I had to stay on base for additional duties. I was gone for a whole week while we had joint KATUSA (Korean Army units embedded in American army forces) - US tactical field exercise since we were less than thirty miles from the border. Still, things were great. I even bought her a small boombox with soul cassettes, which she loaded with Korean music when I wasn't there. This dream world went on for three months, and then I changed. I met some brothers who turned me on to hashish, and I started gambling at someone's hooch in the "Ville." The next month I couldn't pay mamasan for Sue because I had gambling and drug debts to pay off. Yet I still saw Sue as my girl and would dance with her and pay for a short time ($10 / night) at least twice a week. This went on for a couple of months, and each month I wanted to pay Mamasan to have Sue for the entire month, but since I didn't give up the hash or gambling, I never really got together the money to do that.

The next month I had done all right. I had won some money gambling and even scored a little hash that I would smoke in Sue's room. I went to the Club around eight o'clock, but I couldn't find Sue. I asked her friends, but they didn't know where she was. I then went to my buddy's hooch and smoked some hash, getting high and angry at that bitch. I grabbed a taxi to her house and started banging on the door to her room, yelling her name. Finally, she spoke from behind the closed door in a whispered voice, "What you want? You no own me. I have a new yobo now. You leave. I get the police!" This made me madder than hell, and I started using all of my weight to break through the locked door. I pushed the door in, and there Sue stood, holding a large knife and screaming, "Get out. I cut you if you no leave!"

I'm a big guy, and here was a little girl, quivering with the knife in her hand. "Sue, baby. Don't be crazy. I just want to talk to you." "You get out. Mamasan, call police; you go!" I lunged at her, and we struggled with the knife. I grabbed her wrist, she slipped, and the knife went into her side. She gasped, staring at the knife which was sticking to her. "Sue," I cried; everywhere, there was blood on me and all over her; now she fell to the floor, not moving. I just sat down and stared at her, and then I started crying, "Sue, wake up! Sue, get up!" I remember the Korean Police came, hit me, and handcuffed me. The rest of the night was a blurred nightmare that I wasn't waking up from".

Chapter 16: The Chaplain

"Positively 4TH Street" - Bob Dylan

This is a classic song of love and trust being betrayed.

Our chaplain David was a friendly bear of a man, about six feet tall and about two hundred and fifty pounds. Although I didn't attend weekly church services, I got to know him through the officer's club bar. He was a regular, and a lot of us junior officers talked to him because he was friendly and approachable and, most importantly, didn't take the official army line on "hot button" issues.

He asked a few of us over to his quarters for talks and to participate in the Iselin School of Psychotherapy, which he was a firm believer in. These exercises helped individuals to communicate and relate openly. We would sit in a circle holding hands, talking about what was on our minds, looking straight at the person we were opposite, like in a Quaker church service or an Alcohol Anonymous meeting. I had spent many hours talking with him, baring my soul, and we had (I thought) developed a strong bond between us.

One night, I stayed on after the others had left, still engrossed in our conversation, when suddenly, he put his hand on my crotch and leaned over and kissed me. I didn't return the kiss, being too shocked. He proceeded to hold me and gave me another kiss. I became numb, and when he wanted to take me to bed, I undressed slowly, in a dreamlike trance. I somehow still trusted him as I lay naked in the bed. He enveloped me, his body warm and his kisses sloppy wet. He massaged my penis, but it still would not get hard. Then he moved his mouth down and tried to tongue it into erectness. While this was happening, I felt like I was a separate person, hovering above him. I was looking down at him on top of myself.

After about five minutes of sucking me, I still wasn't hard, and I snapped awake. I told him, "This isn't going to happen," and broke free. I got dressed without speaking and left his quarters immediately.

The cold air brought back my sense of reality and left me to reflect on what had just happened. At first, I felt that he had taken advantage of me. All of his touchy-feely exercises were a sham to get me into bed. Then I let the anger go and thought I, too, had been a willing participant. He didn't force me to do anything. More importantly, I didn't feel violated. I wasn't a naïve choirboy being molested by a lascivious priest. In my mind, it was a life experience between two consenting adults that was never even consummated. I never reported him. He was due to retire the following year, and there was no reason to end his career and pension on something like this. However, although we still drank and talked at the club, I never went back to his quarters again. I wasn't angry or feeling vindictive toward him. He had broken our trust; I felt only a deep disappointment toward him.

Chapter 17: Korean Rhapsody

"So kids, did you ever want to become a famous painter? Now you can with my COLOR BY NUMBERS KIT. For a low price of $19.99, I will send you a sketch book with ink outlines of famous paintings; each part of the outline has printed numbers that you match with the included numbered tubes of oil paint. You would have to be a complete idiot if you could not create the perfect masterpiece following these simple instructions. But remember, do not drink alcoholic beverages when attempting to keep within the lines of the painting. We don't want "Mona Lisa" looking like one of the women in Picasso's "Les Demoiselles d' Avignon", do we now."

Jackson Pollack died in an alcohol-related car accident in 1956 at age 44. He was known for his "action" paintings – large canvases tacked to the floor, with Jackson frantically dripping, throwing, and splattering paint on the canvas from all angles.

To me, Pollack represents the twentieth-century American interpretation of nature, just like Albert Bierstadt and Frederick Church represented the nineteenth-century views of nature. In the twentieth mid-century industrial America, the grandiose mountainscapes and light-flooded valleys do not reflect the frantic pace of urban living, with its cacophony of sounds and miles of concrete wastelands. Pollack creates a nature for the modern man: full of irrational movement yet unified in a raw color vision. The colors themselves are the trees, leaves, and rocks: nature redacted to elemental color and movement. Bebop jazz as a pulsating painting: dissonant, deconstructed melodies and sonorous high saxophone riffs.

Many amateurs and artists tried to imitate his paint-dripped canvases but lacked Pollack's frantic energy and controlling unity. Enter the soldier. Being chief of the junkyard, I had access to all of the materials needed to make my own version of a Pollack. I found a rolled-up linen canvas 4 ½' wide by 10' long. I had my choice of dozens of open paint cans and even one old, broken bicycle. I spread the canvas outdoors, holding it down with bricks, and sat in front of it, waiting for inspiration, trying to formulate what I wanted to express. Hell! Pollack was an alcoholic; I think I should have a couple of beers to capture his creativity. After about three beers, images of smoke-filled clubs, with dozens of sweating, gyrating couples thrusting in and out under strobe lights, loud deafening music, smells of garlic-infused kimchi on the breath of Korean workers, the feel of a young girl's body in total darkness filled my imagination - then I started. First, I spattered clumps of paint from all four sides. Then I moved the wheels of the ruined bicycle over the paint, finally dripping more paint, trying to capture the immediacy of my flash-back imagery. After about fifteen minutes, I stopped and walked away, grabbing another beer.

I came back in a half-hour and studied my painting. In the bright noon light, it looked lumpy and haphazard, as if someone had just thrown paint, helter-skelter (Duh!).

I wanted to create an "instant" Pollack and had failed miserably. I tried to duplicate the style without the substance. I wanted to call it: "Korean Rhapsody" but "Korean Rubbish" was more like it. I went back to my room and stared intently at an art print of Pollack's "Autumn Rhythm" - lost in the swirls and droplets. Here was controlled passion: art imitating the forces of nature, the colors abstracting the falling leaves, the leaden skies, the dance of wind, stirring and shaping the landscape.

I found more canvas and tried again; after two more attempts and a six-pack of beer later, I stopped. The last painting, "Korean Rhapsody III", somewhat captures the process but not the overarching vision. My facile, hurried style belies the emptiness of my understanding of the true "way" of nature (all dressed-up and nowhere to go).

"Korean Rhapsody III"

Chapter 18: Comfort Women

"There But For Fortune" - Joan Baez

Rescued Korean Comfort Women tell their stories to US Army investigators in 1944

One of the strangest nights I had in Korea was a night with a half-Korean, half-Japanese girl. I wondered how a young girl of about twenty could speak fluent Japanese, Korean and English too. I asked her about this, and she said that her Korean family lived in Japan, where she was born. Her mother had been taken to Japan just before WWII and served a Japanese family as a domestic servant. Sometime later, she met a Japanese man and had two children with him: her and an older brother.

After her "father" died, the mother and her children did not get any inheritance from the father since he had another legal family. She returned to Korea with her kids in 1955. Although she didn't elaborate on the rest of her life, I could make a heart-breaking guess: her mother had been a "comfort" woman, a forced concubine to a Japanese official or military man. When she returned to Korea, she was ostracized by her family, and the children were teased at school because of their mixed Japanese Korean heritage. With no family to integrate them back into Korean society, the young girl had no alternative opportunities and became a prostitute. Afterward, I went back and researched the "comfort" women and even brought it up for discussion in our history class.

Korea was a "colony" of the Japanese Empire from 1910-to 1945, and they fully intended to make it an integral part of Japan. They forbade the teaching of Korean in schools, forced the men into the Japanese army, and many of the women were abducted and forced into Japanese army brothels. Some of these abductees were as young as 13 years old, and all were virgins. Many were "bought" by the Japanese from poor farmers. Others were promised domestic or factory work in Japan. In total, about two hundred thousand Korean women were forced into becoming prostitutes for the Japanese army camps throughout Japan and Southeast Asia.

These women were raped thirty to forty times a day, never paid, badly doctored, and forced to have abortions if they got pregnant. Many were beaten to death if they didn't "perform" for the army, and many others found ways to commit suicide because of their disgrace. Many of these women were moved with their Japanese regiments and ended up in places like Hong Kong and Singapore when the war ended. Many were killed by their Japanese soldier overlords at the end of the war to silence them from telling their American rescuers what they had been subjected to. The Japanese army tried to burn all records of this atrocity, claiming these women were willing, paid prostitutes.

Due to the daily hardship, the rapes, beatings, and diseases they contracted from syphilis to malaria, almost ninety percent of the "comfort" women died in captivity. The "lucky" few who returned to Korea and told their stories were ostracized as "whores." The average Korean male thought that these women should have committed suicide to avoid dishonor. Many of the returned women were totally silent about the ordeal to save themselves and their families the humility of shame. Furthermore, many of the "comfort women" became sterile because of the constant rapes, and others never married, hating the touch of any man. Now when the surviving women are in their sixties, they are speaking out, telling the truth about their lives. This was a horrific experience, and they felt the world should know what they went through. One of the most heart-breaking real-life stories was Kim Bok-Dong's experience as a "Comfort Woman".

Miss Bok-Dong was only fourteen when she was forced to join other women under the threat of her family being turned out of their home if she didn't accept a "factory" job in Japan. Miss Dong was sent first to Taiwan, then to China, where she was raped and forced to service Japanese military men from 8 am to 5 pm, from 30 to 50 soldiers per day and every day.

She and two other girls tried to commit suicide by drinking high alcohol wine. They almost died but were discovered unconscious and had their stomachs pumped out. She survived and, to avoid future beatings, submitted to the soldiers. She was transferred all over Southeast Asia and was in Singapore when the war ended. She was sent back to Korea, having been gone for eight years. Her parents still thought she had been working in a Japanese factory, and she didn't tell them the truth in the beginning when she returned home.

She told her parents that she didn't want to marry. Finally, her mother found out the truth but the family, including Miss Dong, kept this crime hidden for fear of being humiliated in their community.

Miss Dong was sixty years old when she finally came forward to tell her story. What she wanted, above all, was an apology from the Japanese government acknowledging how they abused these "Comfort Women." If they gave her an official apology, she would forgive them. If the Japanese government were to give monetary compensation to her, she would use this money to fund poor students who couldn't afford a university education because she always regretted that she was not able to get a university education.

Unlike the Nazi gas camp commander criminals, many of whom were convicted of war crimes, no high-ranking Japanese commanders were ever brought to trial for the unknown stories of "comfort women" brothels. These women wanted an official apology from the Japanese government; unfortunately, they still haven't received it. The Japanese continue to deny all of the stories and fragmentary records of their atrocities.

Chapter 19: School Marm'

"Wonderful World" - Sam Cooke

School Marm

Hwa Yi was very intense, rather than pretty, with short, cropped hair, minimum makeup, and boundless enthusiasm for her language and culture.

After a few sessions, I asked her out for dinner. She spoke good, albeit heavily accented English, and we talked about Korea and its struggle to maintain a separate identity from her large neighbors that periodically conquered and occupied her several times in the last thousand years. Yet every time, the distinctive language, way of life, food staples (kimchi), and art survived and thrived. Kublai Khan, the Emperor of China, and Marco Polo fame, conquered it on his way to a (failed) invasion of Japan. Like the Spanish Armada was destroyed by storms before it could invade England, so too a typhoon destroyed Kublai's fleet. The Japanese called this typhoon the divine wind (Kamikaze), which was what the Japanese suicide pilots called their aircraft as they crashed them into American ships in WW II.

The next conqueror was Japan, incorporating Korea into the Japanese Empire as a colony. The last conqueror was the Russians, who swept down through Manchuria in China after WWII. They set up a puppet communist state in the north while the Americans propped up a corrupt but western-friendly government in the South. The Russians got the better deal: the North was heavily industrialized with all the mines, factories, and rail lines, while the South was mostly agricultural with subsistence farmers. Just like in Vietnam, where the North wanted to unite their country, the North built a huge army with communist China's military assistance and training and invaded the South. They crossed the 38th Parallel (a division of north and south) and drove the South Korean and American forces down to the southern tip of South Korea (the Pusan Corridor). Then the UN (mostly American troops) struck back with Gen MacArthur pulling off a brilliant tactical capture of Inchon. This pushed the North Korean army back across the 38th Parallel, and MacArthur continued on until he reached the Yalu River (border of China). Then the communist Chinese army intervened and drove the UN forces back down south again. There were terrible battles; the war see-sawed back and forth. Gen MacArthur wanted to bomb the Chinese mainland, and he publicly bad-mouthed President Truman, who wouldn't authorize the bombing. President Truman then relieved him. It was the right decision; we Americans must have absolute control over the military, or else we are no better than the banana republics of Central America. The stalemate in fighting was cemented by the ceasefire agreement in Panmunjom. The North, meanwhile, keeps building its military state for another invasion.

Hwa Yi and I would meet once a week for dinner and more discussions. It brought back memories of heated college discussions about the war. I was in ROTC and had lost fellow classmates in this senseless war, but there still was a lot of support for the war. What bothered me then and still bothers me is that the antiwar demonstrators picked on the soldiers when they should have criticized the leadership, their local representatives, and senators who helped perpetrate this disaster.

Here the Korean war was still very much alive after a generation of uneasy peace. Hwa Yi was the new Korean: educated, smart, and ambitious, fully aware of the South's fragile position in world politics. She believed the country must industrialize, build up its army and energize the people to want and be willing to defend the freedom they have. South Korea had sent many troops to Vietnam to support our forces. They were hard fighters and skilled in guerrilla warfare, a skill that would be needed given the belligerence of the North Koreans. The parallel between Korea and Vietnam was unnerving: we were losing thousands of Americans' lives to defend a corrupt regime and a disillusioned populace that doesn't give a damn about defending their country. In sharp contrast, South Korea knows its history, that communism is just another foreign invader that must be stopped. Hwa Yi was doing her part, imbuing Korean school children to excel and giving them the tools to strengthen their nation.

I was envious of her- here I was screwing around every night and planning a self-indulgent, self-discovery pilgrimage while we Americans were throwing a whole generation away with bad ghetto schools, drugs, and crime. We were spending more in a month on this unwinnable war than a year's national budget on education. We have a million people on welfare and another half-million junkies in NYC alone. Our prisons are schoolhouses to learn better criminal methods. The joke about prisoners is that it costs as much a year to incarcerate a prisoner as it costs to attend a year at Harvard. The solution: send the prisoner to Harvard and let them show America how it really is on the streets. The business case of running a multi-national drug trade, keeping the supply lines open, the ruthless street distribution, buying corrupt law enforcement, and introducing new drug products would drive our large corporations out of business if they had to compete with these drug operators.

I vowed I would teach public school when I returned, but first, I had to know who I was and what I wanted from life. The Korean principle of Ying and Yang: know yourself before you can teach others to find themselves.

Hwa Yi and I enjoyed each other's company: we visited the National Museum and went to live performances of traditional Korean folk music. She explained the different eras expressed in the painted pottery and funeral urns. I thought the high point of Korean art was the Koryu celadon vase.

KOREAN CELADON

Maebyong design Korean Vase 13th century A.D.

Every country has a period of great artistic flowering. For Korea, this was the production of ceramic celadon in the Twelfth Century AD Koryo Dynasty. Geography favored the Korean potters by giving them fine clay and plenty of wood for firing. Koreans learned their skills by imitating the Chinese, but soon they surpassed their teachers. They learned the techniques of kiln firing control to produce a translucent glaze that is without equal today. They developed a delicate sea foam blue-green that they called "the blue of the sky after rain." They used this glaze on a distinctly Korean vase design called "Maebyong", a broad-shouldered tall vase that tapers down with a slight flaring at the base.

The decorative effect of flowers or flying cranes was achieved by painting designs on the wet clay using a solution of iron oxide. The vase was then dipped into this "magical blue-green" celadon glaze and fired. Incising was achieved by using fine knifepoint to cut the desired design to the wet clay filling the scratched-in design with reddish-brown or even black slip (coloring). Then the piece was fired at a low temperature to preserve the design, covered with celadon glaze, and then fired at a high temperature to give it that translucent crackling appearance. The Chinese valued this celadon pottery; a twelfth-century manuscript praises Korean celadons as "first under Heaven." Korean celadon was traded for silks and imported to China in great quantities.

A Koryo king had his palace roof completely covered with blue-green celadon tiles, designed with a floral pattern that changed colors throughout the day as the sunlight shifted in the heavens. This celadon production lasted for two hundred years until the Mongol invasions ended the Koryo Dynasty, and the "magical" blue-green glaze formula was lost forever.

What started as a platonic relationship soon blossomed into a carnal one. One night after class, we had a late dinner, and it was freezing cold outside. She lived in a dormitory with other teachers and did not want to go back to an unheated bay. We found a hotel room (an extra 200 won for a space heater). We no sooner got into the room when she gave me a strong hard kiss. I helped her undress: she wore a thick woolen undershirt, no bra, and a poured-into woolen girdle that took some time to remove. After she was undressed, there was the obligatory trip to the bathroom while I waited expectantly under warm sheets. She came out and slid quickly under the sheets. I had turned off the light, but the almost full moon shone through the window and bathed the room with a luminescence that set our faces aglow. She constantly stared at me, her eyes intensely focused on me, looking for some assurance that I cared for her. She was giving herself freely. I wasn't taking her. We started kissing; she devoured my mouth with her hard lips and spear-like tongue. I started to move on top. At first, I couldn't get it in; she was so tight. Finally, with her assistance, I was in, and we began our Olympic gymnast's movement. She arched her bottom upwards to accept my thrusts, which she returned with syncopated heaving. I came so hard that I felt I would split her in two. We lay there cemented together, still passionately kissing each other.

I had a weekend pass, so I suggested we go to Kyonju to see the ruins and temples of the Silla Kingdom. She was very excited about this trip; she had not been to Kyonju since she was a little schoolgirl. I picked Hwa Yi up at her dormitory early Saturday morning. She was dressed in a dark gray women's business suit, her hair done up in a permanent with full makeup: she looked very classy. We arrived by train at Namsan Mountain and walked through a fairy tale landscape of rock-hewn Buddhas, solitary stupas, and gaily painted temples, all set in a hilly black pine forest. She told me about the history of the Silla Kingdom. Silla was the first dynasty to unify the Korean peninsula in 688 AD. Buddhism was introduced by Chinese monks in 528 AD, and all the shrines here are Buddhist, constantly rebuilt after one conqueror or another destroyed them. Kublai Khan's Mongols passed through here, destroying the Kingdom on the way to invade Japan. I took photographs of the Silla gravestones and stone guardian mythological creatures as well as Koreans in traditional dress and even Korean Boy Scouts. We visited the main temple, Bulqukia, which is ornate and gaudily painted in rainbow colors. We also viewed the Astronomical Observatory Tower, which also served as a huge astrology guide and as a sundial. I was impressed by the huge bell in one of the shrines, which is still rung for special ceremonies.

Maitreya

While walking around the temples with their stately stoic Buddhas, I thought of one statue that I had seen in the Seoul National Museum that is also of the seventh century AD Silla Dynasty. This is a gilt bronze statue approximately 30" high of a seated Maitreya (future) Buddha.

Internecine wars and foreign conquests had destroyed most of the artistic masterpieces of Korean art, but this Maitreya had survived and embodied all the grace and calmness of Korean Buddhist sculpture. The delicately hermaphrodite figure is in the "elongated style", which is similar to the tall thin Gothic statues that stare out at you with their other-worldly expression on the facade of Chartres Cathedral. Here the Korean figure is lost in meditation, but it is the beatific calmness that arrests you. The future Buddha will come back to Earth in times of trouble to save Mankind. He emanates compassion and understanding and radiates this feminine benevolence that a mother shows her children.

Maitreya (Future Buddha) 7th century A.D. Seoul National Museum

Hwa Yi was very proud of her ancestors, telling me about this king, that valiant princess, and how the Silla Kingdom successfully fought off the Chinese Tang Dynasty armies. We had a great time, but it was not that I had a girlfriend, but rather a respectful tour guide. The taboo of a Korean

girl with an American GI was very strong, especially in this historical city. We never held hands in public for fear that Koreans would ridicule or call her a whore for being with me. After seeing all the sights, we went out for a traditional Korean dinner: bulgoki (strips of beef and pork cooked right at our table, with strong-smelling winter kimchi (fiery hot with chili peppers and tons of garlic), pickled vegetables, and sticky rice, served with rice wine.

We found a good hotel (one with a working space heater). Hwa Yi was a totally different person when we were alone in the hotel room. She was affectionate, relaxed, and happy. "I'm so pleased that you wanted to come here; this is where Korea was born."

"And I'm pleased to have such a beautiful girlfriend explain the significance of what we saw." I went over and kissed her, and she kissed me back, holding me. She went to the bathroom to change, and I undressed, waiting for her in bed. She slipped into bed, and I held her to get her warm. I kissed her nipples until they were rigid, and then I moved down her body, spread her legs apart, and found her private part. My tongue caressed her until she was moist. I came on top of her. She was still tight, but I eased it in slowly, and we started moving, first slowly, then rhythmically faster. She moaned quietly, and I came with a thrust that shook her whole body. We continued moving in each other until we both fell off, sated in our desires. We held each other; she stared intensely into my eyes, but her face was now relaxed, and we fell asleep. I felt very differently on the ride back to Bup Yong. I was with a woman that gave herself freely because she cared for me, not just my money.

We saw each other two more times, our lovemaking a fierce intensity, like two vultures devouring each other in a sexual frenzy. But we both knew that we would need to carry our relationship to a higher level; she did not want just a sexual liaison. She sensed I wasn't serious enough, and she was right. I just wanted a companion to show me the real Korea. She was the real Korea, and I couldn't handle that commitment.

Chapter 20: Korean Countryside

I can see the sun has gone down on my town, on my town, Goodnight. - "Our Town": Iris Dement

Korean Market 1903

After my Korean teacher, Hwa Yi, romance ended, I took long bus trips out to the countryside by myself, photographing the beauties of the country that she had instilled in me. I wandered on dusty lanes, past old farming villages and newly planted rice fields. I saw the slow-paced rhythm of life: men working in the rice fields with their water buffaloes, women making kimchi in large earthen jugs, and children playing and skipping ropes.

In the middle of one field, I came across an old crumbling fortress tower gate, trees sprouting from the top, the entrance cemented shut. The earthen walls had long disappeared. The late afternoon sun suffused the tower in a Turneresque golden hue. I imagined soldiers running on the top of the now gone walls, shooting arrows, defending the village from marauding bandits. The battle must have been furiously fierce, and bloody-the villagers were in a life and death struggle. Unfortunately, they lost the battle: the defenders were slaughtered, the village sacked and burned, and the walls were torn down. But the earth remained, fought over by countless conquerors (the latest being North Korea, just twenty years ago). South Korea is a land of small farms, and this has endured through the love of the rich earth. Today this peaceful farming community is flourishing. This village, unlike its counterpart up North, has a ready market for its produce in the growing city of Inchon, just five miles away.

When I was 13, I read a book my mother gave me that she had read when she was growing up." Markens Grode ("Growth of the Soil") by Knut Hamsun. Unfortunately, it was in Norwegian, so I had to get an English translation of the book at my local library.

"Growth of the Soil" is the story of a farmer: a strong, coarse, uneducated, blood-red bearded, rugged individual who treks off into the wilderness of Northern Norway to carve out a farmstead. He takes up as a helper and common-law wife, a simple woman named Ingrid, who is disfigured with a hair lip. The book describes his struggles to make his farm a success. Ingrid gives him two sons, and then she kills a newborn girl because the baby is born with a hair lip. However, what stands out is the love of the fecund earth.

"He never read a book but often thought about God; it was unavoidable, a matter of simplicity and awe. The starry sky, the soughing of the forest, the solitude, the big snow, the majesty of the earth, and what was above the earth filled him with a deep devoutness many times a day. He was sinful and godfearing; on Sundays, he washed himself in honor of the holy day but worked as usual." (Isak in "Growth of the Soil")

The latter part of "Growth of the Soil" deals with the second generation, the children of Isak and Ingrid. Sivert is the oldest, and he stolidly wants to follow in his father's footsteps and remain a farmer. The other son, Eleseus, is more open to new experiences. He works as a telegraph operator and, even after buying a farm, decides to give it up to better himself by emigrating to America.

Eleseus symbolically became a part of the Great Norwegian Migration. From 1875 to 1914, Norway lost one-third of its population, over 2 million Norwegians who immigrated to America. Most of these immigrants settled in the Midwest, becoming farmers. This was evocatively portrayed by a Norwegian immigrant, Olaf Rolvaag, in his book "Giants in the Earth." The book depicts the struggles of a Norwegian farming family in the Dakota Territory in the 1880s. The lead character, Per Hansa, is like Isak in "Growth of the Soil", a simple but ambitious man who builds a successful farm. But the hardships of prairie life, the loneliness, and homesickness for Norway drives his wife Beret insane.

"Beret had now formed the habit of constantly watching the prairie out in the open. She would fix her eyes on one point in the skyline, and then before she knew it, her gaze would have swung around the whole compass, but it was ever, ever the same…Life it held not. People had never dwelt here. People would never come. Never could they find a home in this vast windswept void."

Per Hansa himself is killed by the unrelenting prairie; however, his children adapt easily and become true Americans, not Norwegians. Rolvaag himself started as a farmer but left for Chicago, got an education, and became a professor: a true American success story.

"Giants in the Earth" may be fictional, but the real-life stories of Norwegian immigrants going insane and committing suicide were graphically chronicled in Michael Lesley's "Wisconsin Death Trip." Here in the haunting photographs of Charles Van Schiak, a local Black River, Wisconsin photographer, who captured images of distraught, disturbed, and genuinely weird Norwegian immigrants. Coupled with these haunting but unrelated images are the real-life newspaper and insane asylum accounts of murder, suicide, and insanity among the mostly Norwegian immigrants.

Taken together, they show that the "good old days" was a lie. The prairie has broken countless immigrants, mirroring Rolvaag's classic pioneer fiction darkly.

The Aunensen Family in New York City circa 1920 (My mother, Magdelana, is the second girl from the left)

My mother's family story was similar with an interesting twist. My grandfather, Ole Aunensen, came to New York City in the early 1900s. He had been a farmer but could not support his growing family on the small family plot. Luckily, he had carpentry skills and found work building the bridges and tunnels of New York City and, in the process, earning a good living.

Here my mother and her younger sister were born (in the Bronx, no less!) but my grandmother could not adjust to life here and forcibly convinced her husband to return to Norway. So, my mother returned there and became Norwegian, always speaking English with that musical Norwegian lilt.

The Great Depression of the 1930s hit Norway badly, and there was no work for my grandfather or his two growing young boys and three girls. Yet unlike "Growth of the Soil's" Eleseus, the rebellious son who migrated to America for a better life, here it was the girls in the family who spunkily re-immigrated to America. My mother worked in department stores and did domestic maid work in Manhattan. Her sister Ingrid attended divinity school and became a life-long missionary in Swaziland, Africa.

WW II started, and my mother became a real-life "Rosie-the-Riveter", making bombs in a small factory in Greenwich Village. It was in the bomb factory that she met my father, who had recently been medically discharged from the army at Fort Campbell.

My father was another immigrant, hailing from Switzerland and working in restaurants. He had been trained back home as a Saucier. Incidentally, my father was the only man I knew in America to have served in both World Wars. He was 16 when WW I started, and they sent him to the border with a rifle in hand to protect Switzerland's neutrality. After immigrating to America, he was drafted into the US army (at the age of 44!) as a cook during WW II. Luckily for me (otherwise, I would be a non-existent figment of the reader's imagination), he caught hepatitis and was discharged at the age of 46. He met my mother at the bomb factory, got married, moved to a newly built house in New Jersey, and a year later, I literally entered the picture.

I shot one of my favorite photographs in this stark countryside. A long, winding dirt road, lined unevenly by Lombardy poplars, denuded by the winter wind and a forlorn Korean farming woman, trudging away off into the horizon. This spoke to me of the harsh, desolate beauty of the Korean countryside; the lone figure, a symbol of the struggles that the Korean people endured, captured in contrasting black and white.

The now peaceful quietude, the distant twinkling of village lights, farm rooms filled with families contentedly eating their evening meal and pervading everything, the heavy, pungent odor of raw waste fertilized rice and vegetable fields (Now that's about as organic as you get – definitely "Wash Before Eating"!).

Chapter 21: The Martyred

I told my teacher that I was reading about the Korean War and wanted to get the Korean perspective on the war. He suggested I read the novel "The "Martyred" by Richard Kim. I got the book, and it was like falling down the rabbit hole in "Alice in Wonderland". "The Martyred" is not a "war" novel, but rather a Christian existential dialogue on faith and free will, set in a war-torn Korea of 1951. The novel unfolds with the shocking revelation that the North Koreans had murdered twelve Christian ministers yet spared two who renounced their faith. The South Korean Army wanted to use these murders as propaganda against the atheistic, communist North Koreans.

The protagonist, Captain Lee, must confirm the ministers met their fate for their faith and interview the two ministers that "renounced" God and were spared. What Captain Lee finds out is that one survivor became insane, and the other, Reverend Shin, refused to renounce Christ and spat in the face of his interrogators. The other twelve ministers renounced Christ but were killed anyway. Reverend Shin was spared because he alone showed courage in the face of death. However, Shin honors the memory of the "fallen-from-Faith" ministers and publicly confesses that he alone betrayed Christ and not the twelve ministers. His philosophy is that the Korean people suffered so much during this War; they must believe that their suffering, like the dead ministers, is not in vain.

The individual sacrifices himself for the betterment of the many; this is Christ's story. Christ, the human, could have forsaken death. By his free will, He chose to sacrifice Himself for the salvation of all mankind. This is remarkably similar to Pericles' funerary oration for Athenian dead soldiers. Here religion and patriotism merge; both Athena and the polis of Athens demand sacrifice to preserve the Ideal: "When the moment came, they were minded to resist and suffer rather than to fly and save their lives." Life only has meaning if you have an ideal: religious, social or political and are willing to sacrifice anything or everything to achieve that goal. Deliberate falsehood, personal degradation, and scorn from your fellow man mean nothing to Reverend Shin if these twelve deaths can inspire, give solace and hope in these dark days of war and suffering. In other words, the ideal, whether it be a free Korea, a defense of Athens, or a false admission of guilt to preserve the communist party, as in "Darkness at Noon", supersedes the free will of the individual.

Growing up, I read Dietrich Bonhoeffer's (a German Lutheran pastor) "Letters from Prison", written while he was in a Nazi concentration prison awaiting execution. His faith sustains him and even calls him to resist by conspiring to get rid of Hitler. His free will triumphs and serves as a symbol of one man's fight against tyranny. What stands out is his universal love for his fellow Germans, giving them hope and urging them to carry on his struggle. "Action springs not from thought, but from a readiness for responsibility." He chose death rather than a resignation to the evils of fascism.

"The Martyred" asks us to condone a lie about faith because it will give spiritual hope to war-suffering Koreans. But how is that different from Mao, who lied to his people about mass starvation or thousands of political executions, all for the greater "vision" of Communism? Lenin promised Peace and Bread as the justification for communism. Dostoevsky's Grand Inquisitor in "The Brothers Karamazov" promised security for the masses; the Church will make all the important decisions for the spiritually weak and guarantee their salvation. Even in North Korea, Kim il-Sung will blatantly lie to his people, promising the good life of Communism, if they blindly listen and obey Him alone.

Free will versus the State, Party or Church authority is the central issue of the book. Reverend Shin refused the sainthood role; he would not betray his weaker clergymen. He sacrifices himself for the "greater good of the Ideal." Dead martyrs are more important as a "shining Ideal" rather than revealing the human failings of the ministers or his lone heroic defiance. The Ideal is greater than the individual, whether it is faith in God or Communism. This is very disturbing because we in the West believe in the individual's free will, the one who stands up against fascism or the Church. A Martin Luther posts his 95 Theses on the Wittenberg church door, risking everything to stand alone and shout out the truth.

At the end of the book, Reverend Shin sees all of Korea as 'the Martyred." So many lives were sacrificed so that the country could be saved. His life isn't important, but the Ideal of sacrifice offers that glimmer of hope to his people.

Chapter 22: Dark Night of the Soul

"Black Magic Woman" - Santana

"See that you are not suddenly saddened by the adversities of this world, for you do not know the good things they bring, being ordained in the judgement of God, for the everlasting joy of the Elect."

Saint John of the Cross: "Dark Night of the Soul"

Portrait of Fanny Eaton" by Walter F. Stocks (Miss Eaton was a black mixed race Pre-Raphaelite model from Jamaica living in London.

It was getting to 11:30 P.M, and I still hadn't found a girl to spend the night with. I was sitting alone (Rick had a night duty assignment) at the Apollo, nursing an OB, when I saw her across the dance floor, sitting alone. She was tall, about 5'9", darkly beautiful with a full body and curvaceous breasts. She also had lightly frizzled brown hair, mahogany eyes and full thick negroid lips. I guessed she was half Black-half Korean, combining the best of both races.

I introduced myself and asked her if she wanted champagne. She accepted and we started to talk. She spoke fairly good English and had haughty confidence that gave the impression that she wouldn't take shit from anyone. Her name was Julie, and as we were talking, I noticed that she had a bad gash on her right arm. I asked her about that, but she was evasive, so we proceeded to the most important issue: how much for an overnighter. She wanted $15, and I countered with $10. We haggled a while, and she grudgingly accepted $12. We quickly grabbed a taxi because it was about 15 minutes to curfew. Her house was down a dark, muddy lane, and her room was bare, except for a small table and chair with a mirror on the table, a small hot plate, a battered wardrobe and a mattress on the floor. There were no photographs or fashion posters on the walls, not even a radio. In the corner was a large suitcase and a pole hanging with the wash, all bathed in the harsh glare from a single light bulb dangling from the ceiling. I asked Julie if she recently moved in, and she said she came from Wi Jun Bo up North about two weeks ago.

I started to undress, loosening the buttons on my shirt when she demanded her money. "Whoa, let's take it slow."

"No, I want my $15 now."

I gave her the money, but she screamed at me, "That's only $12. You give me $15."

"No, we agreed on $12."

Then the tirade started, "You cheap GIs, always trying to get over. My last yobo, he mean, cheat me of my money. We fight, and he cut me. He black, you white. You all same-o, take advantage, but no more."

She turned around, stepped back to her wardrobe and reached down; when she turned around, she had a large kitchen knife and was coming for me. She was screaming, "Get out. I no want you. No fuckee tonight!" I quickly looked around, grabbed a chair and held it as a shield since she was still screaming and charging toward me. She lunged with the knife but couldn't get through the seat of the chair. She tried one more time to cut me but still couldn't get through, all the while cursing me in half English-half Korean.

I tried to calm her, "Hey, let's talk about this. Put the knife down!" After spitting at me and still holding the knife, she sat down on her mattress bed, alternating screams and sobs. Now she was only stammering hysterically in Korean. After about 10 minutes, she stopped, laid back down on her bed, and was quiet. All this time, I was still standing, sweating, and holding onto the chair for dear life. Thoughts raced through my mind, *crazy bitch*. A headline: "American Captain Knifed to Death in a Korean Love Nest", friends I'd never see again, a girl back home, crying at my funeral. Well, given the circumstances of my death, maybe she will just send a Hallmark.

I kept staring at her, making sure she didn't jump up and try to knife me again. Finally, I moved to the far corner and sat down, still clutching the chair. I was still shaky, but I managed to take out a cigarette and light it with one hand while tightly gripping the chair with the other. As the smoke curled up to the bare bulb, I thought about escaping but knew I had to stay here for at least another five hours. If I were caught by the Korean Police for curfew violation, it would be an Article 15 (Court Martial offense), and my military career would be gone.

For the first hour, I was mad as hell: "Fucken bitch! She deserves that gash on her arm; I'd like to give her another." Finally, after the fear and hate dissipated, I thought about her as an individual, trying to understand how it had come to this. She was obviously the daughter of a Korean whore, who got knocked up by a Black GI. Instead of taking her mother back to the States as he promised, he deserted her and his child. The mother continued working the clubs, bringing home dozens of men, screwing them in the same room where she lived with Julie, only being separated by a folding screen or hung sheet. Still, the little girl could hear the arguments and the loud lovemaking.

As she grew up, she had nowhere to turn. The mother, by choosing her profession, would have been abandoned by her parents. Little Julie had a double whammy against her: not only was she the daughter of a whore, but she was also half-black. Koreans are very race-conscious. If you didn't have straight black hair and a chalk-white face, you were ostracized; not even good enough for a day laborer or a push-cart vendor. Even for the poor, pure race Korean girl, there was little opportunity without education. For domestic help, a tailor shop or maybe a factory job, you still need a family to back you and support you. Julie had none of these opportunities, and the only way to make a living was to follow in her mother's footsteps. It was like second-generation welfare in New York. It is so hard to break the vicious cycle of high school dropout, poor choice of friends and lovers, no job and an unexpected child out of wedlock. But Julie had one important feature which made the transition to "hostess" easy: she was drop-dead gorgeous. If she had the opportunity to go to the States, she could have been a phenomenally successful professional model. She had that exotic face, with high cheekbones, coffee colored skin, sensuous lips and a demeanor that could turn you to stone if you looked at her wrong. She could have sold everything from the latest fashion to cold creams and perfume. She would have put all those pale, insipid blond mannequins out of a job.

However, this was Korea and being half-black, the mamasans wanted nothing to do with her. The tee shirts also wanted the stereotypical long black hair, slim body and chalk-white face, the porcelain "china doll" image. So, it was only the black clubs that took her in. Here she stood out, being both young and beautiful. Many of the women in these clubs were older women, only going there after their youthful beauty had passed, and they could no longer compete with the younger women in the tee shirt clubs.

Up north in Wi Jun Bo, life was hard for bargirls. This is the home of the 2nd Infantry, and these grunts are a rough crew. There were more assaults on Korean women there than anywhere else in the whole country. Into this viper's nest strode a proud, defiant young woman who knew the ropes, could sling the lingo and didn't take shit from anyone. The one thing I learned about blacks and their dealings with the bar girls in Korea: they wanted submissiveness and respect. Julie expected them to earn it if they wanted her. This led to endless arguments, physical fights and a knife gash to the arm by an unruly black, who also didn't take any shit from an "uppity whore". So, she packed up and came South to ASCOM, looking for a better life.

This is where yours truly enters the story. She saw me as just another jerk, trying to get over, telling her lies and cheating her of her due money. Looking back, I saw myself as a real schmuck: haggling over her price and then wanting to sample the goods before I paid. All these thoughts scrambled through my head as I sat there, still clutching the chair, afraid she might start attacking me again. Adrenaline, plus a whole pack of Camels, kept me awake and alert.

Finally, I saw the first faint gleam of daylight, peering through the one high, grim-caked window. Curfew was over, and now I must attempt my escape. I gingerly hugged the wall on the side of the room opposite her mattress, reached the door and quietly unlocked it. I opened it quickly, threw down the chair and bolted out to the muddy alley. I ran to the main thoroughfare and never looked back. I woke a sleepy cabbie and told him to take me to the main gate of ASCOM.

As I was riding back to the base, I tried to make some sense of what had happened. Here was a girl that was hurting, and I did nothing to help; in fact, I was the straw that broke the camel's back. I didn't have to be a psychologist to see she was in a deep funk, but she had to go out at night, spreading her legs, just to keep bread on the table. She was beautiful and ambitious, but her inner demons were now in control. I remembered a poignant passage from my favorite author, F. Scott Fitzgerald, who also struggled with his own demons of alcoholism and artistic failure, in "The Crackup".

"Now, the standard cure for one who is sunk is to consider those in actual destitution or physical suffering—this is an all-weather beatitude for gloom in general and fairly salutary daytime advice for everyone. But at three o'clock in the morning, a forgotten package has the same tragic importance as a death sentence, and the cure doesn't work—and in a real dark night of the soul, it is always three o'clock in the morning, day after day."

I never saw Ju Li again: maybe she became a regular in the Dukes, a black club where tee shirts like me were not welcome, or maybe she kept moving south to Taegu, another big GI base, trying to find a place that would accept her on her terms.

Chapter 23: A Reverie: Homage to Coleridge

"Oh, Korea, with your dusty roads and alluring whores, your soft summer nights, your overpowering kimchi smells. The half-drunk meanderings from one bar to another, the countless champagne and OB's, the awkward swaggering, contrived small talk, the bump and grind under strobe lights. The eternal game: deal consummated, the muddy back alleys, the room invariably the same shabbiness, the hurried lovemaking in the dark. Waking to a complete stranger in your arms and always the pale dawn creeping through the grimy, barred window the morning after."

(A fragment of a delirium written down before I fell back into a drunken stupor.)

Samuel Taylor Coleridge

Samuel Taylor Coleridge's "Kubla Khan" is the most famous unfinished poem in the English language. As a Jack of all trades: photographer (say cheese), an artist (painting by the numbers), musician (air guitar), and author (we all see how well this is going!), I thought I might try interpreting this famous poem and, by extension, my own reverie.

The pleasure dome is first a physical place, Xanadu, then a mythological place: the caverns of ice, and finally a phantasmagorical dream of Paradise. The Abyssinian mandolin siren is Coleridge's Circe, bewitching all who hear her hypnotic, enticing song. She especially bewitches Kubla with wild fantasies of conquest and plunder. Kubla is like the river in the poem that runs headlong, swirling everything away in its path of destruction. If Coleridge had finished the poem, I think it would have turned darker. Kubla is a force of nature that can never be tamed. The pleasure dome in the ice cavern is illusionary; it will soon melt. The pleasure dome of the mind (air) is the dream of distant golden lands which await the restless and relentless conqueror.

In my reverie of Korea, I was not trying to imitate Coleridge's vision; however, in rereading it, I can see the parallels to the famous poem. Here in beautiful Korea, the pleasure dome is Sinchon's clubs, and the siren is a courtesan, her alluring song the pulsating rock'n'roll. Her beguiling sweet smile is the pleasure dome of the ice: ephemeral, dissolving in the morning light. Yet the pleasure dome of the mind, the sweet nectar of the gods, is a young girl breathing softly, asleep in the cradle of your arms in the stilling darkness. To quote another Mongol conqueror, the Indian Emperor Jehangir: "If there be a Paradise on Earth, This is it, This is it, This is it."

Chapter 24: A Modern One-Act Morality Play

"Ye think sin in the beginning full sweet.

Which in the end causeth the soul to weep."

- Messenger to Everyman in the 14th century English morality play, "Everyman", anonymous monk author.

ASCOM Main Entrance Gate

The Stage: Bright lights under a huge gate and austerely bare stage set, like a modern production of Wagner's Nibelungen opera. No other decoration.

The Cast: A young GI, his bar girl, and an old Korean woman

The scene opens as the GI and the young girl are talking and laughing.

He: "Did you see his face when I walked into the club with you?"

She: "He seemed upset to see me with you."

Old woman: "Hello, sir! Would you like to buy a beautiful necklace for your girl?"

She said: "I know you. I saw you outside the Apollo, selling whiskey that came from the PX to the bar manager."

The old woman ignored this and showed the necklace to the GI.

He said: "Well, let's see what it looks like?"

Old woman: "Finest light blue aquamarine stones set in real silver. Very cheap for you: only 5000 won."

While the GI examines the necklace in the glaring light, the young girl speaks to the old woman in Korean.

She said: "Where are you from?"

Old woman: "I come from up North, near Wi Jun Bu. I was a bar girl. I stayed there until the camp closed. I have many GIs and make lots of money, but I never found one that would marry me and take me to the States. There was one GI, who promised me that we would get married and move to Oklahoma, but he was fooling me. He had a wife and kids back home."

Aside: The young girl looked at the Old woman. She could see traces of her former beauty. Lines, where there were once sculptured cheek bones and faint traces of jet-black hair, now mostly gray. She was dressed in a tattered grey coat and wore faded Chinese slippers. All of her belongings were wrapped in a bundle, which she carried on her head.

She: "Where are you living now?"

Old woman: "I live under the bridge, just by the stream there. Not too bad; soon come spring."

She: "Don't you have family that you can stay with?"

Old woman: "When I became a businesswoman, my family disowned me. I have a brother, but he won't see me."

She: "Didn't you save any money to start a business?"

Old woman: "When the times were good, I bought fancy clothes and a T.V. But as I got older, I spent most of my money in the Beauty Shop, trying to keep fresh. There are too many young girls, and you have to keep up your appearance in order to get the yobos."

She: (Aside) The young girl was noticeably quiet. She saw her life reflected in the old woman. She, too, had left home in disgrace. She was now in the prime of womanhood, but what did she have to show for it? She had saved some money, but she had no family, children, or everything that was important to her. She asked herself, where will I be in 10 years? She stared closely at the GI. He was a big spender and a lot of fun, but in six months, he would be gone, and I will be alone again.

He: "Well, it sure is a pretty necklace. Do you like it?"

She: "Yes. It would go nice with my black satin dress."

Old woman: "Look at the craftsmanship. You can't find this in the jewelry stores today. I had this necklace for ten years, and now you have this girl who'll look great wearing it. For you today, only 4500 won. Make your girl happy."

He: (to old woman) "You drive a hard bargain."

(to young girl) "As long as you love this necklace, I'll buy it for you."

She: "Oh, this is so beautiful." (Kissing him)

Aside: She held the neckless in her hand. It seemed like a glittering apparition. "How long will I have this before I too will have to sell it, just to survive. I won't make this old woman's mistake: I'll get out before I'm too old. I'll get a seamstress shop or become a mamasan with a stable of girls".

He: "I'm glad I pleased you." (Aside): "Boy, I'm gonna get some special loving tonight for this." (End of Aside).

She: (Aside) "I'll take this and everything else he gives me, but I won't fall for him. He'll go home and brag about what a great piece of ass he had in Korea. Meanwhile, I'll be with another faceless yobo, but whatever I do, I won't become this old woman."

Scene. The old woman packed up her clothes bag and moved on, looking for another GI to sell more of her prized mementos.

She: (Aside) She could see that he was elated, talking a mile a minute, but she was subdued, resolved to inwardly harden her emotions while outwardly showing a carefree sly smile.

THE END

Chapter 25: An Ju: She Said

"The Power of Love" - Jennifer Rush

"I was 18 years old when I left home. My parents were rice farmers, and it was awfully hard living; many times, we did not have enough to eat. We also lived with my older brother and his wife. I had left school at 15 to help with the chores, but there was no future here, so I left.

I first went to Seoul to try to find a job, but the department stores were only hiring high school graduates. There also wasn't much call for an unskilled farm girl in the factories. Like all good country girls, I could sew, but there were no seamstress openings either.

Then I saw the girls in I Tae Won (Seoul's Red-Light District). They were so glamorous; the latest hair styles and their clothes were the latest fashion, but best of all was their free-spirited attitude. They were ambitious businesswomen, and they had a definite air of independence about them. They were making it and flaunting it in a male-dominated society. I wanted to be a part of this. However, even here, there were barriers because I was a poor country girl without fancy clothes, and I spoke no English. I found a mamasan, and she got me in touch with her friend in Bup Yong Dong (30 miles from Seoul). Bup Yong was the home of a big GI depot and a lively club scene.

So, I went to Bup Yong Dong, and the mamasan there gave me a furnished room of my own in her house. She bought me fancy clothes and taught me how to entertain GIs, all for a fee on my future earnings, of course. The mamasan tutored the other girls and me in the house on how to speak basic English and how to style my hair, just like the cover girls in the magazines. She taught me how to pad my breasts to appear larger and taught me how to walk in platform shoes, so I could appear taller. She took special care on how I should make up my face to be chalk white and my lips a ruby red. The other girls in the house and myself practiced dancing GI style, with lots of hand and exaggerated hip movements. And most importantly, use copious amounts of mouthwash and chewing gum to get rid of kimchi (garlic and red pepper infused cabbage, the Korean staple with rice) breath. GIs hate that smell and will not go anywhere near you if you have kimchi breath.

With the preliminaries over, the mamasan talked about how to handle sex. Never accept anything less than 1200 won for a short time and 3000 won for an overnight. Be enthusiastic with him, he is number hana (1), and it makes him feel that way. When you get him to the room, always get the money first, then help him undress, kissing him and massaging his penis before you get him into the bed. After he is in bed, go to the toilet and douche with this cream to prevent pregnancy. Then when you have him in bed, check his penis to be sure it is not dripping, or else you will get venereal disease. This will keep you out of the clubs for at least a week while you are being treated. Also, keep your VD venereal disease card up-to-date, or the health inspector will keep you out of the clubs unless you pay him off.

When you are in bed, help him to mount you. Usually, these GIs have huge penises, and getting in you can be very tight. Also, you don't have to do anything kinky if you don't want to. GIs love having their cocks sucked; if you don't want to do this, make up for it by extra moaning when he's moving in you. When he finished, you give him a tissue (you must keep the bed clean for the next yobo), then quickly go to the toilet and douche again. Then help him get dressed quickly, so you can find another short time or an all-nighter before the 12-midnight curfew.

With all these preparations done, I was ready to lose my cherry, and boy, what a letdown!! My first t-shirt (white GIs always wear white undershirts under their shirts that show) was a drunken private from a farm in the States. He kept raving about how pretty I was. He was so drunk it took me 5 minutes just to massage an erection. He tried to mount me, but I was so tight that I had to hold his penis while he was pumping away. Luckily, it only lasted a minute, and he came. He wanted to marry me and take me to the States with him, but I never saw him again.

My days all drifted together into a familiar pattern. Get up late and shop for kimchi, rice, and an occasional chicken (I only had a hot plate, so elaborate meals were out of the question). Maybe I would buy a new fashion outfit, and the rest of the afternoon I would spend with my girlfriends in the beauty salon, getting my hair and nails done. I spent my off-time going over to Patty's room to watch Korean tv soap operas. Then we would practice English on each other and try on each other's dresses. Afterwards, there would be a quick dinner and the obligatory toilet preparations; I was ready for the evening when the girls and I went to the Apollo to find the next yobo.

I was sitting, chatting away with my girlfriends, and he came over and offered to buy me a drink. He looked older than the privates I usually hooked up with, and he seemed to have money. Champagne drinks for all the girls at the table. We talked as best I could and then danced to a few slow songs. He was always laughing and, best of all, polite. He didn't grab my ass when we clutched together in slow dancing. It was Saturday night, and he offered to pay me for the whole night. We left the club at 11:30 to get a taxi to my house, after a quick stop to get two bottles of Portaju (rice wine) and persimmons. He loved them when they were almost rotted; he said that was when they were at their creamy best, with just a slight tartness to the tongue. We drank wine, ate persimmons, and talked. Then he gently grabbed my face and kissed me. I started to undress him between kisses and get him into my bed. I quickly ran to the bathroom, douched and gargled mouthwash, undressed, and slipped under the sheets. We were lying there kissing while I stroked his penis to erection. He wanted me to kiss his penis, but I wouldn't do it (why do all of these GIs want their cocks sucked, do they think they are lollipops that taste sweet?). We just kissed and fondled each other; then, he came on top of me. He wasn't drunk, so I didn't have to help him, and he wasn't so huge that he hurt me when he penetrated me. We got into a natural rhythm. I was moaning loudly and seeing that I was giving him great pleasure. When he finished, I let him come down slowly. Not yanking him out quickly and giving him a tissue, as my friend Judy does with her yobos.

We drank some more wine, smoked cigarettes, and had sex one more time. Then he fell asleep in my arms. He left early Sunday morning but said he wanted to see me again that night. He was at the Apollo that night, and we went out to my favorite noodle restaurant for chicken and yucca mundo (dumplings). They really make the best yoca munda, light and meaty on the inside. Afterward, we went back to my room with the customary Portaju wine, persimmons, pomegranates, and cigarettes.

This time everything seemed natural. We laughed and sang Korean and American folk songs (he was off-tune most of the time, but it was fun, and he was always laughing). Our lovemaking was also getting better: when we were thrusting together, he grabbed my ass and pushed it up, melding our bodies. We saw each other three times a week; always an all-nighter. My girlfriends were all jealous of me for having such a steady yobo.

After about three weeks, he asked me to be his steady girl, and he would pay mamasan for the whole month. It was a lot of fun, and now I didn't have to worry about the rent. We ate out every night, and he bought me gifts: a cute radio with a cassette player and a smashing pantsuit in my favorite color, emerald green. He often had to go out of town for his army job two or three times a month; now, I could stay in my pajamas and watch Judy's television all day long. This arrangement lasted about three months, and I started to believe that I was his girl; he would take me back to the States with him when his tour was up. We went onto the base for a small party, and he even took me to the officer's club for a fancy dinner. On the weekend, I could come to his room during the daytime. We would play records, sing songs and make love on his creaking bed. He loved to photograph me. One day I was wearing his t-shirt and corduroy pants; he shot a whole roll of film of me, capturing my different moods, he said, propped by a backdrop of comic book art, Korean posters, and his blown-up photographs.

Then one night, he didn't show up, so I went with my girlfriends to the Apollo and then to the Green Door Club to see if he was there with his army buddies. I was shocked and angry when I saw him sitting closely, talking to a Korean woman in traditional dress.

This woman was at least eight months pregnant. She looked so big that I thought she would deliver right there on the dance floor. I went over and confronted him; he awkwardly introduced me to her as Miss Lee. This bitch told me, in Korean, that the child was his and that he was going to marry her. I glared at him as he ordered drinks for everyone, and he told me that Miss Lee had been his friend long before he met me. She just vanished one day, and no one knew where she had gone. I didn't believe him, left the table, and after cursing at him, walked out of the club. I stormed into the Apollo; I was so angry that I danced with this fat private, forced him hurriedly out of the club, and gave him a short time in a nearby hotel. Afterward, I went home and cried. My girlfriend later said that he had left the club with her. That fuck! I really liked him, before I knew that he was really a two-timing son of a bitch!

Then the troubles began. The blacks started beating up whites in the clubs, and I'd heard that there was a white Sergeant killed by a grenade on the base. On the last night before the clubs closed, the Ville was declared off-limits to GIs. It was particularly scary. There were no GIs, only some Korean businessmen in the club. When a champagne cork popped, everyone ducked under the table, thinking for sure it was a gunshot. Then the clubs stayed closed for two weeks, and everyone was hurting for money. It was getting cold then, and mamasan was a pain-in-the-ass with her rent demands. When the clubs finally reopened, it was still slow, with only a few GIs venturing out. I only got one short time in the following two weeks.

I still thought about him, but I knew that our relationship was over. I swore to myself that I wouldn't be one of those girls who cry when they tell stories about GIs who left them behind. "Well, fuck him! I'll move on. There's always another yobo I can screw, and maybe this one will take me to the States."

Chapter 26: On Photographing An Ju

"Everything looks better in black and white."

"Kodachrome" - Paul Simon

An Ju

As a portrait photographer, you are always trying to capture the "soul" of your subject. I remember reading in a National Geographic article that the author/photographer could not take pictures of this particular African tribe. The tribe's witch doctor convinced his people that the photo image of a tribesman "stole" his soul. The pictorial image was the essence of the man, and this was forever stolen in the photograph.

When I photograph the people of Korea, I either try to catch them unaware, or when I snap them directly, they usually glare back at me, sizing me up with stares of indifference, annoyance, or downright hostility. Children in Korea are miniature adults: many times, they give you a soul-piercing stare; other times you can't stop their infectious laughter. Either way, I felt I was capturing a "real" person.

Being in Asia, I was very curious about the people in Red China and couldn't go there to see for myself, so a photography book was the next best alternative. I found a book by a Chinese photographer, which promised to show me the beauty and wonders of this "Forbidden Land" (at least I thought it did since the text was in Chinese with Korean translation). The images of traditional temples and the varied landscapes were awesome, but when the photographer shot the Chinese or ethnic minority people, everyone was smiling or laughing. What had promised to be a real live record of "unknown peoples" turned into a propaganda piece for the communist regime – see how happy our people are under the benevolent communist system: "The farmers happily sing while carrying animal dung to the fields." (actual Chinese Communist song).

To try to capture the "soul" of someone you are close to is even more elusive. Your natural instinct is to put your "best" face forward. A full smile, you are in love with this person, so show it. You mimic the children's song: "Put on a Happy Face."

One rainy Saturday afternoon in my quarters, An Ju and I had just made love; instead of putting on her dress, she grabbed my corduroy pants and white Tee shirt, tying the too-large waist with a sash. I picked up my camera, determined to find the real An Ju behind the smiling mask.

Tina Modotti in Glendale by Edward Weston 1921

First, we posed for the standard arcade photobooth, three prints for a buck. She was seated on my lap, I dressed for the event (being shirtless), and the camera was on a timer. The result was a picture-perfect ad for Colgate super whitening toothpaste but revealed nothing. Then I took random snapshots, using up two rolls of B&W film, to capture her moods and expressions. I was a later-day Edward Weston and An Ju, a beauty equal to Weston's model and mistress, Tina Modotti. Tina was a silent screen actress that was not just another pretty face- she was a communist that saw the synthesis of art and revolution to further the efforts of social justice. Weston, like myself, was in a strange new land (Mexico) and had a new loving relationship. He lovingly photographed her face and voluptuous nude body in chiaroscuro shades of light and dark. Here the natural curves and shapes of her body became one with nature, as organic and free-flowing as his famous closeup of a garden green pepper, passing from the erotic to abstract art (Andy Warhol carried this one step further: enshrining ordinary industrial mass-produced items like a Brillo carton as a work of art. The medieval cathedral was built to glorify God; the Brillo box is designed for the new god: the all-powerful consumer in our secular society).

Weston and Modotti traveled all over Mexico, photographing the people, architecture, and landscapes of this brave new world. The Mexican Revolution reforms were in full swing: the land was redistributed to the poor farmers, foreign industries were nationalized, and unions were given striking powers. There was optimism and hope that the Mexican society could be truly free, and most of the working class lifted out of poverty. This was also a time of intense intellectual ferment: the famous muralists Diego Rivera and Jose Orozco were creating huge masterpieces, exalting the struggles of the farmers and factory workers against the greedy industrialists and bankers.

Weston taught and mentored Modotti in photographic techniques. She was a fast learner, using her newly developed camera skills to document the struggles and living conditions of the farmers, fishermen, and industrial laborers in an acclaimed book, "Beliefs behind Idols". Modotti remained in Mexico after Weston returned to the States, working (and sleeping) with the Mexican communist leaders. She was also Diego Rivera's mistress; he painted her luminously haunting face into several murals on government buildings and universities in Mexico City.

Like Modotti, I felt real love for the ordinary Koreans and tried to document their work and lifestyles. Walking around Korean cities, I see muddy streets; men rigged with wooden harnesses for carrying goods or pushing bicycle carts – willing to do any work to survive. The women pull pushcarts, selling everything from vegetables and fruit to cheap trinkets and plastic toys. The farmers work their small farms with oxen or even by hand; the fishermen are constantly repairing their pre-war vessels and fishing nets. Korea is transforming from a farming to an industrial nation through hard work and a determination to keep its country free from future invasions of the North. I contrasted this unified push with our own society: divided by race and the Vietnam war, poor schools, and a loss of industrial jobs. Do we Americans have the sustained will to rebuild our country as the Koreans are doing? The optimism of "everything is possible" in the Kennedy years evaporated in the steamy jungle of senseless carnage and exorbitant monetary waste.

Did I capture An Ju's "soul" in my photographs? I have included some of these images in my companion book of photographs, and the viewer can make that decision himself. The real test will come if I find she is cheating on me. I will take a cherished photograph of her and stick pins onto the image while mumbling an ancient Haitian voodoo spell… Just kidding!

Chapter 27: An Ju: He Said

"Goodbye My Almost Lover" - A Fine Frenzy

"Her name is An Ju, and since the price was right, she agreed to spend the night with me. We left the Apollo, stopping for wine and ripe persimmons, and took a taxi to her place. Her place was the same as a dozen others: big iron bed, small table with two baby-sized chairs; the only difference was a table light with a mirror for makeup instead of the glaring single bulb hanging from the ceiling. This was an older traditional Korean house, with the floor heated from below by charcoal. The linoleum looked frayed, a great candidate for seeping carbon monoxide poisoning through a small crack in the linoleum. The headline flashed through my head: "American officer found dead in the arms of a dead whore, both victims of carbon monoxide poisoning."

After a perfunctory visit to the hall bathroom, she disrobed and scrambled under the covers. I had been sipping on the wine, and I was now warm and comfortably high. She snuggled under my arm and started kissing me. Wet, hot French tonguing, which roused me up immediately. I wanted her to go down on me, but she shook her head and continued kissing me. She had small breasts, and her nipples were rasped erect by my tongue as I kissed them, but it was her ass that was amazing: hard but pliant to my touch. I rolled over on top of her, and she swiftly guided my erect penis into her vagina with a few deft movements. She was tight, but she arched her back, forcing me further into her vagina. We commingled together as one in long slow thrusts. She kept kissing me, and we fused together. Our bodies are a perpetual motion machine, knowing no beginning or ending: it was just moving under its own volition. When I came, it was like switching on the nitro fuel in a racing car, a burst of semen that made me shutter in a spasm of orgiastic pleasure. I held her in me, savoring the last drops of joy. She was gently kissing me and then cradling me when I slipped out and lay spent beside her.

We drank some wine, ate persimmons, and even sang a few folk songs. She didn't speak English very well, but she was the sweetest girl I had been with. After our lovemaking, she curled up next to me and fell asleep in my arms. I saw her again that Sunday and the lovemaking was more natural; I was getting to know her body. Those precious moments when we were locked in each other's arms, moving inexorably to a burst of semen and emotion. I was hooked. I talked with the mamasan, who "owned" the girls in the house, paying her for An Ju for a month, not even bargaining down the price. For the next three months, I was Mr. Jones (of the suburban Jones). After work, I would go to her house, then to dinner, dance at the club, shop for wine and fruit, and then retire back to her house for lovemaking. I neglected my friends, stopped reading, and thought about her all day: in a word, I was totally pussy whipped!

I would take her back to my Quonset hut on weekends, and we would sing Korean pop standards from scratchy old records. She would alternately begin laughing or crying over childhood memories that these songs evoked. She especially loved watching Korean soap operas on my small TV set. Then one day, when I was alone in my quarters, I heard a knocking on the door. It was my friend, Rick, forcibly dragging me away and telling me I had to go with him to the Apollo. There was someone I had to meet. (To be continued…)

Chapter 28: Admiral Yi: The Man and His Statue

All great cities have a defining symbol that identifies what and who the people are and what is most important to them, above all else. To me, New York City is not the Empire State Building nor the Brooklyn Bridge, nor the pulsating liveliness of Times Square: it is a solitary cast-iron statue of a lady with spikes on her head, carrying a torch. It is a beacon that proclaims: Here is Freedom. Freedom defines us as a country, and the statue is also a welcome: "Give us your poor, your tired masses, yearning to be free." This was the portal that shaped the city and all of America in the last hundred years. New York City was the funnel that created Americans out of countless poor immigrants from all over the world.

In Seoul, you also have a solitary cast-iron statue. This one depicts an imposing bearded warrior in full battle dress, with a Prussian-style spiked helmet, carrying a huge sword. From his stand, he glares out over Gwang-hwamun Square in the center of the city. This is Admiral Yi and what he stands for is Resistance and the resolute spirit of Korea. This isn't a welcome but a call to arms: if you want freedom, then you must fight and, in his case, die to achieve it.

Korea has always been a battleground, fought over by the surrounding China and Japan, each trying to destroy their freedom. Kublai Khan conquered it on his way to Japan. China made it a tributary state, and Japan conquered it in 1910. For Koreans, freedom means fighting and resistance to foreign invaders.

Seoul was destroyed less than twenty years ago in street-to-street fighting with the North Koreans. Admiral Yi showed Koreans that they could defeat superior forces, but the price for many Koreans was death in battle to secure that freedom.

Admiral Yi, the man, was a remarkable military strategist who had no formal training as a Naval Commander. His tiny fleet defeated the superior Japanese Navy twenty-three times in the Imjin War (1592-1598). His most famous victory was the Naval Battle of Myeonganyang, where Yi's thirteen warship fleet beat a superior one hundred thirty-three ship Japanese war fleet, sinking thirty-one enemy warships and not losing a single battleship of his own! How did he accomplish this?

Admiral Yi

Yi took an old warship design of a "Turtle ship" and completely modernized it, specifically designing it for fighting the Japanese. The "Turtle ship" (a vessel shaped like an overturned turtle) was more compact than the Japanese warships but had larger canons and two decks: one for the oarsmen and one for the cannon and fighting men. There were eleven cannons on each side of the vessel and numerous holes for archers and musketeers to fire from. Each turtle vessel had a dragon figurehead, but unlike the Viking ship with its fierce, solely ornamental head, this one concealed four cannons and a smoke-dispenser that masked the ship's movements in battle and thus confused the enemy as to how many ships he was fighting. This was great psychological warfare, and it worked to Yi's advantage, making the Japanese think his fleet was much larger. The top of the turtle vessel was flat, with numerous sharpened wooden spikes, making it look more like a porcupine than an overturned turtle. This was specifically planned to thwart the Japanese style of naval warfare. The Japanese would maneuver their vessel right alongside an enemy ship and then board the vessel with their sailors, who were experts at hand-to-hand combat. The Korean turtle ship was lower than the Japanese warship, but the spikes prevented the Japanese sailors from jumping on board since they would be impaled on the stakes. Meanwhile, the turtle's cannon would keep firing at the enemy's vessel, now directly alongside the Japanese vessel, hitting it below the water line, which caused it to sink quickly.

Yi also sought out the Japanese re-supply vessels, destroying them to prevent ammunition and other war materials from reaching the Japanese Army fighting in Korea. This was the same strategy the US Navy used: sinking the Japanese re-supply ships in the Pacific so that they couldn't reinforce their island and atoll soldiers, thus quickening the end of WW II. Yi also had the home stadium advantage, knowing where to lure Japanese vessels into low-water inlets and when the tides were out, so the Japanese vessels were beached and easily destroyed. Yi died fighting his last victory at Noryang in 1598, a single bullet piercing the chest of his chain-metal battle dress. His famous last words were: "The battle is at its height. Beat my war drums; do not announce my death (give my eldest son my Nike Wingtips)." Korea drove out the invaders and was free from Japan for three hundred years.

Admiral Yi remains vigilant on his cement ship's bridge, overlooking traffic jams and scurrying passers-by. But unlike the iconic scene at the end of "The Planet of the Apes", where Charleston Heston discovers the Statue of Liberty half-buried on the beach and cries out how stupid we were to carelessly throw away our freedom in a nuclear holocaust. I imagined a different scenario. If the North invaded again and destroyed Seoul, Admiral Yi would be buried in rubble, with only his face with its stern visage surviving, a stark beacon and rallying symbol that these new invaders must also be driven out.

Chapter 29: The Troubles

"What's Going On" - Marvin Gaye

ASCOM Depot's daily life mirrored daily life back in the States: there was a clear racial divide between blacks and whites, and sometimes conflicts erupted on the base or out in the Ville, just beyond the gates, in the dance clubs.

In late fall, there were a series of isolated events; a white GI was beaten up by a black over a Korean hostess, and this escalated the next day by a lone black being beaten up by a gang of whites. Now there were roving bands of blacks and whites, shouting racial slurs and fighting in the streets of Sinchon. Two GIs were injured so badly that they had to be taken to the ASCOM hospital.

These animosities were brought back to camp with more fights and angry standoffs. Fortress America closed its gates, no one in or out. The Master Sergeant tried to talk down this situation, but no one would listen to him. The climax came when someone "fragged" (threw) a live grenade into the Sergeant Major's quarters. He wasn't there, but then Martial Law was enacted on the Base. "Fragging" was a deeply troubling problem in Vietnam also. Idealistic Second Lieutenants, straight from West Point or ROTC, would have to implement dangerous or unrealistic missions that got men killed for no good reason. The classic example of this was "Hamburger Hill." Entire companies were ordered to take this hill, which was heavily fortified by the Viet Cong. After a hard-fought battle that saw many GIs killed and wounded, the hill was finally taken. But since there was no logistical support, our troops carried their dead and wounded back to their Home Base. In the night, the Viet Cong returned, recaptured the hill, and started mortaring the Base, killing many more GIs. The Higher Command again ordered that the Hill be taken, so more men were thrown into the fodder to recapture that goddamned hill. The next time a pointless order (from a grunt's point of view) was given by a green Second Lieutenant, just trying to follow his orders, his men responded with "Fuck you" and threw a grenade at the officer, killing him, and the mission was aborted at that point. The official cause of death for that poor officer was: "killed in the line of duty." This became an all too frequent occurrence, and whole sections of the frontline Infantry didn't send out "search and destroy" patrols because of the probable mutinies from battle-weary troops.

The Investigation of The Troubles

Meanwhile, back at the ranch, calmer tempers finally prevailed, and things returned to some semblance of normality. No one had been killed, but the whole incident had to be investigated and, of course, "Give it to Mikey, he'll do it"; the order came down that I would be the Investigative Officer, and I was given a few weeks to research and publish my findings. This was all new to me, but I took it very seriously. How did someone get a grenade? What was the riot's cause? Perceived Injustice? Lax Command? Misinformation? Lack of Communication? Racism? Or "all of the above".

I interviewed dozens of EMs, sergeants, officers, and even the Chaplain to make some sense of it all. The army was a microcosm of our society as a whole, but we saw ourselves as "better". The army was a large family, and everyone in that large family was equal and supposedly given a voice. The blacks I spoke to were angry; they got the shitty assignments and weren't promoted like the whites. Also, they had no real spokesperson who would address these issues. The whites saw the blacks as clannish, always keeping to themselves. There was little communication between the whites and blacks outside of their daily duties, and this led to rumors and men jumping to erroneous attitudes and erratic, irrational behavior.

I saw this firsthand in my hometown of Newark, New Jersey. On a hot summer night, two white cops pulled over a black cabbie for a broken taillight; this led to words and a confrontation, with the cabbie being physically beaten and bleeding for resisting arrest. Rumor quickly spread throughout the community that the cops had killed the black cabbie. This started the Newark Race Riots of 1967, where dozens of people were killed, and the city was in total chaos. During this time, my mother was working in a small Italian delicatessen in North Newark: she looked out of the store window and was startled when she saw a National Guard tank rolling down Broadway, the main street of Newark.

I tried to be even-handed in my evaluations but concluded that the command (and that included myself) needed to do a better job. My conclusions were as follows.

-All duty assignments and any additional duties should be transparent and shared equally by all of the soldiers on a rotating roster (available for everyone to see) of the qualified candidates for that duty.

-The command should have better responsibility and accountability in their weapons storage to prevent the theft of grenades and other deadly firearms.

-The blacks should get together and appoint someone they trusted to meet weekly with the Sergeant Major to voice their grievances.

-The Sergeant Major, in turn, should bring these problems up the chain-of-command for a solution.

-The officers should keep an "open door" and scrutinize the performance ratings and promotions to ensure fairness. They should counsel their soldiers on how to improve their performance when necessary (this was already being done, but with greater emphasis, and monthly, so that each soldier knew how he was performing and if any steps were needed to bring him up to speed, to qualify for the promotion he desired).

-There should be a roving Military Police (MP) presence in Sinchon. Although they had no authority and couldn't make any arrests, just their presence outside of the clubs would be a deterrent to name-calling and fights.

I submitted my findings, and the command did not like the picture it portrayed of the lax responsibilities concerning the control of the Arms Room, nor that they neglected to give the blacks an avenue to voice legitimate complaints; it made them look incompetent and out of touch with their soldiers to the high command in Yongsan. They did not publish my findings, nor did they implement most of my recommendations. They appointed another officer to conduct "further investigations", a whitewash of my investigation. I went back to my junkyard. My thanks for being the Investigative Officer was a career-killing Officer Efficiency Report. However, I promised myself that I would try to implement what I had written in my report with my own men.

Chapter 30: The Return of the Dragon Lady the Enigmatic Miss Lee (Part 2)

"You Ain't Goin' Nowhere" - Bob Dylan

I really didn't know what to expect, but Rick insisted that we go to the Apollo. For a brief moment, I felt like an awkward game contestant, "and behind Door Number 2 is a mystery woman who likes tall men with a good sense of humor." When we got there, he brought me over to see this "mystery woman". To my surprise, it was Miss Lee, the same one who had pulled the disappearing act six months before. However, now she was back, big as a house, maybe eight months pregnant, dressed in a traditional Korean kimono, chatting with friends. We sat down, and I asked her about the last eight months, "Where had she gone? Was she married? And what was the story with this expecting baby?"

Miss Lee told me she had married and went to the States with the GI to Georgia. He lived in a rundown trailer and had no job after leaving the Service. "We fought a lot, mostly over money. I thought everyone in America was rich. They all had cars, maybe two cars. But I had to do all the cooking, laundry, and house cleaning without any help. And I could only go to the beauty parlor once a week to get my hair and nails done. But what really bothered me was the loneliness. I was the only Korean in that small town, and the women folk were not very friendly to me. And what made matters worse was that I was pregnant; however, it wasn't his kid. And besides, my husband wasn't ready for fatherhood. He was always down at the town bar, drinking heavily, and I caught him flirting with the local girls. So, after sticking it out for seven months, I had enough of the "good life" in America and spent all of my savings to get back to Korea."

When she finished this sob story, she dropped the bombshell: "You know you are the father of my child." I thought back that I had met her in January and that she had disappeared in March. It was now late October, but she was also with her American husband for at least seven months in America and certainly more in Korea. To add additional ingredients to the potpourri stew, one of the bar girls told me that she had a Korean legal husband and had been dating still another American GI in Seoul before she left for the States with her husband. This was a real Korean Peyton Place, and I was being set up as the main cuckold in this melodrama. The real question was, what was she going to do now? The kid was due in November. She had no money and was living temporarily with a bar girlfriend in her cramped room in the Ville.

"Was it my kid?" Images kept racing through my mind. And if so, "Whatcha gonna do, boy?" And what about An Ju? We were very close now, and I really cared for her, but whether it was my kid or not, I felt responsible for its wellbeing and wanted to help Miss Lee, at least until the baby was born. I took her to dinner and gave her some money, and then we stayed together in a run-down hotel in Bup Yong. We didn't make love that night, but I held her in my arms until she fell asleep after crying about her life in America. Her baby was very active, and I felt the kicking as I held her. I saw her every day, giving her money for a Korean doctor's checkup and buying the food that she could cook at her friend's place. She was still very secretive about her former American husband and didn't even mention her current Korean husband. My feelings were unresolved, but I was determined to see her through the pregnancy. That was the least I owed her. My state of mind was all jumbled up. If it was my kid, do I marry her and take her back with me? Or do I pay for the child when I leave Korea? Or do I just run out, as countless other GIs did? I flashed back to the half-black Korean woman, Julie, who had pulled a knife on me. Her life was ruined. I also thought about the thousands of half-American-Vietnamese kids wandering the streets of Saigon, stealing or whoring, since they were not accepted by the Vietnamese or Americans. Would I, too, be responsible for ruining a young life? For the next two weeks, I avoided the Apollo, taking Miss Lee to smokey little clubs and out-of-the-way restaurants.

Then the inevitable happened: An Ju found me at the Green Door, sitting with her. I awkwardly invited her to sit for a drink and introduced her to Miss Lee. They briefly spoke in Korean; obviously, Miss Lee told her that I was with her and that she was having my baby. An Ju got up, turned to me, called me a few choice names, and stormed out angrily. I ran after her, trying to diffuse this situation, but everything I said just made her angrier. She accused me of being a two-timing son of a bitch; she never wanted to see me again. I returned to the table, finding Miss Lee with a sly, smiling smirk on her face.

The "Troubles" closed everything. I could not leave the base for two weeks. When I finally got out, Miss Lee delivered a baby girl. The baby was called Hwa Kun (she took the Korean husband's last name, Kun). Hwa was beautiful. Milk-white skin, long silky black hair, and radiant dark brown eyes: a perfectly healthy, purely Korean baby. When I saw Hwa, I was both saddened and relieved that I was not the father. Miss Lee saw the look in my eyes when I saw the baby and knew that she couldn't keep up the charade any longer. She said she was bringing the baby to her Korean husband. I gave her some money for baby clothes and for a doctor's check-up visit. I hailed her a taxi to take her and the baby to her new home. I never saw her again after that. I had also blown it with An Ju; I didn't blame her for not wanting to see me. I didn't know who I was. I had deserted a girl I cared for and threw it all away for some fantasy woman that strung me along as being the father of her child. I retreated to my room, not wanting to see anyone. Then I spent the next three weeks investigating the "Troubles"; after that, I would be out of the army in less than a month.

Chapter 31: "Children of the Dust" Amerasians in Korea and Southeast Asia

"My lovely flower of lily and rose.

Lest you never know

For your pure Eyes, Dies Butterfly.

So you can go beyond the sea without remorse."

Death scene aria (Tu Tu Piccolo Iddio) from "Madame Butterfly" when she ties and blindfolds her child and then kills herself, knowing that the child will be raised by his father and his new family in America.

Giacomo Puccini: "Madame Butterfly"

French Catholic Korean Orphanage 1910

The Korean and Vietnamese Wars left behind thousands of Amerasian children (Amerasians are the children of American servicemen and local national women). This "national shame" hit close to home for me because I was told by a Korean courtesan that I was the father of her child. As I had mentioned before, Koreans are very race-conscious, and Amerasians are not welcomed by the South Korean government nor the average Korean. Between 1955 and 1969, there were about forty thousand Amerasian children born in Korea. A majority of these were children of prostitutes, abandoned by their fathers and shunned by the Korean people. Amerasian children were taunted and ostracized by fellow Korean children.

Luckily because of the good relationship between the South Korean and US governments, most of these children were sent to orphanages in the US or adopted directly by caring parents in the US through Christian adoption agencies. The unfortunate few who remained in Korea were denied access to education, had limited job opportunities, and in the case of young girls, were recruited into prostitution to follow in their mother's occupation. They would start the unfortunate cycle again since that was the only job they could get.

The situation in Vietnam was much more complicated. The French controlled Vietnam from 1945 to 1954. During that time, French soldiers fathered twenty-six thousand French Asians. After their final defeat at Dien Bien Pu in 1954, the French left the country. However, before leaving, they granted French citizenship to all these children and evacuated them to France (Vive la France!).

During the Vietnam War, Americans fathered about thirty thousand children, and when we finally left Vietnam in April 1975, the vast majority of these children were left behind. Before the fall of South Vietnam, President Ford authorized "Operation Babylift", which was meant to rescue Amerasian orphans before the Viet Cong took over. At the time, there were fears of a massacre of these innocents. Tragically, the first plane carrying these orphans crashed, brought down by Viet Cong rockets, killing all 138 children aboard. However, the program continued until the airport shut down due to continuous heavy Viet Cong shelling. A total of three thousand three hundred orphans were airlifted out to safety. Two thousand went to the US, and thirteen hundred went to Canada, Europe, and Australia. The vast majority, about twenty-seven thousand children, were left behind, and they were in limbo. The new Vietnamese government didn't want these "American" children, and to complicate matters, there were no diplomatic relations with the US, so there was no negotiation to bring them home to the US.

These unwanted children were often abandoned by their mothers. Some ended up with grandparents; others ended up living on the streets. The Vietnamese closed the Catholic orphanages, and worried mothers burned any photographs and documents that showed that these children were Amerasians.

The Vietnamese have a saying: "Children without a father are like a home without a roof." These fatherless children were scorned by their fellow classmates, and many were illiterate in both Vietnamese and English. Amerasians were sent to rural farming work camps and reeducation camps along with family members if they had any family.

I blame the US government for not doing more to get these children out of Vietnam before the war was officially over. As a soldier, our credo is: "No soldier left behind". Here we had left tens of thousands of half Americans: "Children of Dust'" as the Vietnamese scornfully call them, without anywhere to turn.

The plight of the Amerasians in the Philippines was just as bad. During the Vietnam War, there were hundreds of thousands of airmen, sailors, and contractors stationed at military bases in the Philippines. These Americans fathered about twenty thousand Amerasians, mostly with Filipino prostitutes. These unwanted children suffered the same discrimination as the Vietnamese and Korean orphans. Yet these children, for the most part, spoke English and were raised as Americans. Yet they could not go to the US unless they were acknowledged by their fathers. These fathers were long gone to the States and had started new families of their own. This was in a country that the US once ruled and should have given preferential treatment to these forgotten American children.

If the American government wants to continue to wage wars in distant lands, then it must own up to its responsibilities to these innocent children. To use an Army term, these children are <u>not</u> "collateral damage" but a living testament of our involvement and our responsibility both on a personal, individual basis and as a collective humanitarian and governmental response. The time to act is now before these children are irrevocably damaged.

Presently the American forces are being pulled back from Asia. There are no bases in the Philippines or Thailand, and Korea is down to 28,000 service members. The Korean Economic

Miracle has thankfully given poor, uneducated women a choice between prostitution and jobs in factories, shops, and restaurants. Consequently, because of this, there will be very few Amerasians born of servicemen and local women.

The Amerasians in America are the last of a special distinctive race: soon they will be absorbed by the larger white, black, and Asian ethnic groups, and we Americans can conveniently forget that this national tragedy ever happened.

Postscript

In 1987 The American Homecoming Act was passed by Congress. This was written by Senator Mrazek from Connecticut. He had read about one crippled Amerasian living alone on the streets of Ho Chi Minh City (Saigon). He decided this abandonment of the Amerasians was a national shame and resolved to bring them all home to America. The Homecoming Act stated that if you could prove that you were Amerasian or even looked half Caucasian or half-black and were born between 1962 and 1975, you and your close relatives could come to the US from Vietnam, not as refugees but as immigrants. This act also included Thailand, Laos, and Cambodia, but not the Philippines. Overnight these children turned from "dust" to "gold". They were the instant "Get out of Vietnam" cards. Suddenly all of these children had dozens of close family members. There were numerous cases of fraud and fake certificates of parentage. A mother who had abandoned her child suddenly showed up and claimed her child. Street orphans had an instant loving family home with, of course, many relatives. The program eventually brought twenty-six thousand Amerasians and seventy-five thousand "relatives", many of whom abandoned their "child" as soon as they got to the States. The children, now in their early teens, were mostly illiterate and had no job skills. Many of these children turned to drugs, gangs, and petty crime. Many couldn't adjust to this new lifestyle with no job skills and felt that they fit in nowhere: neither here nor in Vietnam, and they committed suicide. Others were half-black Amerasians, and they were subject to the same discrimination that they had in Vietnam. However, there were countless "success" stories: young Amerasians becoming lawyers, authors, press secretaries, and engineers. There is an Amerasian "Help Association" in the US, founded by Amerasians to help other needy Amerasians and to assist in getting other left-behind Amerasians home to America. Most of these children desperately wanted to find their long-absent fathers. Unfortunately, for all of the Amerasians that came here, only about three percent actually found their fathers.

I believe that for all of its faults, the American Homecoming Act enabled these children to claim their rightful birthright and have a real chance of productive and happy life in the US, which wouldn't have been possible in Vietnam.

Chapter 32: What Does It All Mean? An Existential Conversation With Myself

She laughed. "It won't last. Nothing lasts. But I'm happy now."

"Happy," I muttered, trying to pin the word down. But it is one of those words, like Love, that I have never quite understood. Most people who deal in words don't have much faith in them, and I am no exception--especially the big ones like Happy and Love and Honest and Strong. They are too elusive and far too relative when you compare them to sharp, mean little words like Punk and Cheap and Phony. I feel at home with these because they're scrawny and easy to pin, but the big ones are tough, and it takes either a priest or a fool to use them with any confidence."

— **Hunter S. Thompson, The Rum Diary**

Soren Kierkegaard 1840

Soren Kierkegaard, speaking to a friend in a Copenhagen café, "You know Sven, they claim I am the father of "Existentialism". I swear by God that I never slept with that woman Philo. But now it's 'Either/Or': 'Either' I marry her 'Or' the Court will force me to pay child support. The thought of living with that bimbo causes me 'Fear and Trembling'. I know if I marry her, it will be 'A Sickness unto Death' for me. Oh, by the way, I know we Danes are eccentric, just look at me, but what kind of name is 'Existentialism' for a kid anyway? What do I know, it's all Greek to me?"

As I sat in my Quonset room night after night, Ms. Lee, An Ju and Hwa Yi, and many others flashed through my mind. Was I just a junkie needing a daily fuck as my fix? Why was I so obsessed with this constant need to find a girl, screw her and then move on to the next one? This wasn't the first time I got laid; I had girls in college and Germany that I cared for, even loved, and yet this was totally different. Why? Is it because of the vulnerability of the Korean girls or the peculiarly American love of the weak and the underdog? Many of the girls are soft-spoken and comforting. They are your understanding girlfriend, not just a floozy whore for one night in a seedy hotel.

Many of these young, enlisted kids were virgins. This was their first time away from home, and here they met a girl who was a glamorous movie star, prom queen, and wholesome girl next door, all rolled into one irresistible fantasy. They would do anything to keep this dream: spend all their wages, sell booze and cigarettes on the black market to get ready cash, or go AWOL (Absent Without Leave) just to be with her.

Being an officer, I made more money, so I didn't have to resort to these extremes. Yet I was just as obsessed as these young privates. Painstakingly, I realized that this whole scene was a community that I was an integral part of. Sure, you could take it as a sexual outlet: "Wham! Bam! Thank you, Ma'am!" but that grows old quickly. What you really want in a relationship is when you can give love and where you can get love in return. Were you fooling yourself? "Sure," said your mind, but not your heart.

When you first start with a girl, you are both lying. You want a long-term serious relationship, you tell her. She, for her own part sees you only as a monthly meal ticket but professes love. Then you start playing house; you come to her room every night, she cooks dinner while you complain about your hard-ass boss, and she comforts you. You meet the other girls in the house, and you talk about their joys and sorrows: Jody, who has been going with this one specialist for six months and is now going to the States with him. Penny, who had been going with this sergeant for eight months, just found out that he had left for Ft. Hood and didn't even say "goodbye." You empathize with their experiences; they make you their secret confidant. You bring your best buddy over to meet one of her friends in the house, and you wind up double-dating at restaurants and clubs. You celebrate their birthdays and take them on long weekend trips. You bring them to your base club and introduce them to your buddies as your girl. Slowly, almost imperceptibly, you begin believing the lie. You view this as the serious relationship that you were always hoping for. For her part, she sees that you are serious and that you will rescue her. Now she is determined not to screw this relationship up. She, too, believes in your sincerity. You buy her clothes, radios, and TVs; she models for you in her new outfit. Slowly, she starts to care for you or, at least, you want to believe this "fairy-tale" love.

I have a dentist friend, Mike, here on base, who was seeing a bar girl. He paid $800 to medically save this girl from complications from a botched abortion, and the baby wasn't even his! He is as kind and sensitive a person as I know; he believes that if he leaves Korea, she will commit suicide, and he may be right. Many of the bar girls in I-Corps up North can't make it down South when the camps close. Either they're too old, not pretty enough, or heartbroken when their yobo leaves for the States, many end up committing suicide. Mike is going to marry her, above all of our objections. This is his first "love", but if you can save just one person in this crazy world, then perhaps you can save yourself. Damn what everyone else thinks about this!

I fell into a similar pattern: some weekends, I wouldn't leave the hooch, watching Korean TV with her or observing her doing makeup for hours. She even looks gorgeous with her hair in curls; the cute way she stumbles, practicing English with some of the girls in the house. I order a huge buffet lunch for everyone to participate in, and we talk and laugh about the small things in our lives. I created my own version of the life that I wanted back home. I took financial responsibility for a pregnant girl that I didn't even love anymore and lost a girl that I really cared for. Now that I'm leaving Korea, I believe that I will miss this close-knit community most of all.

Did I take advantage of these girls, and did they do the same to me? Yes, but I bought the lie. I saw those women as ambitious, proud individuals trying their best to get ahead and leave this shitty life behind. I had become a willing participant in this world, and now I was alone, without a support system that gave me stability and a sense of belonging. This would take me a long time to recapture.

I was sure that this world would change, and Korea would become as rich as Japan. Then there would be opportunities for these uneducated girls to work as hairdressers, seamstresses, and department store clerks. They wouldn't have to become whores, and they would have their own lives, finding suitable husbands and raising families. For this fleeting moment, however, this was a fantasy life that I believed in with my whole heart. "If this ain't love, then don't wake me for the real thing."

Chapter 33: Rick Lewis

"Stand By Me" - Ben E. King

It was four days before I would leave the army, and I was in hiding, lost in a doldrum of self-pity and self-reflection. I was an almost father, a yobo that deserted his loving girlfriend, and a man who wistfully looks back at his time in Korea and asks himself, "How did I screw all of this up?"

Enter Rick stage left. Rick missed our camaraderie and was determined to cheer me up, "You look like shit. C'mon get ready - it's the last hurrah, and you're going to go out with a bang and not a whimper." He almost physically dragged me out of my quarters, and we went to the Green Door Club. Here he plied me with OBs, and we reminisced about our time together. Rick was one of the best friends I ever had, yet he, too, was at a crossroads. Should he stay in the army or go back to a life that offered him nothing?

Rick came from a small, conservative farming community in Indiana. He had just graduated from a small nearby college in Ohio when the draft called his number. However, he was smart and offered them a deal: if he could enroll in Officer Training School, he would volunteer for three years in the army. He got in and graduated near the top of his class; he got a logistics assignment ("you call, we stock, pull and haul") instead of the usual Infantry grunt job. During his Army career, he worked at large depots and forts and earned his First Lieutenant bar at Fort Hood. When it came time to go to the jungle, the jungle didn't need him. So, they sent him to Korea, where he arrived two months later than I did. Now in the next month, he had to decide, should he stay in or get out. He believed that the army was his family, he liked his job, and he was out to find himself, like most young people. Like myself, he was lucky not to be scarred by the horrors of Vietnam. He was thinking of extending in Korea for another thirteen months and then trying for an assignment in West Germany. He wanted a structure that would support his "wanderlust", and the army gave him this confidence, plus the money to enjoy it.

When I looked back at my time in the army, I realized that I learned more about life and people than I ever did in college. The soldiers and, especially, the officers that I met were hard-working (and hard-drinking), intelligent, idealistic, and cognizant of what was going on around them.

This is the "High Noon" of the American Empire. But already, the cracks are visible: a loss in Vietnam, racial strife, a failing education system, and loss of our industrial base and jobs due to foreign competition. People like Rick are the backbone of our country, the ones that do the dirty work to preserve what our American ideals really mean.

I thought how similar we were to the Roman Empire; the one leader that stands out wasn't Julius Caesar or Caesar Augustus, but Marcus Aurelius. He spent his whole life in the trenches – fighting the barbarians to keep the empire intact. In his heart, I'm sure he thought this was a losing cause; but in his "Meditations", we see a man who is committed to being true to himself. You are the Emperor, and it is your duty to fight against all obstacles. He was stoically willing to accept this heavy responsibility. I looked at Rick and the other fine officers I met, and they were a living embodiment of that ideal.

I looked at Rick's dilemma, and I thought, if you don't want to be a doctor, lawyer, or Indian chief and don't have a cushy job that you can slip into your father's shoes and run his business, the army is a good chance to make yourself a satisfying career. This may sound like a recruiting Sergeant, enticing naive farm boys with the idea that they would be the next Audie Murphy (the most decorated American soldier in World War II). Nor is this an advertising poster of a stern, a gray bewhiskered grandfather with a stars and stripes top hat, admonishing his children, "Your country needs you; Join the army." It is not! Being an officer is the hardest job I know – you make "life-or-death" decisions in a split second. If you make the wrong one, like Lieutenant Calley, you are court-martialed as a war criminal, and your life is finished. If you don't look out for your soldiers, there's a good chance you could get fragged for following ill-thought-out command orders blindly.

Rick and I were both sodden drunk, but I was sober enough to tell him that of all the soldiers and women, I would miss him the most. The Hardy Boys had their last adventure, and now he would have to carry on alone, supporting the clubs and businesswomen signally. We hugged goodbye and somehow managed to get back to base before curfew. Jim Carroll, a New York City actor, songwriter, and nightclub performer, wrote a song called "People Who Died", about his friends in New York City and how they died. There was one who was stabbed to death in a bar room fight. "Eddie, I miss you more than all the others. This song is for you. I salute you, my brother." That is how I feel about Rick.

Chapter 34: A Farewell to Arms

When Johnny comes marching home again, Hurrah, hurrah!
We'll give him a hearty welcome then. Hurrah, hurrah!
The men will cheer, the boys will shout,
The ladies, they will all turn out,
And we'll all feel gay when Johnny comes marching home.

"When Johnny comes Marching Home" - Patrick Gilmore, Union Army Bandmaster 1863

"But why think about that when all the golden lands ahead of you and all kinds of unforeseen events wait lurking to surprise you and make you glad you're alive to see?"
— Jack Kerouac, On the Road.

The morning sun shone brightly on the still-frosted rice fields as I walked out of the Personnel Office. I had just signed my last papers, telling the Personnel Specialist that I wouldn't need the one-way air ticket for home because I was getting out of the army in Korea and would see the rest of Asia before I returned to the States. So, after three years and one month, I was a free man. I had served God and country, and now I would see the Asian world firsthand as a true sojourner. I had saved a thousand in cash and twenty-five hundred dollars in traveler's cheques. Armed with my Pentax 35mm camera, thirty rolls of Kodak 35mm color and ten black and white rolls of film, and a duffle sausage-shaped bag that contained: a sleeping bag, five sets of underwear, two dress shirts, two pairs of jeans, a towel, toilet articles and a travel guide to Asia. I was ready to discover a new world.

Would I have adventures as memorable as Kerouac? Asia stands before me: the era of Conrad and Somerset Maugham has passed, and present war-torn Asia will also pass, but I will make my own Asia and record my impressions in words and photographs. It will change me too, hopefully for the better, but I will capture the Soul of Asia, if only for a fleeting moment in time. Move over, Byron and Shelly, step aside, Kerouac; let's get this party started!

The author goes "native" as he leaves the army and heads off for further adventures in Asia

Chapter 35: Babysan

B-A-B-Y - Carla Thomas

Babysan

It was two days before I was a free man. Rick had gone TDY to Tague, and I decided to spend the last night in the clubs. I went to the "Showboat", where no one knew me. I was nursing an OB when I spotted her sitting alone. She was a tall Korean girl, nice breasted, with long flowing, thick brown-black hair. She looked Hawaiian, with a large squarish face and flat cheekbones that radiated like a pudgy cherub, clearly out of place in this tawdry honky-tonk atmosphere. Her name was Kai Yi, but I called her Babysan, and this is her story.

Babysan came from a small farming village near Kunsan. She is the oldest girl in a large poor farming family. Her father doesn't work, and her mother roams the village doing different jobs: washing clothes, helping in the fields, and caring for children; she also has a younger mute brother. She said that often she had nothing to eat. She had left home about a month ago to look for work. She tried applying for work in factories, bus companies, and tailor shops since she was taught sewing at home. No one was hiring: a mamasan found her alone and crying in a bus station. The mamasan offered her a job and taught her the tricks of the trade.

The mamasan took her first to To-ko-ri, the ghost town where the Seventh Division used to play, but now there is almost nothing there. However, she met a Sergeant there and lost her cherry. After a week of little business, the mamasan packed up and brought her to Bup Yong Dong, where I found her. Babysan is still fresh and naively innocent, and I felt that I would give her anything to preserve this.

We went to her room. She was overly enthusiastic but didn't have the experience (or practice) to know how to make satisfying love. It was like a Deja vu to first-time sex with your sweetheart back home. Both of us eager virgins, fumbling in the dark, kissing hungrily, and thrusting our bodies against each other. Finding her vagina and attempting to consummate our excitement; she is tight, you are afraid you are hurting her, and pull back when she cries. You try again. She is still crying when you finally penetrate her. You are so pent up that you come too soon. You pull out, so you don't come in her, and it's over almost before it starts: both of us frustrated and disappointed at what was supposed to be a tender, memorable celebration of our feelings for each other.

I stayed in Babysan's room once I left the army. My flight to Japan was in five days. We spent these days living the high life, shopping in Seoul, and eating out every night. One night we had a special meal: fresh broiled fish, octopus, summer and winter kimchi (your breath could wilt flowers with this one), and copious glasses of champagne. This was "real" champagne, not the watered-down 7 UP strength that they served in the clubs. She would take a sip, sneeze, and then hold her head, saying she saw everything in double. She kept wanting more champagne, and I told her if she could walk a straight line, she could have another glass. Well, she couldn't. On either of the two lines, she was seeing.

We shopped in the high-end stores in downtown Seoul, and I bought her a fashionable aquamarine blue dress with matching platform shoes. As we walked along the main avenue, some young Korean students berated her for being with me, calling her a whore. I was livid with anger and chased one of them for two blocks, pushing aside bystanders, but I couldn't catch him.

Another afternoon, after more shopping, we stopped in a modernistic tea house. There were abstract sculptural pieces in the window, and the walls were decorated with avant-garde Korean artwork; in the middle of the floor was a Japanese wood dripping fountain, water flowing into a small fishpond filled with orange carp, surrounded by stone buddhas and lanterns. The tables were filled with young, fashionably dressed college girls, leisurely chatting and exuding an air of monied confidence. We sat down and ordered, and as I turned to speak with her, I was suddenly saddened.

Babysan's face was crimson with longing, desire, and envy: here was a life she would never have. Was it the money, the freedom, or the careless sophistication of these privileged young girls? She would always be on the outside looking in, like Fitzgerald's "worn shop girls, working late on Christmas Eve, selling clothes and perfumes they could never afford to rich young golden girls without a care in the world".

That despairing stare pierced me, yet I realized that I was the cause. I corrupted her and callously took advantage of her innocence. I must help this still innocent girl before she becomes the hardened pro or the crazed half-black woman that lashed out at the world and almost killed me. When we got back to her room, I asked her what she wanted to do to change her life – did she have a goal or plan to stop this businesswoman's life and move on? She said that her dream was to be a seamstress, to design and create beautiful clothes in the latest fashion. I had said goodbye to so many girls that I had cared for, but this time I was looking for some kind of absolution.

I asked her how much a good used sewing machine costs? She thought about US$30. I offered her a plan: I would give her the money for the sewing machine, another US$50. to pay off the mamasan for her month's rent, and US$70 to get home, where she could do piece work to sell or even apprentice to a dress shop. It would be difficult, long hours at little pay, but it would be her chance at a new beginning.

At first, she was surprised, then she smiled and ran over and kissed me. I gave her the money and wrote my parents' address, so she could tell me how she was doing in her "new" life. We made bittersweet love that night. In the morning, I left for the airport, and she gave me long hot kisses and a tearful farewell. I hoped she would follow through on this chance; at least she had a viable alternative to the club scene.

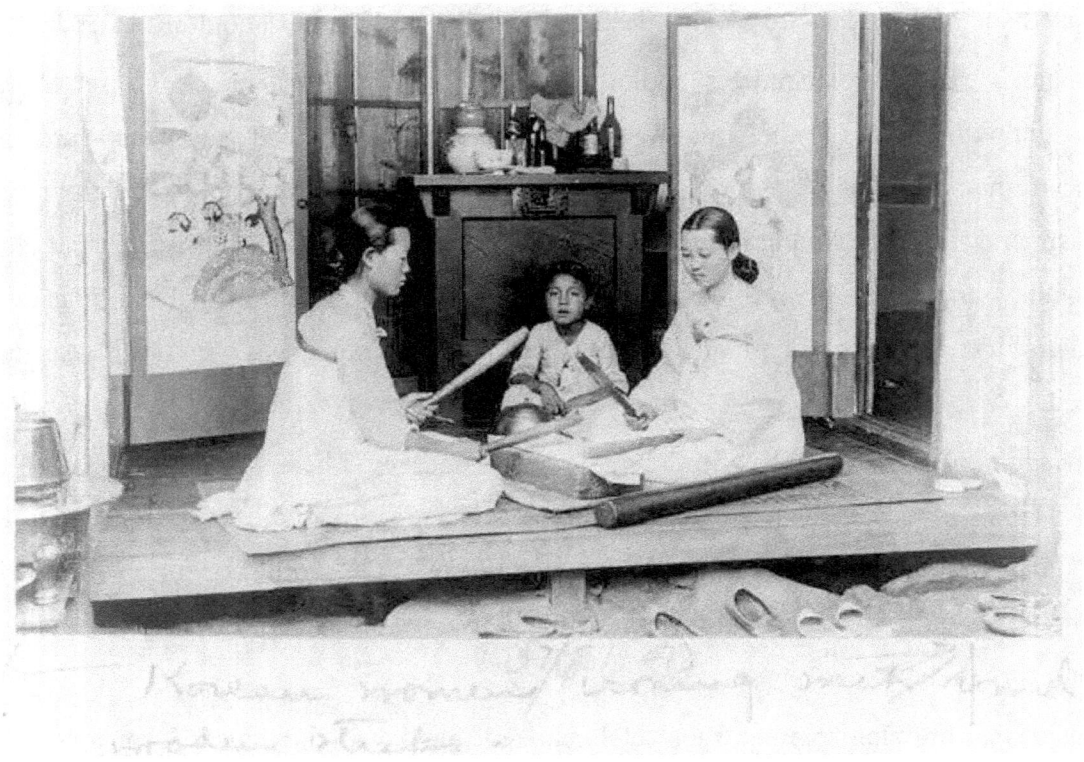

Korean women ironing with wood sticks 1905

"Beat Me Daddy, Eight to the Bar" The Andrew Sisters.

Japan: Home of Samurai, Sony, and Sake

Japanese mother with child 1900. This could be a poster advertising Puccini's "Madame Butterfly"

Chapter 36: Japan

"Sukiyaki" - Kyu Sakamoto

All I remember of this song was that I thought it was a Doo Wop song in a strange language

My plane landed in Fukkoko, at the southern end of the big island of Japan, and I was welcomed by balmy weather and big palm trees. What a change from the bone-chilling, windswept plains of Korea. My first impression was that everything was cleaner; wood replaced the cinder block cement of Korean homes and villages.

I have an ambivalent attitude toward the Japanese. I grew up with cheap Japanese toys, lousy little transistor radios, and cheap plastic toys: back home, it was said that the Japanese were not inventors but copiers of the West. On the other hand, I had a fine Japanese camera (Pentax), a Sony amplifier, speakers, and a turntable. Interestingly, their beer, Ashanti, was better tasting than Budweiser. (Hell! Good beer must be a watermark of a great civilization!)

In college, Japanese films were considered to be "artsy", and I had long, beer-sodden conversations about the inventiveness of "Rashomon". "Rashomon", tells the same story differently from four "eye-witnesses." Was the heroine raped trying to defend her honor, or was she just one randy girl? The viewer must puzzle this out for himself. Also, the medieval Japanese historical dramas with honorable Samurai, treacherous leaders, and endless dynastic warfare were masterpieces of psychological drama as well as spectacular cinema.

I wanted to learn more about this medieval warring period when the Japanese concepts of duty, honor, and loyalty were forged and tested in the heat of battle. I took a train to Osaka and visited Osaka castle, a multi-tiered fortress of one of the more successful warlord shoguns. It is now a beautiful museum with Samurai uniforms, helmets, and weaponry. History comes alive in those somber, wood-paneled, and colorful screened rooms. The world of warriors fighting to the death, yet showing mercy to their fallen foes, the life of a court princess, and the ritualized form of respect practiced by royalty and commoners alike.

Osaka Castle, now a museum

This contrasted strongly with how the Japanese fought a war in the twentieth century. The slaughter of thousands of innocent Chinese in Nanking, the killing of all American prisoners in the Pacific atoll fighting, the enslavement of thousands of Korean women to serve as prostitutes for the Japanese Army, and, of course, the sneak attack at Pearl Harbor. Yet now they are our friends; we oversaw and helped them rebuild into a strong industrial economy that has already captured the free Asian markets. Now they are duplicating this success in the American market with Honda motorcycles, Toyota cars, and Sony electronics. It surely is a Rising Sun for Japan, and that sun is cresting in the United States, with ominous reverberations on our own industrial base.

Could I discover what makes the Japanese tick? I didn't think so, but I can observe how the medieval concepts of duty and respect influenced the modern Japanese. I would start with their spiritual beliefs. This led me to Nara, a beautiful ancient temple city filled with parks and shrines. I found a traditional Japanese house/ hotel with paper screens that fronted a lovely garden with a Japanese stone fountain. The room was bare: a single scroll depicting a bird on a cherry tree branch, a tatami mat for sleeping, and, thank you, God, for a portable space heater (man's best friend on a winter night when he doesn't have a girl).

I visited the Buddhist temples and Shinto shrines – I knew a little about Buddhism, but Shinto was an indigenous Japanese religion practiced by the first inhabitants of Japan. Shinto revolves around "kami" (spirits), which can be human ancestors, picturesque places like waterfalls and groves of trees, powerful animals like the tiger, and deceased emperors. The temple shrines are built to please the kami, and they dwell in a small house model located in the Shrine. Kami have no form and are never pictured. Kami has been tied to the worship of the Emperor since the dominant kami, Amaterasu (Sun Goddess), gave birth to the first Emperor. Every Japanese home usually has a place where the kami of past ancestors can reside and be honored.

There are four Affirmations of Shinto, which don't sound like a religion, but a combination of the Sierra Club (love of nature), Good Housekeeping (family and tradition must be respected), Boy Scouts (physical cleanliness), and the Macy's Thanksgiving Day Parade (festivals must be participated in).

Most Japanese are both Shinto and Buddhist: They register births and get married in a Shinto temple, while they bury and honor the dead in a Buddhist temple because of their belief in the rebirth of souls.

Nara is a walker's city, with dozens of parks, ponds, and medieval architecture. Especially interesting was Nara Park, where there are thousands of tame deer running free and eager for handouts. This stems from the legend that the Japanese" kami "God Takemikazuchi favored Nara and came down to earth riding a white deer. Since then, the deer is considered a sacred animal and allowed to roam freely through the park.

The most memorable "shrine" is located a short distance away from Nara: the bronze Buddha of Kamakura. This giant stands over four stories high and dates from the 13th century. This is not your fat, jolly Buddha you see in every Chinese restaurant in New York; this Buddha has a stern visage, a man who achieved Nirvana (enlightenment) and displays an air of arrogant condensation for the masses below. It is this aloof gravitas that symbolized for me the face of Japan today. The Japanese had achieved their "economic miracle" (Nirvana), and they would now dominate the world with their "superior knowledge". Instead of building monasteries and temples, they are building Hondas and Nikons to proselytize this superior knowledge.

I observed the Buddhist ceremonies, the lighting of incense sticks, bespeaking respect for their ancestors, and the dronelike prayers of the priests. I also endured the endless "Hello, how are you?" and no other words of English from Japanese school kids in the temples.

I was also following world politics by getting the English newspapers that were available in every city. The Vietnam war was almost over, and it was clear that we had lost: a tremendous blow to our national psyche. The other big story was the Indo-Pakistan War over East Pakistan (now Bangladesh). It was the British failure of nerve that let India be partitioned into two Pakistans on either side of India that set the stage for this current bloodbath. Pakistan is a military dictatorship backed by the U. S. that ruthlessly suppressed any self-governance of East Pakistan. The Pakistan Army murdered thousands of unarmed Bengalis and dissolved the elected Bengal Assembly. All that the U. N. and the United States did was endless mouth words about Human Rights violations. The citizen-soldier Bengalis had few weapons and were no match for the well-trained Pakistan Army. Finally, India stepped in and invaded East Pakistan to stop the murders and free the country. While I was in Japan, the Indian Army had captured Dacca, the capital, effectively ending the war. They also helped the fledgling independent country with economic and military aid and then withdrew. This was in sharp contrast to our debacle in Vietnam, where we fought against a Peoples' Movement to reunite a war-torn country. In the end, the People's will triumphed over the world's largest military power. And no one saw the irony of cheering on the Indians for helping the Bengalis become independent while we Americans were responsible for the slaughter of hundreds of thousands of Vietnamese and American lives in a vain and misguided attempt at stopping a nationalist reunification movement that had been going on since 1945.

I left for Kyoto, the ancient Japanese capital, the site of the most famous temples in Japan and their magical gardens. Ryongi-Yu is a famous Zen temple that dates from the third century A. D. Zen monks spent hours each day trying to clear and calm their minds showing little outward emotion, directing thoughts and emotions inward in the attempt to achieve nirvana. Nirvana is the absence of the self or merging with the nothingness that frees them from the cycle of reincarnation. To help them achieve this supra-state of consciousness, they created gardens: forest gardens, running water gardens, and dry gardens. The dry gardens are what we call "Zen" gardens in the West.

Ryongi-Yu Garden in Kyoto

I had spent many hours in the Brooklyn Botanical Garden's recreation of a Japanese Tea House with a "contemplation" dry garden and was moved by the utter simplicity of the creation. At Ryongi-Yu, the large dry garden dates from the fourteenth century and consists of fifteen rocks of various sizes, some vertical, some horizontal, covered in moss on a large bed of finely ground, raked white gravel. The rocks were picked because of their beauty or functionality. The Japanese stole this gardening approach from the Chinese. On every scholar's desk in China, there was at least one naturally sculptural stone on a stand. And the Chinese created gardens from these fantastically shaped rocks. The Japanese now took this basic Chinese concept and transformed it into an abstract art form by combining patterns around the rocks with a special wooden rake. The temple garden at Ryongj- Yu is a public garden made for private contemplation; most Japanese house gardens are walled-in. They are an integral part of the house and are therefore private. Westerners view the garden and try to understand the meaning. Islands in a vast sea of sand (an abstract symbol of Japan) or a lioness with her cubs are just two of many interpretations. Well, congratulations! You just won the hotel on the boardwalk in Japanese Monopoly. Being a Zen garden, it can be anything, or it can be nothing. No interpretation is wrong!

This garden is only a tool that is helpful in achieving Nirvana. Like Christ's sojourn in the desert or Buddha's vigil under the pipal tree: it is a place of solitary quietude. When you view this garden, you are stripping away layers of everyday reality. You are shedding desires, cares, and sorrows; you are emptying your mind from the "maya", the illusion of the material world. The goal is merging with "Nothingness", and the Ryongi Yu Garden is the physical manifestation that your consciousness achieves when you achieve this Nirvana."

Here the idea of "maya" transforms nature into a symbolic, platonic idea of nature synthesized to its based geometric elements. You don't have to be a Zen monk or art critic to absorb the simplicity of design that envelops the mind in contemplating this serene art form. However, Ryongi-Yu Garden is arranged so that only fourteen rocks can be observed from any ground-level position. The fifteenth rock can only be seen when the observer has attained nirvana and can contemplate all of nature as one with the universal soul.

Many museums have Zen gardens; Brooklyn has a particularly beautiful one with an adjoining Tea House. If there is no Zen garden near you, create one. All you need is sand, rocks, and a rake. If you don't have a yard and live in a faceless high-rise or work in a claustrophobic cubical while typing on a computer for eight hours, you can buy a small, boxed Zen garden that comes with sand, pebbles, and a little wooden rake. You can spend your day arranging the rocks and raking different patterns in the sand. This will give you a brief moment to contemplate "nothingness" during your hectic day (unless, of course, that is an apt description of your daily work, then you might need a drink in place of your portable garden).

Tea Ceremony 19th century

I was privileged to witness a tea ceremony and what stood out here and in all of my Asian journeys was the importance of ritual: to perform the tea ceremony the right way, reading the text exactly and in the correct order, or the meaning is lost, and you have offended God. As with the Homeric epics, these rules and incantations were all orally transmitted by singer poets or priests, who spent their lives transmitting this oral transmission of ritual for future generations, exactly as it was practiced hundreds of years before it was transcribed into written language.

In Kyoto, I stayed again in a traditional Japanese-style inn: paper-screen enclosing a bare tatami room; this time too bare, I had to ask for a portable space heater, but the garden of the inn was spectacular. A small running brook cascaded into a Japanese fountain, which was filled with a bamboo stick that made a clacking sound when releasing the water. This was surrounded by moss-covered stones, low bush vegetation, and a small lichen-covered Buddha.

Kyoto is beautiful, with tree-shaded lanes with lovely houses, just like the Inn I stayed in, and small jewel-like temples and shrines at every corner. Perhaps this is the "maya" of the Japanese psyche that makes it difficult to achieve Nirvana.

Now I wanted to see the new Japan: the economic powerhouse that conquered Asia. For that, I had to go to Tokyo, the Big Noodle, and appropriately, I got there by riding the "Bullet" Train: sleek, modern, and comfortable. I sat back in my cushioned seat, observing the "under belly" of Japan: beautiful temples enveloped by suburban tracts, faceless steel, and concrete urban apartment blocks, dismembered autos lying discarded in high stacked junkyards, and an endless maze of T. V. antennae growing profusely from every house: an unkempt jungle of spindly steel run amuck.

Chapter 37: The Nambans Strike Back

As I was riding the Bullet Train to Tokyo, the train passed the port city of Nagasaki. For Americans, this "second" city to be atom-bombed meant the end of WW II. The American high command chose this city because it was a drab, heavily industrialized city. Religious and culturally artistic cities like Nara and Kyoto (as well as Heidelberg in Germany) were spared because of their symbolic and historical importance in the eyes of the Japanese people.

I thought this was ironic that Nagasaki was the first city in Japan to experience the Namban (Western barbarians) and the last city in Japan to be destroyed by these same barbarians. In the fifteenth and sixteenth centuries, Portuguese traders and missionaries were granted permission to use the port of Nagasaki for exchanging silks, spices, and ivory from Macau and Goa for Japanese silver.

Portuguese in Nagasaki by Kano Sanraku 17th century Japan

I remember being fascinated by two huge Japanese screens at the Freer Gallery of the Smithsonian in Washington. Against an all-gold background, these screens depicted a Portuguese Caravel vessel docking at Nagasaki. The Portuguese were depicted with long thin faces, large, exaggerated noses, and pencil mustaches, dressed in colorful billowing pantaloons and loose shirts, all wearing red stove-pipe hats. They walked around the port city, bearing exotic gifts, carrying "fire sticks" (arabesques), and accompanied by coal-black slaves. They are shown bargaining for Japanese goods; black-frocked Jesuits carried crosses and bibles, and even one Namban walking a leashed dog.

The Portuguese were remarkably successful in business as well as religion. They converted the local lords and masses of common people to the Catholic faith. The Jesuits set up religious schools and taught the Japanese Western-style painting with perspective, fore-shortening, and chiaroscuro. These newly taught painters produced religious icons of the Virgin and Child, based on the Buddhist goddess Guanyin (goddess of prosperity and fertility, usually carrying a child in her arms). These hybrid figures had chalk-white Japanese faces, almond-shaped yes, and were painted in High Court fashionable dress.

Christianity, however, posed a threat to the ruling Shogun families, undermining the Japanese moral codes and Shinto beliefs. The ruling Shogun banished Christianity, persecuted, and slaughtered thousands of Japanese Christians, and nineteen Jesuit priests were martyred in 1619. The Portuguese were expelled and forbidden to trade or proselytize with Japan. Three hundred years later, on August 9, 1945, an American B-29 bomber dropped the atom bomb and destroyed the city, killing seventy thousand people; the Namban had their karmic revenge.

A Japanese Virgin by an unknown Japanese Christian artist 17th century Nagasaki

Chapter 38: Samurai and the Evolving Concept of Bushido

"Butterfly" by Smile. dk

A lively bubble gum song about a love-struck girl looking for a real man, a samurai

Samurais have fascinated Westerners for hundreds of years. They have been compared to the Knights in the Age of Chivalry, the John Wayne/ Marlboro Man Western hero, and even the "Hog" outlaw biker. What makes them different from the "rugged individuals "of American myth is the Japanese concept of bushido (the Way of the Warrior).

The outward attributes of bushido are sincerity, frugality, loyalty, martial art skills (use of all types of weapons as well as the body), and honor until death ("seppuka", {ritual sword suicide} which will restore lost honor). The inward attributes are grounded in religion and moral code. The Confucian ideal of filial respect and loyalty to the family is transferred to the "daimyo" (feudal lord). Zen Buddhism teaches the Samurai how to empty his mind to achieve clarity, calmness, patience, and acceptance (of death). They were also literate, trusted advisors, wrote poetry, and performed the tea ceremony (It is a little difficult to imagine John Wayne going into a saloon and, instead of whiskey, asking for a pot of water and tea to perform the elaborate ceremony). When the medieval warring period ended, Samurai administered the estate for his lord and served the Royal Court as administrators and diplomats.

The rise of Japanese militarism in the early 20th century added a new twist to bushido: loyalty until death for the Emperor. Here the soldier sees war as a cleansing of the soul and death as the ultimate goal before any surrender. The Kamikaze suicide pilots were the fulfillment of this bushido.

Between 1937 and 1945, the Japanese murdered ten million unarmed civilians, the most atrocious were the Nanking China massacres and the Filipino wholesale killings of men, women, and children. These tragedies cannot be explained by bushido alone: it was blatant racism. The Japanese saw themselves as morally and racially superior, and these other Asians were sub-human, cowardly beings that did not know honor, and their deaths were of no consequence.

The Tokyo War Crimes Tribunal tried 28 high-ranking military and government officials: 7 were hanged, and the rest were given life imprisonment. Even more important were the lower-level tribunals all over Southeast Asia, where 984 were sentenced to death, 3000 given long prison terms, and over a thousand acquitted of crimes. The Japanese Emperor Hirohito was not tried because of fear of a Japanese uprising. He was, however, stripped of his powers and made a figurehead that endorsed the Japanese Occupation laws.

In the 1960s and '70s, bushido evolved again: it was no longer the Emperor but the corporation or bank that deserved respect and loyalty. This was the beginning of "Happy Harmony", where workers, bosses, bankers, and government officials joined in a web of multi-layered alliances based on trust, respect, loyalty, and profit. Close teamwork, handshake agreements, and broad consensus replaced individual initiatives to achieve the "Economic Miracle".

Bushido keeps evolving. Now, it is a self-help tool, an exercise/practice, and a philosophy like yoga. The principles of bushido are now useful to the ordinary person. They become a guide to train your mind and body to be aware of your potential and live life to the fullest.

A Samurai in the 1860s (photo by Felice Beato)

"Samo the Samurai is here to tell all you kids that you too can be a warrior like myself. All you have to do is buy my video "Samurai for Stupids" and repeat after me, "I pledge on my honor to the Emperor that I will be loyal to my father's company, save my money and only spend it on my new Samo Gucci Samurai outfit, go to the gym and work out with my team, no kicking below the belt. I will be the best: defeat is not an option (bring your sword to the big game: you know what to do if your team loses), practice my bows (watch out for sticking swords) to show respect, and study hard so I can get my lifetime job at the Toyota corporation, help the elderly cross busy streets, even if they don't want to cross, practice the tea ceremony with real tea, not bags, and I will not disgrace myself or my family performing hankey-pankey with the opposite (or same-sex) students, no matter how tempting they look in their cute school uniforms. "Now run off and play but remember not to cut off the heads of any animals you meet in the woods."

Chapter 39: "The Big Noodle"

Stepping out of the train to the nighttime street was like stepping into Times Square on steroids. Everywhere electric blinking lights, neon displays, and blindingly bright streetlights packed with the cacophony of screeching, honking taxi cabs. I felt like a naïve farm boy on my first trip to the big city.

I went to the Japan Tourist Board and got a cheap Japanese-style hotel. No, I didn't have to stay in the small businessman's hotel, where your room consists of a "morgue table" bed that you slide into the wall to sleep. My hotel featured a tatami mat for sleeping, with a generic wall screen and, of course, the ubiquitous space heater. The one bathroom was down the hall. Here I met my first Japanese: two drunk students on holiday from the university who were constantly exclaiming, "Fuck You! Excuse me, Sir!" They wanted to practice their smattering knowledge of English on me, so they took me with them to a live jazz club "Junk" in the Ginza (the entertainment district of Tokyo). The music sounded good, but the sake was even better. Soon we were thrown out for boisterous talking and laughing too loudly. We then stumbled around the Ginza and wound up in a noodle restaurant. The front window of the shop was decorated with fanciful plastic displays of noodle dishes, almost edible pop art. We ordered noodles and dumplings, all very tasty, and it gave me a chance to clear my head. Afterward, we walked around the Ginza to find another jazz coffee bar, where they knew other students. I finally found some Japanese students who could speak passable English. I quizzed them about university life. They said they were all going into business jobs at large companies and banks. They said that going to the university was a hard-won privilege, and they studied for long hours so that they would not dishonor their parents. They would join one company or bank and serve this establishment loyally all their working lives. They only knew America from the movies and translated books. I told them about college life, fraternity beer parties, and casual sex. They were shocked again, asking what my parents thought about all this foolishness. I tried to justify this frivolous lifestyle by telling them of the Vietnam War: the war that hung over every young man's head like an angel of death. I had high school and college classmates that were killed there, and our generation was going to enjoy life before we were hung on the meat rack of the Southeast Asian jungle.

They were very curious about drugs. At that time, I hadn't used drugs, but I knew a lot of young people in my college and hometown that did smoke marijuana. These students never used drugs; they looked upon marijuana smoking like we looked at heroin addiction. As far as causal sex goes, many had girlfriends, but they never had pre-marital sex. They would have sex only when they got married, after graduating and getting their lifetime job. Afterward, back in the hotel, I thought about how seriously these students approached life: they knew their place in society, and that single-mindedness was a major reason for their country's "economic miracle".

The next day I walked around Tokyo alone: absorbing, sponge-like, the mod clothing stores, blaring American Rock and Roll from every storefront; the small Japanese delicatessens, where they make the artistically tied boxed lunches, and the working-class bars frequented by old men, who brought their own bread and ordered curd soup and sake.

The street signs were only in Japanese; I felt like a Soviet tank commander trying to navigate the crooked streets of Prague after the students tore down the street signs during the Spring Revolution of 1967. Luckily, the subway stops were also written in English, and yes, I did get pushed into the subway car by an official train pusher during rush hour. I spent an hour on the subway, transferring three times, to get to the Tonawanda Fish Market, reputedly the largest fish market in the world. Like most of Tokyo, it was well lit and spotlessly clean. There were people haggling over prices, delivery trucks everywhere, and every kind of fish, including whale meat (the Japanese were the only major country still killing whales on a large scale for the ambergris, which they used to perfect perfume essences). The whale meat for sale was only an after-thought.

I was familiar with fish markets because my father worked as a chef at a famous seafood restaurant in New York City, right next to the Fulton Fish Market. Sometimes, I would go with him early in the morning when he bought fish from the market, small storefronts selling the fresh catch of the day. There were delivery trucks hastily loading fish for restaurants all up and down the East Coast. I distinctly remember the putrid smells of decaying fish and seeing the huge rats scurrying the back alleys under the IRT overhead subway line.

My Tokyo hotel was a mini-Chelsea hotel with all sorts of interesting foreigners. There I met a passionate American doctoral candidate working on his thesis. The thesis dealt with the ancient Japanese Noh drama and how such a static art form could command so much attention from the audience. I was incredibly lucky because he offered to take me to a performance. Briefly, Noh drama dates from the fourteenth century A. D. and is a frozen art form in that it has been performed in the same stylized manner for hundreds of years. There are only two actors: the lead, who sings a story based on folklore, and his foil/ sidekick. There is also a chorus that chants poetry and a four-piece orchestra with three different drums and a flute. There are only about 250 Noh dramas, and the cultivated audience knows most of them by heart. The actors are all-male, even if they play women's parts. What stands out are the elaborate costumes and the expressive masks worn by the two actors.

The drama I saw was: "Shuro Mono", about a ghost who bemoans his fate in the first act, and in the second act, he is a warrior defending his lord and reenacts how he was killed in battle. This is all done in a prescribed manner with motions, dances, and songs, which is all judged by how successfully he mimics the original fourteenth-century play. The chorus and orchestra add dramatic flourish, but it is the main actors that define the drama. According to the sixteenth-century playwright Zenobi, the actor must first imitate life, not exaggerate it. Second, if acted truthfully (i. e., correctly based on tradition), then every act and motion is beautiful. Lastly, if he becomes one with the role he plays, he enters a Zenlike trance, which reveals to him the sublime beauty of all nature merging with the godhead (Universal Soul).

Ah, but here is the rub: the would-be American professor is looking at Noh from a director's point of reference. Traditionally the main actors, chorus, and orchestra all rehearse their parts separately, meeting only once with the director before the actual performance. This is based on the medieval Japanese esthetic of "transience:" "one chance, one meeting." This professor really had his work to do, to get into the mind of the Noh director, who, at first glance, appears extraneous to the drama unfolding.

For this art form to survive for so long immediately speaks of the Japanese national identity. The Japanese see themselves as a "unique" society that does not accept foreigners. They may dress like Americans, eat MacDonald's hamburgers, and play Rock 'n Roll, but they define themselves by the old Japanese concepts of "beauty", "honor", "loyalty", and "respect."

Noh performance 1891 by Ogata Gekko

Chapter 40: General Douglas MacArthur and the Japanese Economic Miracle

General MacArthur 1945 in Manilla, Philippines

"I Won't Back Down" - Tom Petty

Whether you love or hate the man, this song defines him.

General Douglas MacArthur was the Head of the Supreme Command of the Allied Forces charged with rehabilitating Japan after the War. MacArthur was a modern-day Jean Jacques Rousseau with a "*tabla rassa*" to do anything he pleased to bring the country back on its feet.

MacArthur was an excellent administrator. He started by stripping the Emperor of all power, making him a figurehead that agreed to all the Allied Occupation laws. He set up a Parliamentary Democracy and prevented former high-ranking military officers and warmongering politicians from participating in this new government. He abolished the Japanese Armed Forces to prevent a resurgence of Japanese military rule by guaranteeing Japan's safety under the umbrella of a U. S. Defense Treaty. He instituted land reform, giving hundreds of thousands of tenant farmers their own small farms.

The biggest challenge he faced was the industrial revitalization. Japan's economy was dominated by huge conglomerates called "zaibatsu" in which banks and large companies crossed shared each other's stocks. This enabled companies to get loans easily and the government aided with lax monopoly laws, tax breaks, and low interest loans for "favored" industries. MacArthur started to dismantle this structure and build up a free trade Western Capitalist system. However, Japan's fledgling industries needed raw materials and markets to sell their products.

Then the Korean War started in 1950, and Japan became the arms and equipment Depot for the Allied war effort. More importantly, there was a change in strategy direct from Washington: Japan must become a bulwark against Chinese Communists abroad and local growing Communist sentiment within Japan. The breakup of the "zaibatsu" was stopped, and the Japanese were allowed to continue this monopolistic policy under a new name: "kuretsa." Large companies, banks, and the government all collaborated to ensure that companies got expansion loans from cross-sharing stocks, and the government continued the policy with "favored" industries by giving tax breaks. This was called horizontal "kuretsa." There was also a vertical "kuretsa", which linked suppliers of parts and machines to manufacturers like Toyota, Toshiba, and Nissan and finally to the distributors of these goods. This worked very well in the auto industry, where there were hundreds of small suppliers that sent parts to Honda and Toyota. Many of these small "kuretsa" companies had only handshake agreements with the big companies, while larger "kuretsa" suppliers were cross-sharing stocks with these big manufacturers. This was a monopoly to control prices, but it worked to build up industries. Japan now had the raw materials from the Korean War surpluses, and they had a market in free Asia and the United States for their products.

This was the beginning of the "economic miracle", and General MacArthur should get recognition for laying the groundwork for Japan's future prosperity. Unfortunately, he was relieved (rightly) for defying the President, and this has left a cloud over his reputation. I imagined President Truman telling MacArthur, "Put this in your pipe and smoke it: you're fired." But MacArthur and his team resurrected Japan without the millions that had to be poured into Europe under the Marshall Plan.

Chapter 41: Yukio Mishima

"Power and the Glory" - Phil Ochs

Yukio Mishima

Yukio Mishima was a tortured and enigmatic literary figure in post-WWII Japan. He was one of Japan's most successful and critically acclaimed novelists. One novel of his that I read, "Confessions of a Mask", deals with a sickly youth, Kacha, who fantasizes about homosexual relations but is too ashamed to admit it, especially in Imperial "masculine" Japan. He keeps these feelings hidden; this is his "mask.". Kacha also believes that everyone hides their true feelings – life has become a "reluctant masquerade". As he grows older, he tries to fall in love with a girl, Sonoko, but his forbidden homosexuality prevents him from any love with the opposite sex.

Many critics see this novel as autobiographical, claiming Mishima to be a homosexual. Whether he was or not, the portrait of the self-tortured Kacha is a sensitive, insightful "bildungsroman", capturing all of the confused yearnings of an outsider wanting to fit into the traditional martial pre-war ethic of Japan.

His later novels and stories extol the virtues of the quasi-military, religious society of the 1930s and 40s. He believed that the Emperor is divine, not in a strictly religious sense, but in a traditional cultural sense: The Emperor is the living essence of Japan. Similarly, Japan had been emasculated by the Occupation Forces: The army was disbanded and became an internal Police Force. Mishima wanted the army to be strong again. Not so much for the external warlike expansion but as a return to the warrior code of honor and duty as exemplified by the Samurai. Mishima described himself in terms of bushido (way of the warrior). A man of bushido has a firm sense of self-respect, takes responsibility for his actions, and sacrifices himself to embody that responsibility.

Mishima looked at the Nationalist Corporate/Bank takeover of Japanese society and felt that everything that made Japan unique was being lost in the hedonistic pursuit of money. He saw the Japanese as losing their National Essence, "kokuti." They would soon become 'rootless' people. "Soon Japan will vanish altogether. In its place, all that will remain is an inorganic, empty, neutrally-drab 'society', a wealthy scheming economic giant in the corner of the Far East." (From Mishima's "A Japanese Essay")

You can see what he is talking about when you look at the typical Japanese "Salary Man" (office worker). He works 12-14 hours per day, dedicating his life to the "Corporate god" of Sony or Honda, which will keep him employed for the rest of his life, while he neglects his family, religious practices, and social obligations. Mishima fervently believed that beauty is an art, and the current Japanese society had lost its values: lack of personality of the individual is reflected in all classes of Japanese society, and this is coupled with a rigid culture of uniformity and dulling sameness.

In many ways, Mishima was a politically naive dilettante. His writings extolled a way of life that had been crushed by the Japanese WW II defeat. Ironically, what Mishima failed to see was that Japan would achieve victory in this "new" war, not of guns and bombs, but of Sony TVs and Honda cars in every home in Asia and America. The Rising Suns of electronics and automobiles would conquer the West more completely and more profitably than any military conquest.

On the 25th of November 1970, there occurred the "Mishima Incident". Mishima had founded a civilian militia, and he and four other ultra-Nationalists took over a military building in Tokyo. Mishima addressed the elite Japanese Forces, proclaiming a coup d'etat: the army would rise up and dissolve the Japanese Peacetime Constitution. He wanted to restore the army's glory and revive the ancient Samurai's code of honor, glory, and hari-kari (ritual death by sword). Instead of rallying to his cause, the army leaders laughed and mocked him.

Mishima had no well-thought-out plan for this revolt, and when he was publicly humiliated, he committed hara-kari, along with his followers. This symbolic form of death was more of an act of "public spectacle" than the duty-bound actions of a defeated Samurai. He chose a "spectacular' death, not to assuage honor but as a symbolic gesture to encourage the return of medieval Japanese values and culture. In the future, Mishima will be judged on his literary works, not by his death, just as Hemingway will be remembered for his great novels and not his ignominious suicide. Hemingway chose death because of his physical disintegration; Mishima chose death because of his society's disintegration.

Chapter 42: Kabuki

Kabuki play in 1858 Edo (Tokyo) by Toyokuni Utagawa III

I first learned of kabuki from the woodblock prints of Toshuai Sharau (Chapter 46 describes this artist in detail). Many of the prints looked like vaudeville actors from the heyday of the Yiddish theater on the Lower East Side with their exaggerated facial expressions and comedic gestures. In the Yiddish plays, song, dance, humor, and florid dramatic monologues were as important as the storyline of the plot. This was a theater for the common man, just like Shakespeare's plays were attended by the lower classes that demanded plays with comedy, blood and guts, and broad characterizations of the principal actors.

Kabuki Theater follows in this grand tradition: a gaudy vaudeville of song and dance, historical and dramatic plays of everyday life. Kabuki goes back hundreds of years. It first started as a showcase for beautiful courtesans, who displayed their talents and strutted their wares to willing customers. Okuni was a famous courtesan who staged a song and dance routine with other courtesans while she parodied Buddhist prayers for the play segment. This burlesque review resulted in shouting and shoving, and fights among the would-be suitors for the ladies' hand. The authorities reacted, banning women and replacing them with young boys. This resulted in the same mayhem with a totally different set of suitors. Again, the authorities stepped in, demanding only mature males be Kabuki actors, which continues to this day.

The playwright Chishingure wrote Kabuki historical dramas. The most famous, "Forty-seven Ronin" tells the tale of Samurais avenging the Ruler who forced their Lord to commit hari-kari. Chikamatsu Monzaemon wrote romantic tragedies of lover suicides, always a great crowd-pleaser (Pass the Kleenex and popcorn).

Kabuki performances lasted all day. People either leave or have their lunch or dinner brought in. The performance starts with a historical play; then there is a long song and dance interlude and finally a domestic everyday life play.

Kabuki is all about the acting – plot or drama takes a back seat to the audience's favorites, who interact and address their enthusiastic fans. Many times, an actor will perform a favorite soliloquy or dramatic piece that has absolutely nothing to do with the unfolding drama, just to show off his acting skills. During the plays, the actors "ham-it-up" with bold poses and exaggerated facial features. Kabuki actors all have stage names, and there are three or four generations of family Kabuki actors, forming a dynasty like the Barrymores or Fairbanks in American movies. When an actor dons a stage name, he must live up to his namesake – he will be judged and compared to the style, spirit, and skill of his predecessor.

Kabuki started as a people's theater: the merchants, townspeople, and laborers were the audience; the nobility despised these "commoner" plays. The name "Kabuki" says it all: "Ka" (song) "bu" (dance) "ki" (skill).

Kabuki attendees were loud, boisterous, and enthusiastic about their favorites, similar to the Globe audiences of Elizabethan drama or the newly arrived Jewish immigrants on the Lower East Side, applauding the "schmaltz" Yiddish plays. Kabuki plays could be highbrow classics, but still, the players needed to spice up these dramas with bloodshed, comedic interludes, and dance and song or feature popular actors.

Today Kabuki has become "classical" theatre-like Shakespeare's plays. It, unfortunately, has also become a "fossil" theatre, where actors strive to mimic and copy the exact style and dramatic pose of famed historical actors. All spontaneity has been lost in this slavish adherence to established canon norms that were set centuries ago.

Chapter 43: "Who'll Stop the Rain?"

Monsoon sheets, straight woodblock lines from Hokusai, deluge the Ginza, flushing away the fashionable denizens and obsessive pachinko players.

Kamikaze gusts dispel fast-food effluences, as with Kublai Khan of yore.

Soaked seagulls huddle together, cooing softly.

Sky and pavement mimic each other in graduations of gray

Neon and blinking electric signs perform in an empty theatre - the show must go on!

Nearby, a yellow ribbon of empty taxis slinks like an unfurled python, waiting to ponce at first motion.

The chonin (shopkeeper) glares at the still streets; his plastic noodle art fails to attract

All is eerily quiet on the Eastern front

A child in a red coat splashes puddles, laughing.

Chapter 44: Yoshiwara

"Streets of Baltimore" - Bobby Bare

The lure of bright lights and the 'good life" destroyed the marriage of a young farm couple.

The Yoshiwara was the pleasure district of seventeenth- and eighteenth-century Edo (Tokyo), the predecessor of the nineteenth/twentieth century Ginza. This was where all the geishas and courtesans lived, along with scores of restaurants, bars, and gaming parlors.

For autocratic, socially stratified Japanese society, this district was a democratic oasis. The customers were drawn from all classes and ranks of society - if you had money, you could enjoy the pleasures. There were no swords or palanquins allowed inside this district. The highbred nobleman and samurai rubbed elbows with vulgar sailors and laborers in the bars and houses of pleasure. The women sat demurely at street level, and for the right price, you could have the night of your dreams. If you think this resembles the girls in the windows in Amsterdam's Red-Light District, you're right. "How much is that girlie in the window, the one with the wavy hair? I do hope that girlie is for sale". The Edo City administration listened to eyewitness reports of how Hamburg handled their sailors, whores, and bars and created this district, patterned after the European model (although there were no scantily clad, overweight Brunhildas wrestling in the mud, like in St. Pauli (the harbor/bar district of Hamburg); the Japanese did have scantily clad, over-weight male Sumo wrestling on mats, which gave the brunhildas a run for the money).

Edo was a city on the move, and young, single men came from the provinces to make their fortune here. Merchants, artisans, teachers, sailors, and other working-class people made good money but had nothing to spend it on. This nouveau riche were prohibited from buying large houses and dressing in fancy clothes due to the social code of Japan, so they spent it on pleasure. Similarly, the rich daimyo (landowner lord) and Court nobles were also prohibited from engaging in money-making enterprises by the same strict code. They, too, could only spend their money on pleasure. The governing Edo fathers also liked this arrangement because it gave them huge tax revenues from the pleasure houses, bars, and restaurants.

The girls were from all classes: the past-her-prime whore, who gave the cheap "quickie" to the commoners for a small price, to the refined geishas, who charged huge amounts of money because they offered witty conversation, dressed in the fanciest silk kimonos, and played a musical instrument. "I play the Pippa (Japanese lute) before I play with your little Pippa." These geishas had their pick of rich nobles, government officials, and samurai (Hey! Take a number and get in line). But it wasn't only money these exclusive courtesans required: the most accomplished geisha chose their suitors based on their lively wit and conversation, their suitors' Beau Brummel clothes, and polite manners.

The flame that burns bright burns twice as fast: by the time these geishas were in their late twenties, their career was over. Most of the older geisha became street walkers, carrying their bedding on their backs and doing hurried tricks under Edo bridges at night.

The Japanese poet-monk Saigyo (1118-1190 AD) gave a presciently fitting eulogy for these older geishas:

"Unknown and unadorned, even I live on in this world.

Why do these cherries then pass away?

So heartlessly from the sight of admiring crowds."

Yoshiwara prostitutes in the early 1900s

Chapter 45: Storyville

"House of the Rising Sun" - The Animals

"A Woman of Storyville" photographed by E.J. Bellocq from his "Storyville Portraits"

The Floating World of geishas and courtesans had its counterpart in America in New Orleans' Storyville. For a brief 20 years, 1897 - 1917, Storyville was the Shangri-la of prostitution. A New Orleans legislator, Councilman Story, regulated prostitution to a single thirty-eight block area in the city. Here were the bars, dancehalls, restaurants, and houses of prostitution, a self-contained city within a city. There were even "Blue Books" published annually at 25 cents a copy. These books were a pictorial guide to the various houses of prostitution, with street locations and maps. House pictures, both interior and exterior, lists of "services" rendered, typical prices from the lowest basement "cribs" at 50 cents a girl to the posh Basin Street mansions at ten dollars and up a girl. There was even a "stable listing" of women at each establishment.

The most exclusive and lavish house was Mahogany Hall, a marble four-story townhouse with a stained-glass fan window over the entrance that led to five parlors and fifteen private bedrooms, all with hot and cold running water baths, fancy chandeliers, potted ferns, and posh Victorian furniture. The amazing detail about this house was that the owner, Lulu White, and most of her forty girls were "octaroon" (racially one-quarter black).

The girls would sit primly in the parlors, where well-healed businessmen and tourists would "walk on the wild side", pick their beauty, be wined and dined, and entertained by musicians like the piano ragtime maestro, Jelly Roll Morton (blacks were not allowed into the houses of prostitution except as cooks, servants, and musicians) and spend the night in the lap of luxurious sensuality.

Storyville was where jazz was born. Buddy Bolden, a black saxophonist, created an improvised version of ragtime, adding black blues riffs and melodies from African Baptist Church Gospel Hymns, all stirred together in a pot to create a musical gumbo called jazz. Louis Armstrong, King Oliver, and the afore-mentioned Buddy Bolden played in these houses as dinnertime entertainment. Mahogany House was even glorified by a swing song: "Mahogany Hall Stomp", which Louis Armstrong performed to great acclaim.

Like Utamaro immortalizing the lives of geishas in woodblock prints, Storyville had a native Creole photographer, E. Bellocq, who glorified the prostitutes in their working houses. His grainy prints show the carefree "live-for-the-moment" attitude and camaraderie of these women of the night. Most of his photographs were of totally nude women, laughing and cavorting in luxurious surroundings.

This golden heyday was closed by the U S Navy when America entered WWI in 1917, ostensibly to protect the sailors from venereal diseases. The houses were torn down, and prostitution fell under the cruel control of organized crime. Today Storyville's site is a run-down housing complex.

Chapter 46: The Floating World

"Living only for the moment,

turning our full attentions to the pleasures of the moon, the snow, the cherry blossoms, and maple leaves:

singing songs, drinking wine, diverting ourselves in just floating;

caring not a wit for the pauperism staring us in the face,

refusing to be disheartened, like a gourd floating along with the river current: This is what we call 'The Floating World'."

- Anonymous Seventeenth Century Japanese poet

Japanese woodblock prints (Ukijo-e) were created for the working class: they served as fashion magazines for the latest designs in women's couture; illustrated scenes of nature; caricatured leading personalities and fanciful Western merchants, and even painted graphic primers for sexual positions. They were mass-produced, cheap, avidly popular with the working classes, despised by the upper classes, and eminently disposable. The West first learned about Japanese woodblock prints when they were used as wrapping paper for safely shipping Japanese ceramics.

While I was in Tokyo, I usually wandered into Japanese bookstores – I don't understand Japanese, but I spent hours looking at the beautifully produced Japanese art books. Three artists stand out; these three took Ukijo-e from common place illustration to extraordinary masterpieces of fine art.

The first was Kitagawa Utamaro (1753-1806 A.D.). Utamaro is famous for his depictions of geishas and fashionable ladies strolling the Ginza, the pleasure district of Edo (Tokyo). He painted women in their toilets, walking with their maids, sitting under cherry trees, and even having sex. He was in love with beautiful, young, fashionably dressed women - the Richard Avedon of his day.

His prints created the Japanese ideal of feminine beauty: porcelain white skin, high pencil eyebrows, small slit almond eyes, full rounded cheeks, straight longish nose, small kiss-button mouth, set in an elongated chin, and coiffured hair in an elaborate bun. This stereotypical face was set on a graceful swan-like neck.

Kitawaga Utamaro: Woman Wiping Sweat 1798

Beauty leads to satire in the next artist: Toshusai Sharau. This enigmatic artist produced all of his work in one the year 1794-1795 A. D. His world was the Kabuki theater actors, and he portrayed them in satirical caricature.

Sharaku was thought to be a Kabuki actor because he was able to paint intimate close-ups of 136 actors. In Kabuki, the actor's role becomes the actor's personality, and audiences judge him on how well he fits into the traditional fixed character. Tradition and not innovation are the actor's goal. In "Otani Oniji III as Edokei", we see a character as frightfully comical as Bela Lugosi's Dracula. The furrowed brow, elongated hawk nose, menacingly curved mouth, and outstretched, grasping, malformed sticklike hands portray not a tragic figure but a laughable evil.

"Otani Oniji III as Edokei" by Sharaku

Sharaku's prints were never popular; the people didn't want their stage heroes denigrated and made fun of.

The last great print maker, Kanagawa Hokusai (1760-1849 A. D.), was primarily a landscape painter. His "Thirty-six Views of Mount Fuji" convey the power of Nature transformed into a mythical vision. Mt. Fuji becomes the Shinto Heaven - unobtainable and unreachable: Nature is pantheistic, portrayed in supra-saturated colors. The effect is like seeing a day-glow poster under a black light for the first time in your life. Here nature dominates man, presenting surreal obstacles, like the clawing wave, preventing him from reaching the dazzling white Heaven of Mt. Fuji.

Katsushika Hokusai: The Great Wave off Kanagawa 1830

The most famous Ukiyo-e and a masterpiece of world art.

"The Lantern Ghost Oiwa" from a 'Hundred Ghost Tales' by Hokusai

The ghost Oiwa shows Hokusai's sense of humor: this ghost would be afraid of his own shadow, a mournful Casper kind of ghost that wouldn't frighten children. However, his artistry stands out: we can immediately visualize what the living person was like through this caricature portrait.

All three artists chronicled their times: from the pleasure quarter to actor caricatures to magical realism landscapes. Japan was a country on the cusp of modernity, but the world these artists portrayed lives on, frozen music of a song long forgotten.

Chapter 47: The Japanese Screen: A Metaphor for Religion and Life

A welcome oasis in a sea of neon, electric lights, and blinding glass skyscrapers is the Tokyo National Museum. Everything that you want to know about Japan can be experienced here. After four hours of viewing, my senses were overwhelmed ("I thought of Gary Larsen's Far Side cartoon where the student wants to go home because he cannot learn anymore, his brain is filled to capacity"). I sat down on a bench, staring straight at a stunning masterpiece by Kano Ectoku (1543-1590 A. D.): an eight-paneled, gold background screen of clouds dominated by a cypress tree coming alive before you. Its branches claw their way to reach all eight panels. It is the living colors that are the cypress: the luminescent almond-brown: the trunk and thrusting branches; the black: shadows on the gnarled branches; the sponge green: the moss; the grey-green: the leaves swaying gently in the breeze. The gold clouds break to reveal a single mountain, a barren mass of inanimate rock, contrasted with the pantheistic cypress.

Japanese screens were used in dark interiors; to see this burst of living color must have been a religious experience, akin to the illiterate medieval peasant entering the cavernous darkness of the gothic cathedral and seeing Christ and angels illuminate the church with shimmering blue and blood red-stained glass. God as pure living color!

"Cypress Tree" by Kano Eitoku 1590

A second two-panel color screen, "White Prunus (plum) In the Spring" by Ogata Korin (1650-1716 A. D.), sets a totally different mood. Here you have the delicate green-black branches of a lightly flowering plum, dipping into a river of swirling stylized waves, squirming and curling as a bed of worms, uncovered while gardening. The delicate, refined branches with their blossoms falling into the frothing, amniotic cauldron of primordial energy: beauty swallowed by rawness. The swirling tendrils of waves served as an inspiration for European Art Nouveau artists in the nineteenth century. They copied these whiplash curls to create a masterpiece like Hector Grimaud's Paris Metro entrance.

Red and White Prunus (Plum) in the Spring" by Ogata Korin

Hector Grimaud's Paris Metro Entrance to the Place de la Bastille, which was demolished in 1962 (Photo postcard)

The last screen that deeply impressed me was a simple black monochrome on white paper of pine trees by Hasegawa Tohaku (1539-1610 A.D). "Pine Wood" is a pair of six-panel screens depicting pine trees with no foreground or background, just the trees enveloped in a foggy mist. The mist covers the pines in graduations of light from gray to black, blurring, shadowing, and hiding the trees. Viewing this, your mood becomes one of contemplation: the eye is mesmerized by abstract images of shadow, lightness, and darkness. The pine trees as a Zen symbol of life's vicissitudes. Starting out as strong, solid, and well-defined, symbolic of the peak of manhood, only to be enveloped by the grey clouds of doubt and nostalgic feelings in a poetic, mystical atmosphere of old age. The pines express the vagaries and intangibilities of life. You are thrust into this netherworld, where youthful hopes and dreams are lost in this dream state of grey compromise. This is a world of simple everyday reality: pine trees enveloped in a fog, yet the deeper meaning is unfathomable, as is the Zen concept of God.

"Pine Wood" by Hasegawa Tohaku

Chapter 48: The Swiss Who Came Down From the Mountain

"Every Breathe You Take" - The Police

In my last days in Japan, I was wandering around the Ginza looking for a sake joint to eat lunch. ("Show me the way to the next whiskey bar, Oh don't ask why": The Doors). I found a small pub in a back alley, and there happened to be a Western foreigner eating his lunch there also. I struck up a conversation with this Swiss German, Rudolf Eisenwehr, who was a manager at an international pharmaceutical company. He was medium built, about 5'10", with fine features: high cheekbones, straight nose, piercing gray-blue eyes, and short-cropped blond hair. He looked to be in his mid-30s and seemed eager for conversation, speaking Oxford English with the musical lilt of a Swiss-German accent. He had been in Japan for five years, spoke Japanese fluently, and even married a Japanese woman, yet he is still considered to be an "outsider" in this society. We talked for hours, fueled by endless bottles of warm sake.

"Japan," he said, "is a closed, homogeneous society; a society built on a network of close spatial relationships built up over generations. On a mini scale, there was the myriad collection of small tool shops that supplied parts for Sony and Honda on a handshake only agreements or, on a macro scale, the collusion of big banks, government, and huge industrial companies, that crafted fiscal policies and easy loans to build the 'economic miracle.' It was this personal loyalty and the sense of not 'rocking the boat' that held the Japanese together. On a professional level, the decision-making process was always a group product. There was an initiative, but it was channeled through the group, always showing respect to the supervisor by giving "suggestions" rather than solutions. On a personal level, the sense of "fitting in" was based on a core system of ritualized etiquette and unspoken emotional restraint. As in the Noh drama, where an eye twitch could trigger the catharsis of a deep-felt emotion, so with his relatives and coworkers, this innate 'restraint of feeling' closed him off from belonging to the Japanese 'superior' society."

I told him about my encounter with the university student, and we both agreed that the universities were producing the next generation of loyal automatons who knew their place in society: filling the desired niches of respect for parents and absolute loyalty to companies with their lifetime tenure. I listened intently. He was pouring out his heart to a passing stranger; the loneliness he felt must have been overwhelming. I tried to imagine the personal relationship with his wife. The Japanese, like the Koreans, were extremely racial, and this prejudice must have affected his intimacy with a traditionally-minded Japanese woman.

When a westerner marries, each partner sees themselves as equal in the relationship: love and intimacy are shared openly, without any restraints.

Japanese women are outwardly subservient to their husbands, but inwardly they control the household. Traditionally, marriages were arranged by parents, and intimacy and love develop slowly, each partner knowing their role in the relationship. This emotional restraint that Rudolf felt at work must have been experienced in his home life. Was he "A Stranger in a Strange Land" there too? I reflected on my own experiences with Korean women: I projected on them love and protection, but was I just a misogynistic meal ticket in their eyes, even after months of intimacy?

I said goodbye to Rudolf, leaving him as he nursed a last bottle of sake. He looked relieved as if he had just left the confession booth after baring his soul (now say three Hail Sonys, you are absolved, but remember Sony is watching you).

As I stumbled out of the bar into the late afternoon sun, I thought I had learned more about the Japanese this afternoon than I had in reading any books or talking with any Japanese people about their own culture.

Chapter 49: Yoko Ono

"Hold On" - John Lennon/Plastic Ono Band

Yoko Ono and John Lennon in 1969

While riding on the subway back to my hotel, I thought of Rudolf and his wife, Miko, and the gulf between Eastern and Western cultures. This "restraint of emotion" that typifies a traditional Japanese marriage is totally alien to what we expect in a relationship. We want to know everything about the person we love, and we want that person to know us as well. How do we bridge that gap?

Yoko Ono is one individual that lived a symbiosis of East and West, and I believe that this was through the expression of art. Her lingua franca and connection to people was through her artistic vision. Yoko was a child of privilege, but WW II changed that. Her banker father was imprisoned in Saigon, and she survived the Tokyo firebombing of 1945. However, her family was destitute, begging and selling prized heirlooms for rice. Here she developed her "aggressive attitude" and realized what it meant to be an "outsider" to her culture. Seeing the horrors of devastation convinced her to be a Peace activist against the Vietnam war. When her father was released, the family soon regained their wealth, and they moved to New York, where her father was transferred by his bank. The family lived outside the city in Scarsdale, and she attended Sarah Lawrence but soon moved to a loft in Soho to become a part of the New York art revolution of the 1960s. Here she brought her Eastern sensibilities to filter and infuse (yin and yang) Western avant-garde art. She saw herself as neither Japanese nor American but a World citizen, communicating through her art. She started as a conceptional artist, almost burning down her loft as she destroyed a piece of her art by fire as part of her show.

She attracted John Lennon by creating an art "sculpture" that the spectator creates: a blank wooden board with a box of nails and a hammer. The viewer is invited to pound nails into the board at random, creating an "instant" art piece. She used her body to do performance art and wrote music imitating bird calls and other nature sounds. She and John Lennon found each other in the swinging art and music scene of 1960s London but soon moved to New York City for personal freedom and artistic opportunities. New York City in the 1960s was the chaotic center of the world for artistic expression, the anti-war and free speech movements, women's and gay rights' liberation, the sexual revolution, and a vibrant folk and underground music scene.

John Lennon had found an artist that was his equal, a partner that converted him into a Peace advocate, a songwriter that collaborated with him, and a conceptional artist that showed him a new form of creativity. Yoko went on to make experimental films and new forms of performance art and even formed a successful music group, The Plastic Ono Band. Yoko and John supported and challenged each other: art was the medium that allowed them to overcome the East/West divide and encompass the world with their message. I remember seeing a photograph of the Movie Marque in Times Square installed by the Lennons with the bold but simple statement: "The War is Over". This was not just an anti-war slogan but a monumental performance piece: art can change life in a symbolic and literal sense.

Chapter 50: A Modern Geisha Tale

"Foxy Lady" - Jimi Hendrix

A Traditional Geisha 1870

Walking back to the subway one night, I came across some colorful Japanese hippies: girls with pierced noses and straight-cropped hair and styles dressed in multi-colored India-print skirts. Guys with flowery shirts, long straggly hair, and that faraway, drug-induced stupor on their faces. I wondered if this was the chink in the armor of Japanese society or just a play-acting diversion, like the straight suburban Long Island kids, who become instant hippies for the weekend to score drugs and get their kicks in Greenwich Village.

The next day I returned to the Ginza. This was the original pleasure center of Edo (Tokyo), as depicted in the woodblock prints of Hiroshige. Here were the sake bars with their geisha hostesses, the beautiful parks with flowering cherry blossoms, and the girls dressed coquettishly in their best kimonos, each carrying a colorful parasol. This looked like a sea of mushroom tadpoles when viewed from above.

The Ginza was still the pleasure center, but now it was all flashing neon, mod clothes shops, pachinko machines, and countless eateries and bars. In the small pocket park off the main square, I encountered more of the counterculture Japanese. I went up and talked to them because I was curious if they spoke English and if I could understand what they were doing and why. The girls spoke broken English, but the guys looked like immobile zombies and only grunted when I approached. The girls, like all Japanese, were intensely curious about all foreigners, especially Americans, since they were copying them in hippie clothes and hairstyles. They had seen many foreigners: smartly dressed businessmen, American sailors from the naval base nearby, and foreign exchange students. I was different: my clothes were scruffy, and I always carried my camera around my neck. One girl talked with me. She had a nose ring and half blond hair, wearing a short skirt and a t-shirt with the logo: "I Love NY", half-covered by a short denim jacket with multiple patches sewn on the front and back. She was short and chubby, with a pug nose and high cheekbones, and had a fresh and energetic countenance that gave her a bubbly cuteness. Her name was: Su Ju, but she only spoke a few words of English. I introduced myself, and she repeated "Goldon" (like most Asians, the Japanese have trouble pronouncing "r", which comes out sounding like "l". I offered to buy her lunch at a nearby noodle shop, and she accepted. She ate ravenously, and I managed to understand that she was a "panhandler" and lived with a friend away from the center of town. I told her, through hand signals and language, that I was traveling all over Asia, and she said that she liked traveling. After lunch, I offered, through signs, English and a little Japanese, to take her to Ueno Park Zoo. We had a lot of fun. She kept running from one cage to the next, wide-eyed and enthusiastic. I saw for the first time a red panda (a small foxlike creature, not like the giant pandas in China), and I also saw many ostrich-type birds that I'd never heard of or seen before.

When we finished the zoo, it was late afternoon. Somehow, I got through to her, asking if she wanted to come with me to my hotel, which was a half-hour away on the subway. To my surprise, she said "Yes," and we started our trek. It was getting dark when we arrived, so I got a boxed dinner for two with rice wine and some sweet cakes she indicated she wanted. The hotel manager was nowhere in sight, so I had no trouble getting her into my room.

As I mentioned, the room was pretty bare, but I did get the space heater going, and it was getting warm as we ate dinner on the low table. We talked as best we could. She had a mother but apparently had many problems with her. She moved out, and now the street people are her friends. She asked all sorts of questions. "Where you live?" "What you do?" "How long you stay?"

After about half an hour of this, I put my finger to my mouth and said, "Shhhh." Then I leaned over and kissed her. She responded, and soon we were in each other's arms, kissing and fondling. I tried to get her t-shirt off, but she jumped up, turned out the light, and undressed in a corner. I also undressed and waited under the sheets. She came into the bed, and we embraced. Her body was chubby, but her breasts were larger than most Korean girls, and she was enthusiastic. She worked slowly, kissing me all over and then grabbing my penis with her hand. I was stroking her vagina, and we were kissing each other hungrily. Soon we were at a fever pitch, and I penetrated her wet blackness. She wrapped her legs around me and pushed up as we rocked back and forth. She moaned, and I gasped as we climaxed. Afterward, she lay cradled in my arms, and we fell asleep. When I awoke, "this bird had flown", along with all of the cash in my wallet, about US $25. Luckily my camera was locked in the small chest by my bed, along with my traveler's checks and passport. It may have been an expensive night, but I had my "modern-day" geisha. Although Su Ju dressed and acted like a Hippie, she definitely didn't believe in "free love!" I returned to the Ginza the next day, looking for her, but I never saw her again.

On my last night, I walked all over the main commercial district, amazed at how the god of capitalism was being honored. Everywhere were huge blinking shrines dedicated to Rolex, Honda, Sony, and Chanel perfume. Most of the billboards depicted American or European models driving BMWs, drinking Santori Whiskey, or demonstrating the operating ease of a Hitachi washer/dryer. You worshipped this god by buying this brand-name product, thus ensuring your place in "consumer heaven".

"Tokyo at Night" Photo by Andre Benz (UNSPLASH)

Nationalist China

A river scene in old China 1905

Chapter 51: Taiwan: China in Miniature

"Twenty-Six Miles (Santa Catalina)" - Four Preps

Taiwan was discovered by the Portuguese while searching for China. They called it: Formosa, a "beautiful island", and it surely lives up to its name. It was fought over and ruled by the Dutch and Spaniards in the 17th century, by the Chinese in the 18th and 19th centuries, and from 1896-to 1945 by the Japanese. It is a lush sub-tropical paradise of mountain gorges, picturesque lakes, and friendly people. Yet this is a society undergoing a revolutionary transformation from agrarianism to industrialism. A little history helps to understand this transition. By 1949 Mao's Communist Army had consolidated its control of mainland China. The nationalist government of Chiang Kai-shek, a former warlord general, had been defeated. Chiang, in the last desperate days before the communists took complete control, stole China's gold reserves, looted 5000 years of Chinese art from the Forbidden Palace, and fled with two million soldiers, businessmen, and intellectuals to Taiwan, 75 miles from mainland China. Here he set up a fortress state, armed and protected by the US. His portrait is as ubiquitous as Mao's is in China. He is, in his own mind, the last defender of traditional Chinese culture. Although he doesn't call himself "Emperor", he perpetrated a one-party state under martial law to consolidate and control his island kingdom. To his credit, he destroyed Taiwan's landlord class, giving the land back to the people and encouraging the traditional practices of Chinese culture. This is in sharp contrast to the turbulent time in mainland China: Mao's "Cultural Revolution" was destroying shrines, forbidding religious practices, sending intellectuals and teachers to rice fields and prisons, turning children against parents, and uprooting 5000 years of Chinese tradition.

Chiang had the vision to remake Taiwan into a prosperous ideal China, *albeit* in miniature. The Nationalist Party government controls the banks, forcing them to give loans to small businesses. The State focuses on encouraging high-quality technical and electronic products for export. The "Taiwan Miracle" is setting the example for free Asian economic resurgence after World War II. The keys to this success are a stable political and social environment, an educated and cheap workforce, and the absence of trade unions. The US encouraged companies to invest in production in Taiwan and offered a ready market for these high-tech products. But it was the Chinese people who were remarkable here; everybody tried to help you. They told me not to take an expensive cab, because a city bus went right by the hotel I wanted to stay at. They even put me on the right bus from the airport to my traveler's hotel: "The White House."

At the White House, I met Paul Batchelor, a college drop-out from New York City who had gone to Paris to study French and had been traveling for the past two years outside of the U.S. Together. We sampled the myriad Chinese cuisines and nightlife in Taipei, the capital. Having grown up in the excellent Cantonese Chinese restaurants of New York's Chinatown, it was a gourmet's delight to try all of the other Chinese regional cooking: the fiery Sichuan chicken, the Haakan seared fish, and delicate Fukien pork dumplings. Again, the Chinese people were very helpful. When you asked what they were eating, they made you sit down, translated the menu, and told you what the price was, the same price for foreigners and Chinese.

Paul and I also visited some Confucian shrines, watching the priest officiate a ceremony and lighting candles for ancestors. Afterward Paul and I discussed the nature of Confucianism. "Outwardly," I stated, "it seems to be a religion."

Paul disagreed, saying, "The central premise is an ethical and philosophical system. Human beings can improve using the philosophical 'Ren', loosely translated as 'humanness.' The rituals of Confucianism are all ethical: behavior, politeness, loyalty, and self-cultivation are all internalized in the individual. You want to do good because it is the right 'social' thing to do. If you do not, you will cause shame on yourself or 'lose face' among your family, friends, and society. Self-cultivation creates actions that make you a good man and is the mark of social correctness. Confucianism expresses our golden rule in a passive voice: 'Do not do unto others what you would not have them do unto you.' Filial piety, respect of children for father and mother, by extension, to all of your ancestors, is a central tenant of the system. By paying them respect, you respect yourself. Social harmony and knowing your place in the social and political order are of the utmost importance.

Similarly, the same rules are applied to the King, General, or Ruler; these people must have 'Ren.' Loyalty extends from the family to friends to the Ruler of the State. The Ruler must show 'Ren' to his subjects. He takes care of his people because he knows what's in their best interest. Therefore, he should be obeyed. He has 'the Mandate of Heaven.'

Chiang Kai-shek has practiced 'Ren' to his people, even though he is a dictator in a One-Party State system. He gave the people land, fostered economic growth by controlling the banks, and leveraged his anti-Communist stance to get American military and economic aid and a free-trade market for his country's products. Consciously or unconsciously, the Taiwanese people have given Chiang the 'Mandate of Heaven.'"

Poster of Chiang Kai-Shek on a Taipei Street

(Author photo)

Chapter 52: Chiang Kai Shek

The Man Who Would Be King

"Oblivion" - M83

This title song from the movie "Oblivion" tells of the destruction of our planet by alien invaders, just like the "Old China" was destroyed by the victorious Communists in the Civil War in 1949.

His huge, serious face hung everywhere in Taipei. His personality cult was only surpassed by that "other China" leader. His story has been China's story for half a century. He was a loyal lieutenant to Sun Yet Sen when Sun overthrew 5000 years of Chinese history. Chiang worked tirelessly to unite the country, fighting the warlords and collaborating with the Communists to achieve a united China. Afterward, Chiang abandoned the Communists and fought them in a civil war. Then he held the Chinese army together to fight the Japanese and saved at least part of his country. After the Japanese defeat, he again fought the Communists to preserve the traditional Chinese way of life.

He was an enigmatic figure - many called him a corrupt warlord; others an opportunist that played Russia against the United States. But he was a true patriot, putting China first and, in the end, tragically lost it all.

I first read about Chiang Kai Shek in a novel where he was never seen, nor did any of the characters interact with him. He was the bogey man in Andre Malraux's "Man's Fate", which imaginatively chronicled the abortive Shanghai Insurrection of April 1927. Malraux wrote the novel from the communist point of view, but he also captured the decadent *fin de siecle* of Shanghai in the 1920s. Here you had a city that was divided into two parts: the international settlements, where British, American, and French businessmen made millions, exploiting China, backed up by British and American warships. These businessmen built the impressive Bund, which defined the city in the popular imagination all over the world. They lived like royalty; they had their own racetrack, casinos, exclusive shopping areas, and airy mansions with troops of servants. This was all separate from the other Shanghai: the poor, teeming masses of Chinese in China's largest city.

Shanghai was a melting pot of wealthy European and American businessmen, Christian missionaries, White Russians (refuges that had fled Red Russia after the failed 1920's civil war), Communist Trade Unionists, vicious Chinese gangs (the gangs-controlled opium, prostitution, and gambling in the city) and Nationalist Chinese soldiers, that kept nominal order.

This was the fabled Shanghai of exotic nightclubs, Chinese and White Russian singers, and prostitutes. The era of formal balls, where champagne and opium flowed like water, and you could indulge in any vice, as long as you had the money.

Shanghai's Bund in the 1930s

Malraux's novel deals with the struggles of Chou-en-lai's communists struggling to overthrow the Nationalist Army under Chiang Kai-shek and take over the international settlements. The main protagonist is Kyo Gissors, a half-Japanese half-French leader that is leading this revolt. His forces, the Communist Trade Unionists, were ordered by Chiang Kai-shek to surrender their weapons (at that time, Chiang Kai Shek was an ally of the Communists). With the help of a Soviet agitator, Katow, and a dissolute French black marketeer, Kyo, obtains guns, storms the nationalist arsenal, and briefly captures the city.

Malraux was a communist sympathizer and fervently believed in the communist ideology of a united brotherhood of men, struggling vainly against overwhelming odds.

The revolt ends quickly once the superior Nationalist Army under Chiang retakes the city and gruesomely kills thousands of Communists by boiling them alive in a steam locomotive stack. Kyo is betrayed on all sides: the Russians, the Nationalist Army, and his dashed hopes that the bulk of the peasantry would rise up and join the insurrection. His philosophy is that you make your own moral choices, and you live and die by these decisions. "What would have been the value of a life for which he would not have been willing to die? Dying could be an exalted act, the supreme expression of a life which this death so much resembled." He then takes cyanide and dies.

Katov also has cyanide and plans to kill himself, but his two young Chinese Communist companions are terrified of being boiled alive, and, in a last act of brotherhood, he gives the two his cyanide, and he faces the boiling death, knowing he has helped his comrades in their desperation. This is his last act: affirming his humanity and stoically going to his death.

Chinese Communists being led to execution by Chiang Kai-Shek's Army in 1927

In the aftermath of the revolt, life in the international settlements went on as usual. A New York reporter, Irene Khun, living and working in Shanghai, wrote naively about the insurrection, "Even though the tremors of approaching violent change were occasionally felt, it seemed the land was so vast, the civilization, the people and their ways too ancient for change ever to be successful."

Chapter 53: Taipei National Museum

All great museums overwhelm your sensory perceptions. Some because you see the totality of man's creative energy in one place, like the encyclopedic Metropolitan Museum of Art. Here you can see the earliest cave art of pudgy fertility goddesses to the Soho Loft paint-spattered canvases of Jackson Pollack. Other museums show the aesthetic vision of a cultivated collector, like the Isabella Gardiner Museum in Boston, where every room is a jewel-like microcosm of a specific epoch. Still, other museums like the Taipei National Museum concentrate on one culture and immerse you into a time warp of five thousand years of Chinese civilization. You see firsthand how civilization developed, matured, and flowered, and unlike Western art, you follow an unbroken continuity of that culture.

You absorb this unique collection of oracle bones from 3000 BC, asking, "Should the king sacrifice thirty oxen to satisfy a wrathful ancestor?" The Chinese-lettered prophecies scratched on cracked tortoise shells, a five-thousand-year-old Chinese script that is still readable by the average Chinese person today! Try reading "Beowulf" in the original Anglo-Saxon and see how far you get.

This is followed by depictions of dragons as water gods (based on fresh-water crocodiles, which were abundant in Chinese rivers thousands of years before Confucius lived). You see how the horse was the supreme catalyst of change throughout endless dynasties. Endless hordes of invaders conquered vast areas of China with their small pony-sized horses, only to be absorbed by the superior culture of the conquered. This was the true "melting pot" as Americans envisioned their own culture. The invention of paper facilitated the beautiful calligraphic scrolls. The secret of silk manufacture spurred world trade and created the most intricately beautiful clothing and wall-hangings that the world has ever seen. Similarly, the white-glazed porcelain was the envy of Europe for hundreds of years because they couldn't duplicate this uniquely Chinese process. The Chinese religion of Tao (The Way) enabled painters to achieve a symbiosis of man and nature. This nature could be admired both for outwardly beauty: gnarled trees set in picturesque cloud-covered mountains and for the inward beauty of absorption into the oneness of the universe. You experience how religion, nature, and art are fused into a pantheistic monism: God is everywhere and is in everything.

"Immortal Heaven Hall in the Mountains" (10th century A.D.) by Tun Yuan

This Taoist sense of nature comes to life in the tenth century Southern Sung dynasty and the fourteenth century Yuan dreamscape paintings. Two paintings that I particularly enjoy stand out as the epitome of this Taoist ideal of the world: the first, a black and white brushstroke painting,

"Immortal Heaven Hall in the Mountains" by Tun Yuan (10th century A.D.) (above), depicts cloud-shrouded scholar-stone mountains overlooking a limped lake, surrounded by huge spruce trees, with their single brush stroke branches. There is a small temple on the mountain top, but this is only a token reminder of how insignificant humans and manmade structures are, in comparison to the dynamism of the landscape (the Way). A feeling of awed calmness envelopes you. You feel the clouds moving over the mountain. You are drawn in, floating in this dream world, in harmony with God and Nature.

"Forest Grotto in Juku" by Wang Meng

The second painting by Wang Meng (1309-1385 A.D.) is a colored painted scroll, "Forest Grotto in Juku". Here we see a phantasmagorical Chinese scholar rock mountain-scape, swirling and writhing as if it were the scales of an awakening dragon. The mountain is alive in all its rawness, lunging out at you from the scroll, swallowing everything in its path. The tentacles of creeping rock are thirstily lapping at the Water of Life. Here we see the inexorable movement of the cosmos, a lifeforce of primordial creation.

I spent a whole day there, and I only saw a part of this great collection. Later I found out that the museum could only display 1% of its vast collections because of a lack of space. Furthermore, my time in the museum was enriched by two Republic of China soldiers who paid my entrance fee, walked around the exhibits to guide me, bought me lunch, and even paid for my bus back to the White House.

Chapter 54: The Right Way, the Wrong Way, and the Tao Way

"Go Your Own Way" - Fleetwood Mac

The Taipei Museum was an enriching experience. However, all culture and no play make Gordon a dull boy. So, Paul and I went to the Chinese Disneyland called "World." This funhouse, located in the center of Taipei, has six floors of eateries and entertainment. The first floors have cuisines from all over the world served by local Chinese youths in native costumes. It was mildly hilarious to see petite Chinese girls in gaudy low-cut dirndl blouses, loaded down with huge platters of bratwurst and beer that they balanced in each hand. The third floor was for kids: pinball machines, German fuss ball machines, and slides that dumped you into a sea of multi-colored rubber balls. The fourth floor featured a Chinese cabaret with Rockette-style dance routines. On another stage on this floor were Chinese torch singers in a dark smokey cabaret. The fifth floor had a Chinese vaudeville show with such exaggerated slapstick acting that even I could understand the simple humor. The top floor attracted all the teenagers. There was a men's band: young Chinese in leather jackets doing fast Ramones's rock, and on yet another stage were pony-tailed girls, dancing to a loud Chinese rock group, performing the latest American and British pop tunes. The pony-tailed girls were very pretty, and we had a good time dancing with a few of them. After that, we went to a Chinese "businessman's bar". These bars are usually filled with middle-aged Chinese office workers. The atmosphere was similar to an American Cocktail Lounge, only here there were half a dozen beautiful young girls behind the bar offering geisha services: pleasant conversation, plying drinks and compliments, going out of their way to make you feel important. These geisha types aren't whores; in fact, some of them are university students. If they liked you, they might dispense their favors freely on a personal basis. Unfortunately, Paul and I weren't among the "chosen few", but the atmosphere was friendly, and the girls bantered jokes with us about our scruffy appearance. We stayed until the bar closed and then got a taxi back to the White House. Unfortunately, as a by-product of the National Law and the curfew, the hotel and all of the shops were closed until 5 A.M., and we couldn't get into our rooms.

The city was eerily quiet, and the nighttime chill forced us to keep walking. We passed a darkened temple, which Paul explained was a Taoist shrine. He had been studying Chinese philosophy and religion on his own for about a year when I met him. He was deeply into Taoism, which isn't a religion in the Western sense, but a way of looking at life, stripping away the external ritual and ceremony of daily life to actualize the flow of the Universe, the force that is behind the natural order of the world.

One of the goals of Tao is "Wu Wei" best described as "effortless effort", placing your Will in harmony with the universe, not losing yourself to the Universal Soul that the Buddhists seek. Complimentarily with "effortless effort" is "pu" (passive reception), where you free your mind of past knowledge and personal experience to let the "awareness" of how the Universe works and allows you to live in the present, absorbing your surroundings in order to become a part of the Tao ("Wei"). This is pantheism, where God is in everything and You are within this nature or Godhead, but the Wei is in everything but not of it, pervading nature but supra-natural and ultimately "unknowable."

The nature of Tao now merges with Taoist philosophy: knowing others is wisdom; knowing yourself is Enlightenment. The three main principles of theoretical Taoism are compassion, moderation (in the West, we would call this simplicity), and humility.

The Yin Yang is a Taoist symbol; when both sides are equal, all is calm. When one is outweighed by the other, there is chaos. The philosophy of Taoism is laid out in the "Tao Te Ching", written by Lo Tzu. The book details the nature of Tao and how to attain it, but it starts with "The Way that be described is not the True Way." This cryptic warning is like saying, "God is in everything but apart from it." You can't describe God because He is unknowable, pervading the order of nature but surpassing it. The goal of man is to return to the simplicity of the flow of Nature. Compassion and humility towards your fellow man allow you to be aware of the perfect balance of the universe. (This was a pretty heady discussion at 4 am; I had read about the hippies, who had wanted to get back to nature, but this was taking it to a whole new level!) Paul told me that Taoists are persecuted in Communist China because they are seen as being against progress. Even if it helps people, a dam should not be built because it's the Way of the river to flow unimpeded. Self-actualization through meditation allows one to discover this inner way, which in turn allows you to outwardly observe the true rhythm of the universe.

I disagreed, "It is the Individual that makes and shapes our world. All of my heroes were individuals who took the initiative against a great injustice. Christ defied the Jewish hierarchy by bringing his message of eternal salvation to the common people. Martin Luther, in posting his Ninety-five Thesis, tried to stop indulgences, which give you a free ticket to Heaven; you stand or fall by your actions before God. We Americans are a "Can Do" nation, and that is what makes us great. The Individual can make a difference. Dr. Tom Dooley in Laos was a modern-day saint who used his medical skills to save one life at a time and, by his selfless work, to promote Christianity.

Paul countered that "These "Individuals" knew themselves in the inward Tao meaning. Therefore, they sought to help to restore the balance of Nature by helping their fellow man, applying the Taoist principles of compassion, simplicity, and humility. If someone is in "need", help them (compassion). Here the example of a great individual would be Gandhi (representing simplicity) through his nonviolent "effortless effort" against the oppressive British overlords. Moses struck the ground, finding water; his oneness with God exemplifies compassion: to save his people, who were dying of thirst in the desert. Mohammed, showing how to achieve paradise through his role as a humble servant of God, exemplifies humility". "All of these 'Individuals' Paul said, "are part of the Tao." Only if you are at peace with yourself can you spread the Way of the Tao.

I had learned so much from that early morning walk, and there were so many other questions I wanted to ask him. I wished that he would come with me on my travels in Asia, but Paul was on his way to Japan to study Zen Buddhism in a monastery in Kyoto. I told him of my visit to the Zen gardens in Kyoto, and I told him what I felt: a sense of calmness, the emptying of thoughts, and the inner stillness that I felt is the key to meditation. I saw Paul as the "poster child" to all of those restless searchers looking for meaning in our lost generation. He chose the hard path, studying and practicing the ancient wisdom, philosophies, and religions of Asia; not the easy path that so many in our generation took, the instant enlightenment that drugs falsely give.

Chapter 55: A Visit to the Countryside

"Country Roads, Take Me Home": John Denver

I took off for the provinces, and my first destination was Sun Moon Lake. This was like those Chinese scroll paintings you saw in the National Museum: a placid lake with an island in the middle, crowned by a small Chinese wooden temple. That night at the lodge, I met some Chinese students who invited me to a dance party. They were excessively friendly, almost forcing me to dance with the girl students. We did the tango, waltz, and cha cha cha, and it was a lot of fun, although they put me to shame with their graceful movements. The next day they took me to a temple they were building around the lake and treated me to sugar cane, which you chew for the sweet sap stalk and spit out the pulp.

I asked them about their views on school and communist China. The students told me that their teachers would tolerate no argument from them – they would fail the student who challenged the teacher's views. Most of the students were very curious about communist China. Most of them wanted to visit it, and no one wanted to fight their mainland brothers if there was a conflict. They didn't particularly like their own government because of its restriction on personal freedom or the inability to travel freely. Talking with them, it seemed like the ideological separation of communist China from nationalist China was as if they were the republicans in our Senate and Mao's communists were the democrats.

Then I went to Taroko Gorge. This was obscured by clouds most of the time, but you caught glimpses of beautiful ravines, waterfalls, and lush vegetation everywhere. Again, it recalled those beautiful paintings in the National Museum, where nature has a mystical Taoist atmosphere.

Taroko Gorge: Nationalist China

Everywhere I went, I rode on Chinese buses, and it was a trip: you ride for an hour, then you stop for an hour. Everyone rushes out to the eateries to grab snacks and drinks; then, they take their picture next to anything that looks the least bit impressive. Several Chinese girls took off their shoes to walk out on rocks to the middle of an ordinary pond, just for a picture of themselves in the great outdoors.

I arrived back in Taipei, where I met a Chinese Sergeant who invited me to a party. I hesitatingly went with him, thinking to myself: either I'm going to be rolled or get completely plastered on rice wine with other soldiers. Instead, I found myself in the midst of a 1950s American sock hop, a scene complete with parent chaperones, Coca-Cola, and peanut butter cake. I danced with many pretty young Chinese girls, showing them how to do the American "jitterbug". It reminded me of all the sweetly innocuous parties I'd had as a teenager back home. I especially remembered the dances sponsored by the local Catholic Church. When you slow-danced with a catholic schoolgirl, you held each other a good foot apart: that was the space left for the Holy Ghost, according to the chaperoning nuns (somehow, I always thought the Holy Ghost would be bigger).

Chapter 56: Motorcycle as Metaphor

Richard Thompson: **1952 Black Vincent Motorcycle**

"I don't want to eat a pickle. I just wanna ride my motorcycle."

Arlo Guthrie: **Ride My Motorcycle**

BMW Motorcycle (Similar to the model that Ian was riding for his around-the-world trip)

BSA Motorcycle similar to my own motorcycle that I purchased in Germany

I first met Ian McQueen, a tall, lanky Canadian dressed in black leather, looking like an extra from the Marlon Brando movie, "The Wild Ones", in the lobby of the White House. I had a couple of bottles of beer and offered him one. We sat down and started talking. He was on a motorcycle pilgrimage: to circumnavigate the world on his motorcycle and sell his story or write a book about this adventure. He had traveled all through Canada, shipped his bike to Hong Kong, and then onto nationalist China for the second leg of the journey.

Before he told me, I guessed he rode a two-stroke 650cc BMW. He did! This is a great machine for touring. It has two precision carburetors positioned on each side of the engine that gives a smooth and stable ride. I had the identical machine, complete with a matching side car, for about one week. When my commanding officer saw this, he told me to either get rid of it or he would ship me out; next stop: Vietnam. He had lost too many officers in motorcycle accidents on the autobahn. Deutschland or Vietnam, it was an easy choice: Auf wiedersehn BMW!

After my commander transferred out, I bought a BSA one carburetor 650cc Thunderbolt from the Canadian PX (Canadian and American forces were co-located in the southern part of West Germany). This bike was perfect on a Sunday afternoon, cruising the small medieval towns that dotted the Rhine, but after four hours, your back was aching badly from the reverberations. I thought this was because of the single carburetor, but I spoke with other bikers who had the two-carburetor Lightning model, and they suffered from the same problem. Also, the BSA had one glaring deficiency for American riders: everything was opposite on the gears because the English drove on the "wrong" side of the road. With American, German, and Japanese bikes sold in the States, you accelerate with your right foot and brake with your left foot. With British bikes, it is just the opposite. Many American bikers were killed on British bikes because they thought they were braking; instead, they were accelerating.

The BSA motorcycle looks sleek, with volumes of shiny steel, an almond-shaped gas tank, and a long black seat just made for you and your girl (the platonic ideal of a motorcycle). The appeal is middle-class: office 9-5ers, teachers, and small business owners, all having a feeling that they are non-conformists, a notch above their peers. In the States, they would be the "sunny afternoon" riders: "Rebel with a Weekend Cause". The mystic, not the substance, of bike riding. In the U.K., this type of rider was called a "Mod" – always dressed in black suits with long thin ties. They attracted slightly rebellious, well-dressed girls and projected an image of "calculated coolness".

The Harley rider was defiantly working class; he is the real-life rebel, glamourized in the 1950s by Marlon Brando in "The Wild Ones" and in the 1960s by Peter Fonda in "Easy Rider". Here we see the natural successor to the cowboy, the lone hero riding his "hog" into the sunset. There is a true camaraderie among Harley riders, and they always project that edgy outlaw mystic – you were not to be messed with. With their distinctive gang names embosomed on their well-worn leather jackets to their scruffy appearance, they epitomize the American "rugged individual". They ride in packs, dominating the highway like wolves, answering to no one except the alpha leader. It was not surprising that the Rolling Stones chose the Hell's Angels as security for their Altamont rock concert. They would kick ass first and ask questions later. Horrifically they savagely killed an argumentative black youth, and this tragically and symbolically ended the Woodstock dream of Peace, Love, and Music.

The BMW rider takes it to a whole new level. This is not a sport or hobby but a way of life. He is serious and performance-driven. He sees his BMW as a touring, workhorse machine, the "only" motorcycle for that NYC to San Francisco road trip. It's all business with this rider: eight hours a day in the saddle in any kind of weather; then, you can have your beer in the biker joints.

I asked Ian about life on the road. He enjoyed the solitude and the visceral awareness of your surroundings that you can't get riding in a car. Besides English, he knew French and was picking up some Chinese. I asked him about the maintenance and availability of German parts. He told me that Chinese mechanics were Wunderkinds. They could even prefabricate hard-to-get parts. He also told me that the Chinese were courteous to motorcycles, giving them a wide berth. He was on the road for about eight hours a day, driving without a Plexi shield and hunched over due to the German short-cropped handles. American bikes have standard bicycle handles which allow you to sit up and straight back, but you get a good deal more wind without a shield.

He really liked the Chinese, but he was now headed for Japan. Japan the homeland of Honda and Suzuki. The Japanese were already the world's largest manufacturer of motorcycles. They had captured the Asian market for low horsepower work bikes and off-road bikes. Now they were gunning for the big "kahuna", the high-performance superbikes. They were winning the international competitions, and because of cheap non-union Asian labor, they were half the cost of American or German bikes. The Honda 750cc was a dream: it outperformed the Hurley, had extraordinarily little maintenance problems, looked very glitzy, and, did I mention, it was cheap.

The Japanese took Henry Ford's assembly line and revamped it. They brought together supervisors and workers weekly, emphasizing quality inspections and listening to assembly workers' suggestions to improve routines. Assembly lines were stopped if there were defective parts or incorrect assembly. Workers were proud of their performance; they were not just a cog in the wheel of American factories. We Americans should be rebuilding our industry to meet this competition; instead, we are throwing away billions of dollars on a war we already lost.

Ian and I talked of Japan, debating if they would overtake America as the world's largest economy. I looked at Japan as a closed society that could never overtake the West. For a country to be truly great, you need to have a culture that is all-embracing, not only in economics but socially, militarily, and politically. The Japanese social model is very race-conscious and gender prejudiced. There is very little immigration permitted, and they see themselves as superior to all their Asian neighbors. Women are second-class citizens and have few opportunities in the male-dominated business, political and cultural spheres. Militarily, they need to be self-sufficient and not rely on the US to defend their country. Politically, this government's favoritism to certain industries stifles initiative and ultimately prevents the regeneration of a stagnant state-business-run economy. Culturally, they borrow and ape the West in their quest for a new international identity.

After about three hours of beer-infused discussion, I wished Ian the best of luck on his journey and called it a night; I was flying out at 7:30 A.M. If we only had another hour, I'm sure we would have solved world hunger, but as the Beatles sing "Obla Dee, Obla Da, Life goes on".

Hong Kong: "Go Your Own Way"

Street Scene in old Hong Kong 1900

Chapter 57: Hong Kong

"Hong Kong Garden": Siouxsie and the Banshees

Hong Kong in the 1850s: engraving by Thomas Allom,

Hong Kong was a sleepy little Chinese village that the British took over in 1842. The British were importing vast quantities of Chinese tea, and their balance of payments was hemorrhaging the empire. They needed an export to China that would offset the losses from tea buying. The answer was opium, and they fought two wars with the Chinese to make them accept this lucrative, addictive product, which was produced in British-controlled India.

The British wanted access to the vast Chinese markets, and Hong Kong, with its natural deep-water harbor, was the perfect location to facilitate this trade. Conversely, Hong Kong was also China's window to the world, and so this arrangement satisfied both countries.

There is a great comparison to New York City: both manufactured and traded goods from their respective heartlands. Both were lively, get-rich-quick cities that supported vast sweatshops that exploited their own citizens. Both had vast slums, and both had a growing heroin/opium-addicted populace. Both had large banks that financed and controlled their industries in their respective countries. Both had natural deep-water ports that supported a flourishing import /export maritime trade. Both also had organized crime bosses (the mafia and the Chinese Tongs) that controlled drugs, prostitution, and all other corruptions. Both were the most vibrant culturally, artistically, and innovative cities in the world. People came to both cities to buy, trade, and sell everything. On a personal note, I found them to be two of the dirtiest cities in the world: people throw garbage out of their windows whenever they want in both cities.

Dock Workers striking in the old Hong Kong port in 1897

Like New York City, there are protests and demonstrations almost daily in Hong Kong

CAPTURING A CITY

Walking on the crowded streets of Hong Kong, I felt at a loss on how I could portray this vibrant city in photographs. Do I search out images that reflect London in miniature? There are the staid English administrators and businessmen, the privileged Chinese, the intellectual Anglo-Indian, or do I roam the streets to get a glimpse of old women playing mahjong, the sweating rickshaw drivers, and grandmothers practicing Tai Chi in parks in the early morning hours?

What struck you immediately was the cacophony of music: American and British Rock & Roll, whiny Chinese erhu (violin), syrupy Chinese pop music, and English brass ensembles playing on hot Sunday afternoons in the parks. I stayed in Kowloon, the Brooklyn of Hong Kong, the bedroom community for the commercial island of Hong Kong. Hong Kong feels a little like London at first glance; double-decker buses, English cars, motorcycles, and Victorian buildings, but the energy is different. It is interesting to see how they ape the English. Nattily dressed Chinese, with cricket bats in hand, St. Paul school uniforms, and Oxford accents. They all belong to the English clubs, and they all attend the English racetrack in their finery. They really enjoy their arrangement, that they are under England instead of China because they're making money and living well. The Chinese girls are better dressed and more open than in Taiwan. The lifestyle here is definitely Western, with pop music, tight body dresses, and heavy makeup: everything one needs to become a "beautiful person." Like New York, there are many other nationalities: Indians, Anglo-Chinese, and Europeans, small islands in the vast sea of Chinese faces.

Everyone in Hong Kong is out to get the tourists. People constantly hassling you to buy things, meet women or men (if you're disposed of that way), or "ride my bicycle rickshaw". Since I wasn't a "buying" tourist, I tried to find the real Hong Kong in the back streets, harbor, and countryside. One day I did find the old China when I was walking around a crowded market. The market fronted a small square where they had set up a small stage; they were performing a Peking Chinese Opera that evening. Mr. Wu, our landlord host, offered to accompany us to the opera. We caught a double-decker bus to the market, not knowing really what to expect. Previously, my only experience with opera was with the New York Metropolitan Opera on television. At that time, I was not a big fan of fat women in blond wigs wearing Viking horns, shrieking and sobbing hysterically, periodically drowned out by a bombastic brass orchestra.

So, I fortified myself with a few huge bottles of Tashtego beer and wasn't feeling much pain when we left for the show. When we got to the market, Mr. Wu explained the opera to us as we waded through wave after wave of colorful humanity. The Chinese Square was packed solid, but we managed to elbow our way into seats where we could see the stage clearly. The show was a historical drama about a prince who was to marry a princess, but she was kidnapped and then there was a war, and everybody was running around trying to find her. There were skilled gymnastics and exaggerated sword fights throughout the performance. The prince also had a comic sidekick, whose broad facial expressions put the audience in stitches. This must have been a popular opera because the audience always knew what was going to happen next and kept cheering on the actors or laughing before the well-known joke was made, just like we start laughing every time we hear Abbot and Costello begin their "Slowly I turned" or "Who's on first". There was a small musical ensemble that featured a Chinese harp, erhu (Chinese violin), flutes, drums, and cymbals. The musical accompaniment set the mood for the audience and prepared them for a tragic or fighting scene. There was no singing in the traditional Western sense, but highly stylized intonated speeches, which had a lilting rhythmic appeal. Needless to say, the prince reunites with the princess, and everyone goes home happy, except for the aficionados, who claimed that the prince was not as good as Liu Wan, a noted Hong Kong Opera performer. I enjoyed the performance: the colorful costumes and the strangely mesmerizing Chinese orchestra. We capped off the day by eating Peking duck in a small Chinese restaurant (washed down by more Tashtego beer) that was unbelievably succulent and followed by fresh lychees for dessert.

Chapter 58: Peking Opera

On the double-decker bus back to the hostel after dinner, Mr. Wu told us about the opera. The performers go through a vigorous training program that starts as a child. Unlike Western classical opera, where the singing is everything, Peking performers must be versatile acrobats (for their fly-through-the-air sword fights); masters of facial expression to show moods and character; dramatic actors (to keep the audience's attention); skilled make-up artists (the "masks" the performers wear are all hand-painted); and, of course, be skilled in singing and voice modulations.

Peking Opera Performance: scroll painting by Xu Yang 1759

This is a traditional, even fossil, an art form, but great performers are able to enliven their roles by superior acting, updating the variety of facial gestures, and singing in their own unique style.

These were the reasons why the audience was, in turn, enthusiastic and disappointed at the street performance.

Mr. Wu continued, "Peking Opera was originally intended only for the emperor. All Peking Opera has two main melodies as musical accompaniment and only four primary character roles. "Sheng" is the lead character (many times the Emperor or Senior Military figure); "Dan" is the female role (played by a man). "Jing" is either a primary or secondary role demanding a strong voice and exaggerated gestures. "Chou" is the male clown role".

The elaborately applied makeup masks identify attributes of character by color. Red is bravery. Black is boldness. Blue is steadfastness. Green is impetuous. Yellow is cool-headedness. White is treachery. Gold and silver are for gods and spirits.

Originally many operas had up to 24 acts and took several days to perform. Nowadays, they're concentrated on one-act plays. Mr. Wu said there are now only five popular operas that are performed today. The First, "Drunken Beauty", is about a beautiful Princess who is stood up by the Emperor and gets drunk: "Oh, Emperor dear! Don't you know that girls just wanna have fun?" The Drunken Beauty role allows Dan (the female character) to show great acting and acrobatic skills.

The "Heavenly Maid Scatters Flowers" is a Buddhist test of faith involving a fairy princess ("Fairy tales can come true, It could happen to you if you're 'pure' at heart").

"Lady Wang Zhuojan Goes Beyond the Frontier" is about a beautiful princess that must become a bride to a "barbarian" to save the kingdom. ("Paris is worth a maiden.")

"Lady Mu Guiying Takes Command" is about a female general that was disgraced but swallows her pride and comes back, kicking ass to save China in true Sigourney Weaver "Alien" fashion.

The last and most popular opera is: "Farewell My Concubine." Emperor Xiang Yu is fighting for the unification of China but is defeated by Liu Bang, the founder of the Han Dynasty, which truly united China. Xiang Yu knows all is lost and orders his favorite horse to leave, but it stands fast. Xiang then tells his favorite concubine, Consort Yu, to flee, but she refuses and pledges to die beside him (He then complains to the director that nobody listens to him, but the director also refuses to listen to him and tells him to get on with the play). Yu kills herself with Xiang's sword, and he dies fighting to the end.

"Farewell My Concubine": The Film

There is a beautiful 1993 film about Peking Opera, "Farewell My Concubine", by director Chen Kaige. "Farewell", tells the story of two Peking Opera stars and their relationship spanning fifty years of turbulent Chinese history. It is a great introduction to the rigors of training required to becoming an opera performer. The lead star, Douzi, has a feminine nature and thus trains for the Dan roles, particularly Consort Yu in "Farewell My Concubine". His close friend, Shitou is rough and masculine and is cast as the Emperor in the Sheng role. Together they are a success and become the "movie stars" of pre-Mao China. Douzi really loves Shitou in a homosexual way, but Shitou runs off and marries a high-priced courtesan named Juxian. This new love triangle causes a rift between the two stars. To compensate for his hurt feelings, Douzi finds an abandoned baby, Xiao Si, which he raises to be a mature opera performer to replace him. China, meantime, was invaded by the Japanese, and afterward, the communists took over.

Here we see how the Cultural Revolution (1966-1977) affected, among other aspects of culture, the Peking Opera. Douzi's adopted son fervently believes in the Revolution and becomes a performer in the new communist revolutionary opera. Both Douzi and Shitou are subject to "Struggle Sessions": public humiliation and torture for performing "bourgeoise" anti-revolutionary opera. They are forced to denounce each other. Douzi tells the Red Guard Inquisitors that Shitou's wife, Juxian is a prostitute and Shitou is forced to denounce her to save his own life. He must leave her; Juxian is devastated and commits suicide. Douzi's son Xiao Si is also tortured by the Red Guards for practicing "Farewell My Concubine" secretly by himself in front of a mirror.

Douzi and Shitou do not see each other for ten years. Their friendship seems irrevocably destroyed, but now it is 1977, and the Cultural Revolution is over. The actors come together to rehearse a reunion performance of "Farewell My Concubine." On the surface, everything seems like the old days have returned: two friends rehearsing their signature roles. However, at the end of the rehearsal, Douzi takes Shitou's sword and cuts his own throat, paralleling the fictional consort Yu's suicide. Shitou has now lost everyone he cared for, and as the curtain falls, he walks away a broken man. The film is important in that it really gets into what it takes to be an opera star and examines the inhumanity of the Cultural Revolution. The heart-wrenching denunciation of Juxian recalls George Winston's actions in Orwell's "1984", when he denounces his lover to save himself from the rats. The film starkly accuses the "Cultural Revolution" of destroying the friendship and even the humanity between the two close friends. What makes this film even more poignant is that the Douzi character, played by Leslie Cheun, a wildly popular actor, also committed suicide in real life in 2003.

On a positive note, Peking Opera is widely popular today, and like the performance, I saw on the streets of Hong Kong, Opera stars have a fervent and enthusiastic following.

Chapter 59: Mao's Little Red Book

Monotones: "Book of Love"

Photograph of Mao Tse Tung from "The Little Red Book" by Mao Tse Tung

I spoke with Mr. Wu about communism and expressed an interest in Mao's Red Book. He went into his office and brought out a thin pocket-sized book. "Read this, and we can discuss it if you want to." I started reading it and was amazed to find that it was only a compilation of quotations, sophomoric in tone and message. This was the "Sesame Street" introduction to communism. The only quote that resonated with me was, "Political power only grows out of the barrel of a rifle."

I approached Mr. Wu after dinner, telling him of my feelings about the book. He sat down and sighed," This is a simple, easy-to-read book that reinforces and justifies communist ideology. An easy primer to memorize by an illiterate farmer, an effective catechism for idealistic students, and a call to action for every soldier. It is the most widely read book in the whole world. The Communist Party printed hundreds of millions of copies- enough for every worker, farmer, and especially every soldier. China is now going through an upheaval – a political, moral, and economic crisis. People in the hierarchy of the Communist Party were questioning Mao's leadership, the economy was faltering, and people were losing hope, returning to the traditional ways, looking for answers in religion.

Mao still had unwavering control of the army; he mobilized these ultra-idealistic Red Guards to enforce and double down on the communist message. This was called the "Cultural Revolution": temples and shrines were destroyed; intellectuals and teachers were sent to communal farms for "re-education", forced to work the fields with the farmers. Everyone was expected to carry and have read Mao's book. Red Guards confronted and tested millions on the book's message.

I was amazed and dumbfounded at what the Little Red Book accomplished. You were kept in line and had to be enthusiastic about the message. This message could be twisted at will: if you identified America as a reactionary evil nation, you could mobilize the whole nation against America, the landlord class, or any other people or institution. It was the perfect vehicle to spread any message or direct any hate by simple association and constant repetition.

Chapter 60: Hong Kong II

(ROBESPIERRE)

"Kowloon Hong Kong": Reynettes

Kowloon is the "Brooklyn" of Hong Kong

One night after dinner, we decided to sample Hong Kong's bar scene. We found that it was remarkably similar to Korea's, but the girls are far more aggressive, almost dragging you forcibly into the club and then making you buy them expensive drinks while pulsating music deafens you. Hong Kong is doing very well because of the Vietnam war. Every serviceman (sailors, GIs, and airmen) is given seven days off from their wartime duties around the middle of their year serving in Nam). This is to let them blow off steam and is called Rest and Relaxation (R&R). Bangkok, Tokyo, Australia, and Hong Kong were their favorite choices. The lucky ones chose Hong Kong. Slick agents met the incoming service flights and persuaded willing servicemen to come back with them to the mamasan for a planned holiday. For a stipulated fee, she gave you a girl of your choice from a lineup of all of her ladies, and you kept this girl for a full seven days. These girls all had their VD cards up to date, and with the girl came a nice clean hotel room. All you had to do for your seven days was to spend money on food and entertainment. (For many of these war-weary kids, a bottle of whiskey and a big comfy bed with this girl was all of the entertainment they needed). At the end of your time, they even gave you a framed photograph of you and your girl as a parting memento. Nice graduation present!

A Chorus Line of Chinese courtesans in the early 1900s

The part that I enjoyed most about staying at the Hong Kong hostel was the conversations: staying up until two or three in the morning, talking about everything – politics, religions, traveling, and what we wanted to get from the road and life.

The big news one morning was the arrival of two blonde California hippie chicks and how everyone was fawning over them (round blue eyes floating in a sea of almond-shaped brown eyes). We went bar hopping that night: Jean Pierre, the Swiss traveler that I had befriended at the hostel, myself and the two flower-power girls. First, we went to the Scandinavian Bar (I think the last Nordic left with Leif Erickson on his way to discover America, but there were a lot of Chinese call girls) and then on to a Chinese nightclub, where we danced wildly for hours to a Chinese rock band. Afterward, we bought a couple of large Tashtego beers and returned to the hostel. The hippie girls had a beer and then said they were tired and retreated to their room (all flower and no power!), but we were joined by Glenda, a short, dark-haired Brit with thick horn-rim glasses, who was reading in the lounge when we arrived.

I had read Mao's "Little Red Book" and was eager to talk about communism with Jean Pierre and Glenda, particularly Mao's control of the world's largest country (the 500-pound gorilla next-door).

I started the conversation, "But don't you need a period in the revolution when the old order must be totally swept away? Just look at the French Revolution and the Reign of Terror under Robespierre."

Jean Pierre now spoke up, "Yes, but Robespierre was stopped."

"Yes," I answered, "but what happened next? You had a tyrant like Napoleon, who threw all of Europe into chaos and killed hundreds of thousands of people. Who really benefited from the revolution? The rich bourgeoise and the old nobility, the common people, were just as bad off as before the revolution. In China, the people are now in control, and they are building a new society: a Utopia where every man has a new beginning."

"Yes, that's true," said Glenda, "but I value my individual freedom. In England, we fought kings for the Magna Carta, Lords and noblemen for the Charter Movement, and patriarchal parliament for the women's right to vote."

"You're absolutely right. I, too, value individual freedom, but in America, we have so much poverty, a permanent underclass, a horrific drug problem, and a government-controlled by big business. Who is profiting from Vietnam? Big business, in collusion with our government, and we, the common people, are the expendable fodder who fight their meaningless wars. Just look at Hong Kong; there's individual freedom here, but at what cost? Organized crime, prostitution, drug addiction and hundreds of thousands living in poverty, exploited by rich Chinese bourgeoisie."

"Yet what system would you want to live under?" retorted Jean Pierre. "I was raised in America and still believe in the capitalist system; I think you can better yourself, be better off than your parents were. That is the American dream. The key is education and hard work. The flawed American system is imperfect but still offers the individual hope for a better life, but I was given a lot of opportunities by hard-working parents that put me before their own desires. The 'opportunities' are not there for the average Chinese peasant, nor would they ever have been without the revolution."

"So, you think communism is the answer to all of the world's problems?" asked Jean Pierre.

"For third world countries like India, yes, I do believe that. India is the world's largest democracy, but what did that do for the mass of the people there? There's unbelievable grinding poverty; isn't it the goal of the government to provide an opportunity to live a normal decent life for all of its citizens?"

I asked them if they thought China was better off under communism. Glenda piped in, "Yes, but all of the killings, reeducation camps, and repression really bother me."

I asked Glenda to elaborate on the "re-education" camps because I remembered the stories that the escaped North Korean prison guards told.

Glenda spoke passionately, "The Chinese have just gone through a terrible famine in the 1960s. Reputedly between ten and twenty million farmers starved to death because of the mismanagement of the communal farms. The party leadership didn't know the enormity of the disaster because the provincial governments falsified production figures. Everyone was afraid to admit that they had not met their farm goals or that there was any starvation in the countryside. The common people were now disheartened and angry. There were stories of uprisings, people returning to the old ways, Confucianism was secretly practiced, and the Communist Party was losing its grip on the masses. Mao realized this, and he mobilized the army to force the people back to the "original" vision that had united the country in 1949. All vestiges of religion were swept away, and millions were sentenced to hard labor in 'reeducation camps'. Mao's 'Little Red Book' became the gospel that every man, woman, and child must know and believe in. Intellectuals, teachers, and provincial government officials were seen as reactionary, corrupt capitalists and subject to hard labor and forced indoctrination. The army carried out a Reign of Terror, destroying temples, executing 'capitalist leaders' and creating chaos: sons informed on fathers, students on teachers, and workers on their bosses. When I think of all of this human misery, how can I really say that China is better off under communism?"

I was dumbfounded! "I knew about the 'Little Red Book', but the level of indoctrination and repression was way beyond anything I was aware of."

Mao called this "the Great Awakening", and it was in full fury while we were idly debating philosophies over beer across the border in "free" Hong Kong. Here was a "religion" that was being forced on a quarter of the world's population, and everything else, from Buddhism to the rampant capitalism of Hong Kong, seemed insignificant and meaningless. I felt like a fool. I had been extolling communism as an easy answer to poverty and injustice and now realized this is a lie. China was no better than any Banana Republic dictatorship.

This is the great battle for the "Soul" of Asia. China had been forced into capitalism by the Western powers in the nineteenth century. The English instigated two "opium wars" to force that poison into China. Now the communist Chinese were doing the same thing to their own people. This time it wasn't opium but an all-pervading ideology that kept everybody subservient and crushed individual freedom. Lenin won over the masses in Russia by promising "bread and peace." Today it seemed like China had neither of these to give its people, and the Chinese people had nowhere to turn to escape this nightmare.

The conversation on this subject died since no one had an answer. But now I brought up Bangladesh. "I want to travel to Bangladesh – this is a brand-new country. I want to see how they handle this opportunity. Here you have a poor country that just overthrew an oppressive military dictatorship, and now they are on their own. Will it become a success like the American Revolution against Britain: a "beacon on the hill" for all other nations? Or will it fall into chaos and corruption, with no end to the poverty that engulfs this country?"

"We here in the West have to help them, to ensure that they will really succeed," Glenda again passionately spoke up. I countered, "I hope Europe will band together and help them, but I don't see America stepping in. We are mired in a costly war in Vietnam, and besides, we even supported West Pakistan in this genocidal independence war because they are our "allies" against "socialist" India, which is supported by Russia. It's all a political chess game for us; we really don't care for fledgling democracies; we only want to stay one chess move ahead of the Russians."

It was now pressing 3 a.m.; the beer was long gone, and I felt dejected and embarrassed. I had no idea to support; it seemed that communism and capitalism were just a two-sided coin that couldn't buy freedom or well-being for the peoples of Asia. We called it a night, discouraged by the grim reality right next door.

Chapter 61: Baby Slippers, Dragon Eggs, and Ivory Soap

As I wandered around the back alleys of Hong Kong Island, I came across a whole row of antique shops. I stepped into one store that was particularly dusty, cluttered with relics that spoke of a China that is forever gone. In one corner of the shop was a large, elaborately carved bed, with a platform you step up to pair of gilded and carved doors, which could be closed for privacy. The bed was about 8 feet high and enclosed in carved wood on three sides. The wizened owner saw my interest and told me (in Oxford English, no less) that this was a "marriage bed". The bride in old China brought the bed to her groom's home as part of her dowry and spent most of her day in it-eating meals, doing her makeup, and just lounging and conversing with family members.

Then he showed me a chest full of what looked like baby slippers. I have friends whose parents tied their child's first shoes to the overhead mirror on the dashboard of their cars, proudly proclaiming a cherished celebration of the baby's first stage of maturity. However, the shop owner told me these were adult shoes worn by upper-class Chinese women who had their feet bound as a child so they would not grow larger. Foot binding was a mark of status and even considered beautiful in old China. It showed to the world that the family was so rich that the women would not do anything in the household; servants would do all the chores.

Rich Chinese woman with foot binding

I thought of my own mother, struggling to support herself, first as a household domestic, next as a factory worker, and finally, as a housewife, doing her chores, pinching pennies, putting food on the table, and saving for my education as mistress of the household expenses.

Now in red China, women are equal to men: serving in the army, managing collective farms, and serving as party political leaders. Whatever I may feel about red China, it has given women a status that we in the West have not achieved (in my father's Heimat, Switzerland, women were not given the vote in all the cantons (states) until 1967). In New York City, women were not content to be secretaries, rising to lead the garment workers and the teachers through hard-won unions. Eleanor Roosevelt is a shiny example of a woman that used her position for humanitarian goals, selflessly working to improve the lives of her fellow citizens. However, contrasted to her are the Eva Peron and Imelda Marcos of the world: women who project a glamorous Hollywood lifestyle, a glittering foil to distract the masses, while their husbands continue to rape their countries through corruption, bribery, and repression.

As I walked out of the shop, I saw some dirty brownish "eggs" and asked what they were? He answered they were fossilized "dragon" (dinosaur) eggs from the Gobi Desert in Inner Mongolia (a part of China).

Fossilized Dinosaur eggs

Instantly, I was back home in New Jersey. I asked my mother what we were eating, and she replied, chicken ala king. Without thinking, I told her, "I don't want to eat that shit." I was amazed at my self-asserting effrontery, and, of course, my mother stopped dead in her tracks.

"What did you just say to me!" Needless to say, I took off on the run (I was pretty fast for a ten-year-old), and she was not far behind. In our house, you could make a complete loop from the dining room through the living room to the kitchen and back to the dining room. I knew if she caught me, I would get my mouth washed out with a bar of Ivory soap across my teeth for my cursing (I still believe today I have such gleaming white teeth because of my periodic soap cleansings. And besides, Ivory is 99 and 44/100 percent pure). I was way in the lead at the quarter turn; as I rounded the turn and entered the kitchen, I knocked over a pot of boiling string beans, which spilled on my feet. I started screaming, my scalded feet swelled enormously, and I had to be hospitalized. (The doctor expressed some concern that I might walk with a limp for the rest of my life, but with extensive physical therapy, I won that one for the Gipper). However, when I was in the hospital, my visiting mother (sans the soap) brought me some National Geographic magazines to read.

I remember being mesmerized by the issue where Roy Chapman Andrews discovered fossilized dinosaur eggs in the Gobi Desert. Hundreds of million years ago, dinosaurs roamed the swampy lowlands of the Gobi. They laid their eggs in the marshy mud, which was covered by sediment or ash. Over eons, the eggs turned to stone, and Andrews's team unearthed them in the 1930s. The discovery was sensational, but even more interesting to me were the adventures that led to the findings. Andrews endured sandstorms, Chinese bandits, truck breakdowns, corrupt officials, starvation, and frustrating excavations that yielded nothing. Here was a genuine American hero who persevered against all odds to achieve this great discovery. Now I was in Asia, following in the footsteps of this great explorer, visiting firsthand "lost cities", ruined fortresses, overgrown temples, and encountering exotic peoples.

Roy Chapman Andrews (The Real "Indiana Jones")

I didn't buy a "dragon egg" because I thought they were cleverly made fakes for the tourist trade. Back home, my mother gave me two stone "rocks". She told me that they were petrified fruit from the dinosaur age. They were given to her by her brother, who had been a coal miner in Svalbard Island, above the Artic circle. Svalbard was part of the huge continent Gondwanaland and, like the Gobi, was a tropical swampy marsh. I examined this "fruit" closely; to me, it looked more like dinosaur poop than fruit. When I showed them to my friends, I told them that they were two pieces of petrified dinosaur shit. (I can say that now without fear of getting my mouth washed out with soap).

Chapter 62: Hong Kong III

THE NEW TERRITORIES

"Undercurrents": Faye Wong

This popular Chinese torch singer sings of broken love in Hong Kong

One bright morning Mr. Wu, owner of the hostel, took a few of us travelers on a car trip to visit the New Territories. Mr. Wong was educated in communist China, and he, like all Hong Kong residents, can go back and forth at will to the mainland. He even told us that drug addicts, who really want to kick the habit cross over because there are no drugs in mainland China. Once they are "cured", they return to Hong Kong.

One of my fellow passengers was Terry, a Malaysian Muslim who had been traveling throughout Europe and Asia for six years and really saw himself traveling for the rest of his life. He had many funny stories, but I noticed he excused himself, went outside, and came back noticeably high. After touring some farms and small fishing villages, we found a small restaurant near the bay. This is where I finally understood why Hong Kong is world-famous for its cuisine. The floating restaurants of Aberdeen are always chock full of tourists, but they couldn't come close to the variety and types of sauces that this small, cheap restaurant served us. From black garlic bean to fiery chili to mellow coconut-based sauces, everything was a delight, especially since we washed it down with copious bottles of Tashtego Chinese beer.

While we were eating, the background music was choral singing with strident musical accompaniment. I asked Mr. Wu what this music was that I was hearing, and he answered, "Chinese communist revolutionary opera." He explained that the people were singing in unison against their oppressors and how the Communists saved them so that they could build a new China together. I thought of the great Russian choral work: Sergei Prokofiev's "Alexander Nevsky". Here Prokofiev handled a similar theme, writing his choral work about a valiant Russian patriot who defeats a foreign invader, the Germanic Teutonic knights; only this has stirring melodic choral singing and dramatic orchestrations. If the Chinese communists wanted a replacement for Peking

Opera, which represented to them the old corrupt regime, then they had best compose something better than this atonal propaganda piece.

We returned to the hostel, and I went out exploring the back streets, to see how the Chinese got rid of all of their tensions from living pent-up and so close to each other. After school or work, ping pong tables sprang up everywhere, like green seaweed squares, and these kids were great players – this was not a sport but mortal combat. The opponents, standing three feet from the table, smash the ball across the net.

The other sport was martial arts: judo, jujitsu, or kung fu. There were storefront clubs everywhere practicing these arts, and Hong Kong was the leading producer of kung fu action films. A young handsome Chinese American named Bruce Lee was a famous kung fu movie star here. He was all the rage, and every kid was trying to imitate his moves. Chase, one of our hostel roommates, had come to Asia to study martial arts. He called his quest "The Endless Flip", a clever take on the popular surfer film, "The Endless Summer". Chase, like the surfers looking for the perfect wave, was searching for the "best" martial art, so he could start a school in California teaching that martial art discipline.

"I'd walk a mile for a Camel."

As I was walking around Hong Kong, I noticed that everyone was smoking. All the Chinese shopkeepers had a cigarette dangling from their mouths; both men and women puffed away at restaurants and clubs. Back home, my favorite attraction in Times Square (besides the peep shows and XXX-rated movies) was the huge billboard showing this handsome stud puffing on a Camel and real smoke coming out of his mouth.

It seemed that everybody smoked; both my parents smoked, but I didn't start smoking cigarettes until my senior year in college. I had a night shift job in a Newspaper print making factory, and after set up of the printing material, there was nothing to do except watch the huge rolls of paper go round and round (20 years of schooling and they put you on the night shift), so I started smoking like the rest of the crew. This habit increased in the army (as John Wayne said to his embattled soldiers in a World War II movie: "If you've got 'em- smoke 'em."). Cigarettes in the PX were dirt cheap: $1.70 for a carton of Camels. In Europe, I tried the French cigarette "Gaulois", which I swear is one-part tobacco and two parts horse shit (Merde!).

In every Asian country, I bought the local brand since American smokes were prohibitively expensive. Here in Hong Kong, someone told me that communist China's fearless leader Mao chain-smoked American capitalists produced Marlboros. I had this wild vision of Mao, dressed in his trademark gray Chinese leisure suit, visiting a commune pig farm in eastern China, sporting a ten-gallon Stetson and Frye leather cowboy boots with spurs, riding a huge water buffalo, puffing on a Marlboro, herding and yodeling to the pigs: "Get along lil' doggies."

Chapter 63: Revolutionary Opera

"Night at the Opera" 1935 film starring The Marx Brothers
Movie Poster photo

Driftwood (Groucho Marx): How much does Mr. Lassparri get?

Gottlieb: $1,000 a night.

Driftwood: A thousand dollars a nacht? What does he do?

Gottlieb: What's he do? He sings!

Driftwood: So, you're willing to pay him $1,000 a night just by singing? Why, you can get a phonograph record of Minnie the Moocher for 75 cents. For a buck and a quarter, you can get Minnie.

After my initial disdain of Chinese communist revolutionary opera, I completely forgot about it until one morning. I was eating dim sum in a local restaurant when this strangely hypnotic singing started playing over the owner's radio. I asked him where it came from, and he told me it was "The White-Haired Girl", a revolutionary Opera. The plot of this opera is simple and didactic. An evil landlord takes a beautiful but poor peasant girl from her father as repayment for a debt he owes him. The evil landlord rapes her and keeps her captive in his large mansion. Meanwhile, back at the farm, her former farmer boyfriend tries to rescue her but fails. He then enlists the "big guns", the Red Army, to help him. Meanwhile, back at the mansion, the girl manages to escape, living in the mountains on roots and nuts and suffering so badly that her hair turns white. In the end, the evil landlord is killed by the Red Army; the girl is rescued; she marries her hayseed boyfriend and lives happily ever after.

Meanwhile, back at the hostel, I asked Mr. Wizard (Mr. Wu) to explain to me revolutionary opera in all its gory and didactic splendor (in three-part harmony, no less, please). He told me that there were six operas and two ballets created by Jiang Qing, the actress wife of Mao-tse-Tung. These products were called Yang Ban Xi (Model Works), which combined Hollywood Bushby Berkeley dance routines, Peking Opera stylized acting and exaggerated facial gestures, elaborate set designs, highly skilled acrobatics, and colorful costumes.

Scene from the Revolutionary Ballet, "Red Detachment of Women"

These were produced during the Cultural Revolution (still going on while I was in Hong Kong). revolutionary opera's purpose, according to Mao, was "to serve the interests of workers, peasants, and soldiers conforming to the Proletarian ideology." What it did was spread a message of hate with arias like "Hatred Blazes When Enemies Meet." This, combined with Mao's "Little Red Book", taught all of China, mostly illiterate peasants and gung-ho soldiers, to hate the enemies of communism: greedy landlords, invading Japanese soldiers, and corrupt capitalistic Americans.

These operas were the only game in town. Throughout China, there was no music, stage performance, or films other than these eight models' works. Everywhere you went in shops, factories and schools, this was the only music you heard. It became an integral part of your life. I tried to empathize with the Chinese people, but all I could think about was listening to an entire album of David Seville and the Chipmunks over and over for years, nonstop. I would go bonkers, standing with a chain saw over a chipmunk hole, leering and waiting like Jack Nicholson in "The Shining" ("Honey I'm home, Come Out"), to kill everyone of those damn critters.

The famous Chinese novelist Anchee Min, author of the novel "Red Azaleas", wrote of this period, "Every day I listened to this when I ate walked and slept, I sang the opera, knowing all of the lyrics by heart, wherever I went." What saved these operas musically and artistically were the great actors, dancers, songwriters, and producers. They could not find other work, so they wholeheartedly created an art out of a lifeless propaganda piece. At one time, there were three thousand theatrical troupes performing these operas and ballets throughout China. They performed in factories, collective farms, and schools (Broadway goes to the Boondocks). In a real sense, the people were empowered. Millions of young Chinese students learned to play musical instruments or to perform dramatically on stage. The stories weren't about upper-class warriors and emperors but about ordinary people who fight back against oppression. Theater and life became one in China for millions of uneducated peasants, soldiers, and factory workers. Incidentally, when the performers fly through the air, attacking their oppressors, they carry a rifle instead of the sword of Peking Opera, reinforcing Mao's famous aphorism from his "Little Red Book": "Revolution is only achieved through the barrel of a rifle."

Growing up in the 1950s and 1960s, I saw lots of movies with beautiful rich people: Doris Day and Rock Hudson in romantic comedies and Tab Hunter in beach heartthrobs. I felt like the Chinese peasant: life stories of rich carefree couples or beach bums were not my life. Our family was struggling. My father had two jobs, and my mother would babysit children for husband and wife working families. Then I saw "On the Waterfront." Here was a hero I could identify with. Terry Malloy was uneducated, inarticulate, and a palooka, but he was "real" in that you could empathize with his struggles because these were your hopes and dreams too.

Macau

St. Paul Church Ruin – Old City Macau

Chapter 64: Macau

Aimee Mann: "Save Me"

This film noir movie poster of "Macao" says it all: world-weary hero falls for tough cookie singer in steamy Macau

Macau is one of those magical places where the name conjures visions of exotic intrigue. The hero, a strong, chain-smoking, world-weary character dressed in a rumpled doubled-breasted linen suit, always gets involved with smuggling a priceless, stolen Chinese antique, seduced by beautiful mysterious Eurasian femme fatales, hounded by sinister Fu Man Chu Chinese gangsters and balding, fat European antique collectors and arrested by bungling Portuguese colonial police. The heroine, a sultry, tough-cookie brunette, is usually an out-of-work singer who bounces from one seedy bar to another, singing her heart out, waiting for Mr. Right. After many plot twists, the hero does the right thing: he returns the gold idol to the temple it was stolen from, makes the singer an "honest woman", and they go off to Marionville, Ohio, and raise five kids.

But what you remember from these B-Grade melodramas is the decadent noir atmosphere of Macau. All the characters wear crumpled white linen suits, spend their time in high ceilinged, crumbling stucco houses, drink bourbon straight up to keep their minds off the steamy humidity, sit sweltering in white wicker chairs under slow-moving ceiling fans, listen to fados (Portuguese lament ballads) and torch songs in dark, smokey Chinese nightclubs, get pulled all over the city by sweaty Chinese coolies and invariably have a climatic shootout on a picturesque junk in Macau's congested waterfront: the triumphant hero and heroine walk arm in arm into the sunset (Wow, I said all that in one long run-on sentence without stopping to breathe!).

This Macau I described is born of Hollywood fantasies. There is an earlier "imaginary" city which was the threshold between the West with the dynamic seafaring Portuguese exploring the unknown world for geld and God, and the mysterious East, the reclusive Chinese with their isolationist closed society. It was this cross-cultural interchange that made Macau so fascinating. Yet it was always hidden, a Petrie dish for the Chinese to spy on the "barbarians" from a distance.

Macau is an "invisible city" to use the criteria of Italo Calvino's extraordinary novel "Invisible Cities". This book describes the supposed conversations of Marco Polo with the Mongol Emperor of China, Kublai Khan. Kublai wants to know everything about all the cities in his vast realm and tasks Marco to visit them and report back to him what they are like. Marco obeys and visits all the large cities, dividing them into eleven categories: memory, desire, signs, thin, names, ear (hearing), dead, sky, continuous and hidden. He reports back to Kublai and describes all the cities in phantasmagorical detail. Kublai finds these cities more fanciful, wonderful, and believable than the "real" cities. They now become the magical cities of his own imagination. But in the last conversation he has with Marco. He tells him that there was one city he did not describe: his hometown Venice.

Marco smiled. "What else do you believe I have been talking to you about?"

Marco answered: "Every time I describe a city, I am saying something about Venice."

In my travels, I see Asian cities as a point of comparison with my own hometown, New York City. Unlike Calvino, I do not use surreal images to conjure pulsating, multi-faceted New York but dredged up, long forgotten figments that now appear as a camera obscura, a cache of old crinkled photos rediscovered in the attic of your collective conscious mind. One of the greatest "invisible" cities in modern fiction is James Joyce's Dublin in "Ulysses". This was written in exile in Zurich (my father's heimat), a cold (physically and emotionally) Northern European city, but Joyce transports the reader to a vibrant, mythical place that exists only in his mind as a magical realism vision of a long-gone city. This "city of Memory, Desire, and the Dead" now becomes a part of the reader's subconscious, more real and fascinating than the actual Dublin.

I first found Macau, another "City of Memory, the Dead and the Hidden", to be disappointing: a few brightly painted colonial customs and revenue buildings, peeling badly in the tropic humidity, and Chinese restaurants that serve Portuguese food, desserts, and demi-tasse coffee to the tourists.

Macau has become an easy weekend getaway, where wealthy Hong Kong Chinese gamble away their newfound riches in glitzy Las Vegas-style casinos. Communist China now sets the policies while keeping the anachronistic Portuguese administration nominally in charge.

However, you can still find the Portuguese colonial city in the historic old Centro. Here are brightly colored baroque churches still in service, set-in tree-shaded plazas, cooling wrought iron fountains with mudejar tiled bases, imposing ionic columned Portuguese administration buildings, a large stone fort overlooking the city and the icon of Macau: the magnificent ruin of St. Paul's Church. All that remains of this large baroque church, which burned in the nineteenth century and was never rebuilt, is the wide, steep steps and the ornate stone façade –propped from behind by steel girders, reminding me of the fake Western towns of cheap spaghetti westerns, only facades held upright by visible wood struts. Yet this is the meeting place par excellence for students, lovers, families, and tourists.

Wandering the back lanes of the Centro, you find the old merchant mansions, pastel-painted, peeling two-story stucco townhouses with long verandahs, wood shutters pulled tight over the huge, rounded windows, all coolly shaded by bougainvillea vines, tall palms, bamboo and tree ferns.

However, Macau is a mere shadow of its former greatness. The Portuguese came to Macau during the Age of Discovery in the 16th century. The riches of China were fabled: silks, porcelain, jade carvings, and spices. The Portuguese wanted in and gained Chinese favor by eliminating the coastal pirates, which plagued the Chinese merchant junks. The Ming government allowed the

Portuguese to trade in Macau harbor but would not let them stay ashore on the Chinese island. Eventually, they were allowed to take over the whole island, paying an annual rent to the Ming government. The Jesuits came to build churches and schools to convert the native Chinese, which is over 95% of Macau's citizens. For a hundred years (16th to 17th century), the Portuguese had the sole monopoly of the China trade and became fabulously wealthy.

Two Jesuits, Matteo Ricci and Adam Schall, hold a map of China, before starting on their proselytizing mission to convert the country to Catholicism

A Jesuit from Italy, Matteo Ricci, left Macau after learning Mandarin to convert to the Ming court. The Ming Emperor was impressed with Ricci's mathematical and astronomical knowledge, but the Jesuit was not able to win any royal converts to Catholicism. Macau was also a starting base for trade with Japan. The Portuguese grew even more wealthy, trading Chinese silk for Japanese silver through the port of Nagasaki, where they had the sole trading outpost for the Japanese trade. Here the Jesuits were actively proselytizing the Japanese, spearheaded by Saint Francis Xavier. Jesuits taught the Japanese Western-style painting figures in Chinese Court clothes and oriental faces, a fascinating hybrid of cultures (see my chapter on "Nambans" in the Japan section). The closure of Nagasaki was the beginning of Macau's decline. Another trade blow was the Dutch capture of Malacca in Malaysia, an important Portuguese trading colony, which had traded heavily with Macau, sending spices and ivory for Chinese silk and jade.

The final spike on the trade coffin was the Chinese leasing the British Hong Kong Island in 1842. Hong Kong had a natural deep-water port, and the large trading vessels would berth there, bypassing Macau, which became a sleepy time capsule until the gambling casinos arrived in the 20th century. After imbuing the old colonial mélange, I found a small Portuguese restaurant (run by Chinese) that served paella-Macau style –a lot spicier than the traditional Spanish paella, made with varieties of shellfish that I had never seen before, washed down with a carafe of vinho da Portugal. Desert was a Chinese variant of Flan (Spanish custard pudding in a caramel sauce) with strong café negro - Bom Dia!

My last stop in Macau was the Protestant Cemetery. From the very beginning of its founding, Macau was a Catholic stronghold. The Portuguese would not permit any Protestant churches nor allow foreign cemeteries. However, from the 18th century on, the bulk of the China Trade vessels were manned by Dutch, English, and American seaman, most of whom were Protestants, who had no place to bury their deceased merchants and seamen. Finally, the British East India Company was able to buy a plot of land in Macau that they converted into a Protestant cemetery in the late 18th Century.

Old cemeteries are literally masterpieces of art. While visiting a friend who lived on a farm in New York State, we stumbled on an early 19th Century graveyard. The church was long gone, but in the overgrown weeds were crooked crumbling sandstone markers decorated with primitive doves, willows, and sun symbols, carvings that were peeling away, along with the names of long-dead forgotten farmers. In Macau, there were leafy willow trees, manicured lawns, and many elaborate stone memorials to former governors and distinguished merchants, but the most poignant were the narrow fading stone markers of long-dead sailors who perished on China trade or whaling vessels.

Gravestones of sailors and merchants in the Protestant Cemetery, Macau "Ebenezer Cowles from New York, Age 26

Died from a ship's mast fall, August 14, 1826

May God Rest His Soul"

"My dearest Bethany,

It is a stormy August night, and the men are grumbling since it has been three weeks since we were in a port and off this foul-smelling ship. We had picked up a cargo of calico and pepper at

Cochin, India, and we're headed for Canton to buy black tea. It has been five months since we sailed from Salem, and it looks like another six months before I am back in your arms. I miss you so much, but the proceeds from this venture should give me enough money for a cabin with a small plot of land near Rochester. I have not wasted my money on rum or gambling, and our bonus on a successful voyage will go straight to the bank.

Our ship chores are not odorous, and the First Mate looks out for us, making sure our food is not wormy and saving us from the wrath of our surly captain.

The worst duty is to look out mast watch, which I will have to perform shortly. I will not be able to see anything in this storm, but at least the strong wind and rain should keep me awake during this monotonous tour of duty. The first mate has called my name for duty, so I will close for now. When I return, I will tell you about all the wonderful places and strange people that I encountered in India. Goodbye for now, my love.

Your Loving Eben."

Macau is an "imaginary city", according to Jonathan Potter in "Macau: The Imaginary City": "Dreamlike as though sustained by the effort of some powerful imagination, continuous, but everchanging." The exotic East versus the capitalist West, the battleground of Confucianism versus Christianity, and complacent stagnation versus go-getter optimism. Yet it is primarily a memory of a lost empire; the dead are more important than the living. A 97-year-old Jesuit priest toils daily in his monastery on his history of Macau. The Sacred Museum is stuffed with angular, blood-soaked, suffering crucifixes, a sobering reminder of Christian hopes dashed in an attempt to convert the Chinese masses. The name Macau will still conjure desires and fears, but it will be as hollow as the empty space behind the facade of St. Paul's.

I caught one of the last ferries back to Hong Kong; the low-roofed, red-tiled port buildings, doubled-masted junks, and small freighters glowed rusty orange in the fading light—soon, the incandescent brightness of Hong Kong would banish the darkened horizon.

Chapter 65: Hong Kong IV

(Titling this as #4 shows a glaring lack of imagination on my part, as bad as the "ROCKY" movie franchise; I'm waiting for "ROCKY" X: The Wheelchair Fight, Duking It Out at the Senior Citizen Home". However, if you slugged through the first three Hong Kong's (You're a better man than I, Gunga Din!), this one is mercifully short. Also, I usually try to select songs "of great political and social importance" as Janis would say. But the following song is dedicated to all those "lucky individuals" blessed with the moniker II, III or IV after your last name (if you're German, I will include anyone with a "Von" between your first and last name'') and not to neglect the girls: to those distinguished fairer sex individuals whose first name is "Mercedes", here's honking at you, baby.

"Does Your Chewing Gum Lose Its Flavor": Lonnie Donegan

When I returned to the youth hostel after an afternoon of serious drinking, I met some familiar faces: Brad and Arlene Morris, the married couple from my army duty days in Korea. They were on a whirlwind tour, having already visited Australia, New Zealand, Indonesia, and now Hong Kong. They enjoyed their trip, but they were eager to get home. Brad had to prepare for his law school boards, and Arlene just wanted to get on with her life and career. We had dinner together, where I got even more drunk, discussed our mutual friends (in a heavily slurred speech), and wished them well (between hiccups).

I was a little jealous, in that they knew what they wanted and were doing it, whereas I was still wandering, without any real plans or ambitions for my future. However, that night I thought about the Chinese Ying and Yang: know yourself before you go home and "save the world". Wait let me get my speech... now where was I? Oh yeah: there is still so much to learn and experience. This is my time, and if you elect me, I will bring jobs, improve our schools, a chicken in every pot... wait, that wasn't on my teleprompter screen. Whose been messing with my well-rehearsed justification-for-not-going-back-home-now-speech?

The next afternoon my plane took off for Manilla. It was a beautiful day; you could really see the magnificence of the city nestled into the bay and the surrounding hills. The jigsaw sky-scraper mass on Hong Kong Island, with the cargo ships stacked up by the dozens in the harbor, the endless gray concrete block apartment houses of Kowloon, and the green farms and open vistas of the new territories.

Hong Kong in 1972

Philippines: Santos and Uncle Sam

Manila Street scene 1900. This could be a street in San Francisco at the same time: the streetcar, English language signs, horse drawn buggies and colorful wooden buildings

Chapter 66: Welcome to Blue Jeans, English and Rock and Roll

"Hey Joe": Jimi Hendrix

Every foreigner is called "Hey Joe" by the Filipinos

I arrived in the Philippines, the only Christian majority country in all of Asia, and was greeted by a sea of humanity wearing tee shirts, loose summer blouses, and everyone in blue jeans, all enveloped in the sticky, humid heat. The people are basically Malay: short, black-haired, chocolate brown with fine features, infused by strains of immigrants from China, Islamic countries, Spain, and the US. They speak over three hundred languages, spread out through 7000 islands. Tagalog is the principal language, strongly infused with Spanish and English vocabulary. English is widely understood and spoken by all strata of Filipino society, but every American or foreign traveler is greeted by the ubiquitous "Hey Joe".

I really knew nothing about the Philippines, but what amazed me was that America had "owned" them for half a century, and besides a little English and rock and roll, we did nothing to really help these people. I went to the Manila library and got a book on Philippine history to try and understand our failure at colonialism. We bought the Philippines from Spain for twenty million dollars in 1898 as a spoil of war after defeating the Spanish in the Spanish-American war. Ostensibly, we wanted to free these people from the despotic, anti-democratic Spanish government and give them a real democracy like we have. But the politicians in Washington believed that these people did not have the experience to govern themselves and that everything would degenerate into chaos. Also, we were afraid that in the aftermath of this chaos, the European powers would step in and carve up this country and exclude us from its potential riches and deprive us of a strategic foothold in Asia.

We would tutor them on how a true American democracy works. And then let them establish a self-governing system based on a presidency with two houses of congress. Unfortunately, the Filipinos didn't see it that way, and they declared independence under the leadership of a small-town mayor turned resistance fighter, Emilio Aguinaldo. Emilio Aguinaldo had fought the Spanish, and now he declared himself President of the Philippine Republic and fought the Americans.

The Filipinos could not hope to beat the better-equipped American forces in conventional battles, but they were adept at guerilla tactics, inflicting many casualties on the Americans. To counter this, the Americans set up concentration camps, euphemistically labeled "zones of protection" that separated the "good" Filipinos from the "bad" guerilla Filipinos. Unlike the similar "classification" policy in Vietnam, this worked, but the camps were so cramped and unsanitary that hundreds of thousands died from dysentery and other diseases. Again, like in the Vietnam war, there were powerful voices objecting to our imperialist policies. The most famous was Mark Twain, who wrote: "I thought we should act as their protectors, not try and get them under our heels...we relieved them from Spanish tyranny to set up a government not under our ideas but a government that represented the feelings of the majority of the Filipinos."

Filipino Freedom Fighters 1898

We captured Aguinaldo, ended the war, and set up a government under our system. We brought in schoolteachers from America to teach English and instituted free, universal, public education." The Filipinos learned fast, and they quickly established democratic self-government. However, just like in the U. S. at that time, it was controlled by rich businessmen, and there was cronyism and corruption at the highest levels. The Filipinos finally gained independence in 1946, but today the country is still controlled by corrupt politicians, like the current president, Fernand Marcos. Marcos was widely popular when I arrived in the Philippines. He had taken over businesses owned by the Filipino Chinese community and given them to his "native" Filipino cronies, enriching himself along the way. Meanwhile, the vast majority of Filipinos remained in abject poverty.

After arriving in the Philippines, I stayed at a small rundown hotel in the heart of the Old City, Quiapo. Quiapo in the daytime was teeming with life: beggars, cigarette girls selling single cigarettes, young jobless men idly smoking and drinking beer on the streets, Chinese shop owners, and street vendors. There are horse-drawn carriages unloading produce and multi-colored jeepneys (a jeep modified to have 6-8 seats, the unofficial taxi servicing all of Manilla, clogging the crowded and filthy streets.

The architecture in the Old City was old Spanish-style buildings, painted in pastel colors but peeling badly due to the tropic humidity, crumbling wooden-latticed balconies, huge wrought iron gates, and wash hanging from strings across the ornate windows down into the streets. This Spanish colonial area was interspersed with ruined churches and derelict old forts, divided into town squares, watered by graceful fountains and broad shade trees.

I walked into Manilla's Chinatown, dominated by a huge Pagoda Emporium, which sold everything from Chinese medicinal herbs to cheap clothing, toys, and electronics and had dozens of noodle shop eateries. Here, the Chinese had set up their own temples, benevolent society, tea shops, and restaurants: a separate city within Manilla.

The Chinese were part of the great outward migration from mainland China, coming to the Philippines as rice farmers, merchants, restaurant owners, and jewelers. They prospered, sending money back home to their poor families in Fukien and Hakka provinces in China. They also intermarried with the Filipinos and created a small subculture from the fusion of the two races.

Native Filipino teenagers hanging out in their version of the Brooklyn stoop

The Chinese controlled most of the small businesses and restaurants in Manilla, and there was a sharp contrast between the hustling Chinese and the languid Filipinos, who wandered listlessly on the street corners, trying to pick up the local girls. I had also been warned at my hotel that there were a lot of pickpocket thieves and to be careful at night. However, I found most of the people to be extremely friendly and eager to talk to me and find out about life in America. We had instilled our American culture: movies, pop music, fashion, and cars, but they had no jobs or money to obtain this much-desired lifestyle. Almost everyone I spoke to wanted to come to America. As I mentioned before, Marcos began a campaign to marginalize the Chinese influence, pushing for native Filipino ownership of major industries and increased taxation on non-Filipino small businesses. The government also required that only the Filipino language be used in schools, religious temples, churches, and on all public lettering on store front signage. This caused mass outward emigration of the Chinese and the Chinese Filipinos. The native Filipinos also left the country in droves because of no jobs; one out of every ten works abroad. The jobs they took overseas were desk workers in Arab oil fields, domestic help in Europe, and doctors and nurses in America. These hard-working immigrants sent back money to their families, and this has become a major pillar of the Filipino economy.

The huge gap between the rich and the poor was embarrassingly evident in Makati, an exclusive enclave in Manilla. Broad avenues, tall skyscrapers, American style, air-conditioned supermarkets stocked with foreign delicacies, and posh hotels and restaurants. This was the good life for the privileged few; you don't have to be a communist to see that this couldn't go on forever. A true democracy must bring the majority of its citizens into the middle class, a sharing of the wealth to forestall a revolution of the "have-nots".

Chapter 67: From Soldier To Shopper: The Jeepney

Born to be Wild: Steppenwolf

Jeepney

You can't look at the passing cars in every district of Manilla without seeing dozens of jeepneys; as I mentioned before, the original jeepney was an American jeep that was modified with a steel roof and an extended truck body. This body was fitted with two long fitted wooden benches opposite each other, and the rear was modified with steel stairs so that you could get in and out. These jeepneys can transport 6-8 people and serve a basic transportation need: public buses are few and overcrowded; jeepneys serve all Manilla neighborhoods with fast, cheap, and reliable service.

Enterprising Filipinos bought up hundreds of American military Jeeps after the war, modified them to be minibusses, and now they are everywhere. Jeepneys are also being manufactured locally by small Filipino companies and sold to transport companies and individuals as taxicabs. What makes them special and fun are the painted decorations that individual owners and drivers lavish on their jeepneys. You have cartoon heroes, movie stars, and religious icons, all painted in garish psychedelic splendor. Riding in a jeepney is also an experience; you're thrown together, with a chance to meet new people, and the sights and smells of the city are viscerally alive and, in your face, since there are no glass windows. Instead of fighting the Japanese, you are now fighting traffic, with blaring horns and colorful language from the speed-crazed drivers. Hold on to your seat; you ain't seen nothing yet!

Chapter 68: Jesus Has Still Not Come Home

"One of Us": Joan Osborne

This song imagines God as a tired worker, getting on the uptown bus to go home.

The square was a vast sea of multi-colored umbrellas and brightly lit candles. The loudspeaker blared out a prayer, while on an adjoining street, a band was playing a military march. The devotees took off their shoes and formed a procession line to the Quiapo church, a huge, blue, peeling stone edifice in the heart of Quiapo, the historic center of old Manila. All along the approaches to the church stood where everything from candles to incense to hot noodle soup was for sale. The selling was most intense right at the entrance to the church. This was the shrine of the Black Nazarene. Legend has it that there was a fire in the church, and everything was destroyed except the Christ statue, which was only blackened by the smoke. The Black Nazarene is now a miracle worker, curing illnesses and granting good fortune to true believers. This is how the Cult of the Black Jesus sprang up. Its followers' number over half of a million within the Filipino Catholic Church. The life-size, somber wooden statue of Jesus was carved in Mexico by an anonymous Indian sculptor in the seventeenth century and arrived in Manila as part of the Acapulco to Manila Galleon trade. It is now bedecked with jewels and dressed in purple velvet robes.

The festival consists of carrying Jesus out to the people and around the Old City for the yearly festival. It is borne on an elaborate gold and leather litter, carried on poles by the faithful. These pallbearers are all young Jesus lookalikes: dark, finely featured, Botticelli-pretty young men. The Nazarene moved slowly in the heavy rain. Always there were new devotees who stepped in and carried it a few hundred feet before yielding to other young men, everyone wanting the honor of carrying the Christ. If the image drops down or slips from an upright position too many times, it signifies bad luck for the coming year. Today, the rain makes the carrying tough; so many superstitious people predicted a bad year. The procession waded through crowds of old men with gold teeth carrying pictures of the Nazarene. Young men, sporting a picture of the Black Nazarene on their tee shirts, were smoking, cursing, drinking, and trying to pick up every young girl along the route. There were groups of old women wrapped in shawls, some with crowns-of-thorns on their heads, clasping hands while chanting Ave Maries and supplicating the Christ for favors.

Schoolgirls and other young women in short-cut summer dresses were out to woo the crowds. There were young kids everywhere, setting off firecrackers, selling single cigarettes, and creating mischief in the crowds. Even the rain couldn't dampen the holiday spirit and religious adoration.

I followed the procession, and finally, the blessed image came into sight, with the people holding umbrellas over it to protect it from the rain. I tried to get close to take some photographs, but the shoeless throng kept shouting at me, "No zapatos" (no shoes), afraid that I would step on their feet.

The "Black Jesus" moving through the streets of Quiapo

(Author photo)

The Nazarene moved slowly, the young barefoot boys struggling as they hosted it on their shoulders while others tugged on ropes to help keep the image upright. The whole Quiapo area was cordoned off from traffic, and the people in the main square of Miranda Plaza were hanging out everywhere: out of high ornate plastered windows, clinging to fences, or holding onto the plaster robes of the Catholic Saints that surrounded the Quiapo church, just to get a view of the blessed image. Vendors were doing brisk business, and toward the evening, a wooden platform was set up in Miranda Plaza, hosting a talent and comedy show.

While watching some incomprehensible Tagalog slapstick comic, I meet a 20-something, stunning Filipino girl, Miramum. She spoke American English like a college student, with a lilting accent, and was very lively and funny. She dressed like a flower child hippie: long black hair, straw bonnet with flowers, worn blue jeans, loose tie-down, embroidered blouse, and leather sandals. She translated the comic for me and made jokes about the sincere but terribly awful singers performing in the following talent show. We talked about life in Manila; she wanted to become a nurse, but her family did not have enough money to send her to nursing school. She was ambitious and trained as a midwife to learn medical practices. She had plenty of work: most Filipino women have their children at home because they cannot afford hospital care. It was great to talk to a normal girl and not a whore, that was just out for your money.

I wanted to get her address and thought we could get dinner together, but before I could get this information, these two overweight ogres arrived. They claimed to be her sisters, yelled at Miramum in Tagalog, and whisked her away with only a hurried goodbye. I was left alone in the street, without even a single sandal left behind, so I couldn't search the streets of Quiapo looking for a match.

The rain formed a big puddle in front of the church, but planks were set up over the puddle and allowed dry access into the church. The church was crowded, but it seemed spiritually empty without its Nazarene. Around 10:30 at night, Christ had still not returned from the procession. The rain had finally let up, and a Fourth of July festive mood stirred the crowd. More fireworks were shot off as the people crowded around the church, waiting for Jesus to return. I left around 11:30; the festivities were still going strong, and Jesus had still not come home yet.

Chapter 69: Sacred Images

In every country that I visit, I seek out the art of the country as an expression of their national consciousness. In the Philippines, this national art was the exquisite religious carvings in wood, stone, silver, and ivory. The Spanish missionaries brought catholicism in the 16th century. They established churches and encouraged the newly converted to have individual house shrines. All these churches and shrines needed religious images, so they set up sculpture schools of indigenous craftsmen to carve the religious figures. What makes this statuary unique is its fusion of Spanish religious fervor with the native animistic influenced faces and symbols. The native artisans used the European models and imbued them with their Filipino sensibilities to create works of luminous piety. I saw an ivory figure in the National Museum depicting Christ as a Filipino peasant: swarthy and bloodied, stoically suffering crucifixion.

These missionary schools also trained immigrant Chinese artisans. Here the Chinese looked to their own artistic heritage and saw that the Virgin Mary and Christ child were very much like depictions of Guanyin, the Chinese goddess of good fortune and fertility, usually shown with a young child in her arms. Here you had a hybrid art of the catholic Virgin and Christ Child, with Chinese faces and dressed in regal Asian clothing.

"Our lady of La Naval de Manila" Ivory face and hands, silk costume and precious jewels, late 16th century, National Museum, Manila

Ming Dynasty Ivory Guanyin with child (late 16th century), Walters Art Museum, Baltimore

Here in these two examples of the Virgin with a child, you can see the influence of the Chinese carvers: the rounded face, almond eyes, and serene gaze. This is typical of the Chinese depiction of the ivory Guanyin with a child carved in China at the same time.

Contrasted to this quiet beatitude are the native Filipino carvers, which show Christ bloodied and anguished in his suffering on the cross or on the way to be crucified. Here also, you see the pictorial representation of the native Filipinos' reaction to the oppressive Spanish rule. They have made Christ an Indios: life is suffering in the indios' world, and their Christ suffers with them.

A Bloodied Christ: St. Augustine Church, Manilla

I was fascinated by this fusion art of European, Chinese, and native Filipino animism and purchased a one-hundred-year-old, armless Jesus from a small antique shop. This Jesus had an Indios face and a sense of resignation in the face of death. This Jesus adorned a private house altar in Spanish colonial times. The face and body of Jesus were worn down by continual veneration of holding and kissing the image. The face had lost its sharp contours, and the polychrome colors had long since disappeared. It was a beautiful, though ruined, religious figure that had given hope and succor to many generations of devoted believers and still had the power to make you feel and experience the agonized suffering of the dying Christ.

Chapter 70: Reading, Ritin' And Rithmatic

Another Brick In the Wall
by Pink Floyd

Middle-class schoolgirls in Manilla being taught embroidery by the American school system, which emphasized "useful" skills

Teacher to students: "Now that you learned how to make dinner placemats, let's try something different and make some money: "Victoria's Secret" wants 1000 see-thru negligees in all different sizes- here's the pattern, so let's get started. Remember, do not take a sample home to wear around the house or wear in front of your boyfriend. This will be our little secret."

As an American walking around the streets of Quiapo, seeing the shoeless children, the rundown wooden slum houses, and the garbage in the streets, I felt ashamed and then angered. This was America's only "colony" in Asia. What did we do to better the lives of ordinary Filipino?

In America, we are taught that to "get ahead" in life, all you need is an education and hard work. The Filipinos, unlike the Chinese in Nationalist China, had no jobs that would raise them out of poverty. There were the rich and upper-middle-class in Makati, who ran the country, while the rest of the people had nothing. Education was the key; what had we done after we "bought" the country in 1898, a prize of the Spanish American War? The American Consulate library had an extensive section on Philippine history, and I spent an afternoon there, reading about our efforts to educate the country.

The Spanish possessed the Philippines for nearly four hundred years, setting up schools and universities, all taught by church priests. They instilled the Catholic religion and the Spanish language in their educational curriculum. In the mid-nineteenth century, the Spanish instituted free mandatory public education, a first in Asia, even before the Japanese instituted it. Spain sent the brightest students to their universities in Spain; among the students educated there was Jose Rizal, the "Father of Philippine Independence." However, Spain was a poor country and had little money to build schools and pay civil teachers. So parochial education continued to be the main teaching tool. By 1898 the American war department estimated that only 25% of Filipinos were literate.

The first American teachers were idealistic soldiers turned scholars. Their task was formidable; they had to build schools and start teaching almost simultaneously. Back home, Congress appropriated money to establish free universal education, with free textbooks and a civilian teaching corps. The first boatload of certified teachers arrived in 1901. There were originally 365 males and 165 female teachers; they were called "Thomasites" because they arrived on the passenger ship USS Thomas.

By 1903 we had over 1000 teachers here and established a program called the "Pensionado Act", where we sent a few hundred of the brightest students to America for higher education. The goal was to "educate and find current and future leaders for the American Colonial Administration." These teacher precursors to the Peace Corps faced impossible odds; they had to learn Spanish, then teach English. They were sent out to the countryside, where they lived in primitive conditions, without electricity, running water, or a support structure. In the larger cities, the Americans established boy and girl separate schools, which later became independent universities. They trained the future leaders, instilling in them the American value system. However, this widened the gap between a thin educated upper crust and the vast majority of Filipinos, over 80% of whom never went beyond the fourth grade.

The teachers' philosophic approach to learning emphasized "industrial skills:" improved farming techniques and mechanics for boys and embroidery for girls. The poverty was so overwhelming that the majority quit school to help their families with farming or to perform menial jobs.

We taught them the American democratic process: a president and bi-cameral bodies of the legislature, but couldn't stop the corruption, cronyism, and greed that still bedevils the country today.

The "American experiment" failed, just like it is failing in the American inner-city and on American Indian reservations today. Yet like today's Peace Corps, these dedicated teachers were trying to make a difference "one village at a time." The Thomasites and later teachers did their best with limited resources from Congress. The rural poverty, like in Appalachia, forced even the brightest students to leave school for even the slightest low-paying jobs just to survive.

If there is anything "good" about the Vietnam war, it was that a vast number of rural poor, white, black, and red, were exposed to new ideas and different lifestyles. Many developed skills that got them good jobs when they returned home; others used the Services as a steppingstone to get a college education under the GI Education Bill. There is a Brave New World out there and a way to escape poverty back home. The Services offered them "a little help from my friends" (unlike the IRS, which also claims they are here to help you).

Chapter 71: Old Manilla

"Sympathy for the Devil": Rolling Stones

A busy street in old Manilla 1911

Manilla was once called: "The Pearl of the Orient", a shining example of the fusion of Asian and Western influences. There were lush, fountained parks, stately Spanish mansions with wrought-iron balconies, a colorful Chinatown, and gleaming white-columned Greek Revival municipal buildings built by the famous American architect Daniel Burnham. The broad avenues were lined with fashionable department stores and bustling San Francisco-style street trollies. The streets were swarming with businessmen in white linen suits and straw hats and ladies in the latest Parisian fashion.

Unfortunately, this jewel city was totally destroyed at the end of WW II, along with over 100,000 Filipinos in one of the war's worst massacres: a horrific Japanese war crime. The Japanese, in a last-ditch effort to keep control of the city, went on a rampage, raping, mutilating, and outright killing thousands of Filipinos. They broke into convents and churches, killing priests and raping and mutilating nuns. They took over schools, raping young girls and then killing them. There were mass executions in the streets. To secure the area north of the city, the Japanese attacked and burned villages, killing 55,000 more men, women, and children. Fleeing pregnant Filipino women were raped, their bellies ripped open, and the mother and unborn child were killed. They even used Filipino women as "human shields" to protect frontline Japanese positions. If the women survived, they were then murdered.

U.S. troops fighting in the Walled City of Intramuros, Manila, 27 February 1945

The urban warfare to retake Manilla was one of the most savage in the war: street by street had to be taken at great loss of American, Filipino and Japanese lives. When the city was finally in

Allied hands, the Americans and Filipinos discovered thousands of dead Filipino men, women, and children in the rubble, killed by retreating Japanese soldiers. Six hundred American prisoners of war were found starved to death in the Santiago prison.

Justice came belatedly; the Supreme Japanese Commander of the Philippines, General Yamashita, was captured, prosecuted as a war criminal, and hanged in 1946.

Chapter 72: Fort Santiago

Farewell, sweet stranger, my friend, who brightened my way;
Farewell, to all I love. To die is to rest.

Jose Rizal: Excerpt from "Farewell To My Country"

(This was the last poem Rizal wrote before being executed)

The Revolutionary Poet Jose Rizal

Many great cities can be rediscovered by peeling back the layers of previous cities that had been built over. New York City was originally a Dutch city with guild houses, taverns, and warehouses for the fur trade. The familiar names of streets belie their true origin; for example, Wall Street marked the boundary of the old wooden Dutch fort. Canal Street was an actual canal, and Bowling Green was exactly that: an outdoor bowling space used by the old Dutch burgers for a relaxing pastime. When the foundations of new skyscrapers are dug in downtown Manhattan, old Dutch artifacts such as clay pipes and broken Delft China are discovered under deep layers of soil.

Other cities like Rome absorb their glorious past with monuments that survive almost intact, like the Coliseum, a throwback to the Roman Empire, now an island surrounded by traffic jams. Manilla is one of these cities built around a fort that has survived for over five hundred years. The original Spanish wooden fort replaced an earlier Malay Raja fort. This fort was burned by Chinese pirates while fighting the Spanish Conquistadors. The Spanish rebuilt it with volcanic tuff stone and added gun turrets, and made it the capital of the newly found colony, calling it: Fort Santiago, after St. James, slayer of the Moors. The British captured it in 1762, beefed up the fortifications of the original Spanish fort, and then returned it to Spain after the Seven Years' War. The fort fronts the Pasig River, and it was the loading area of the famed Manilla Galleon trade, where armadas of vessels were loaded with spices, Chinese silks, and carved ivory, bound for Acapulco. These same galleons returned six months later, laden with Mexican silver.

Fort Santiago is steeped in history: there, the father of Filipino independence, Jose Rizal, was imprisoned and executed by the Spanish for treason in 1896. Rizal was an intellectual, physician, and poet. He wrote revolutionary manifestos and advocated for Filipino independence. His martyrdom started the struggle to free the Philippines from Spanish rule. From 1896 to 1898, native Filipino armies fought the Spanish and captured Fort Santiago. However, independence was stymied when the Americans bought the country from Spain.

The Americans, in turn, took over the fort, using it as the U. S. Army headquarters. The U.S.'s one big improvement was filling in the moat that surrounded three-quarters of the fort and creating an exclusive golf course ("Man's gotta know his priorities").

The Japanese conquerors took over in WW II and used it as an infamous prison, a "killing field" for executing thousands of Filipinos.

Ruins of Fort Santiago

Today I walked around the fort, exploring the ruined walls, crumbling buildings, and bare, eroding foundations. Here I felt the multi-layered fort come alive. Traces of Spanish, English, American, Japanese, and now Filipino culture could be found in this historic edifice, a symbol of the resilient Filipino people. Although the fort is named after St. James, who rescued the Spanish people, it has not helped the Filipinos today. This time they are suffering under the tyrannical, corrupt government of Ferdinand Marcos. How long before the people rise up, storm this "Asian Bastille", and like St. James, slay the unjust politicians to finally achieve true freedom for their beleaguered land.

Chapter 73: A Little Trip to The Country

"Thank God I'm A Country Boy": John Denver

American School teacher Mary Cole teaching in Visayas, Philippines 1900

After a week in Manilla, I was determined to visit the countryside of Luzon Island. My destination was the Banaue rice fields, one of the natural wonders of Asia. The Manilla Bus Station was a sea of humanity, rushing here and there, and I finally found my bus. I was wrong! I said the only thing we left in the Philippines was English, blue jeans, and rock and roll – but I found another legacy: old Chevrolet buses from the 1930s. Somehow these buses were still running, held together with spit and bubblegum, spewing dark plumes of diesel smoke. After an hour of loading, we finally sputtered off, leaving a black cloud trailing behind us. The bus was packed with farmers from the Manilla produce market: mothers with crying babies, shopkeepers with goods strapped to the top of the bus, and older couples returning to the country after visiting their children in the "big" city.

Everyone was friendly and outgoing. I was offered food and shared my cigarettes with some of the passengers. The scenery was breathtaking, especially as we climbed the winding dirt roads through gorges and along mountain tops. These dirt roads had room for only one vehicle at a time; this caused me some consternation since the driver thought he was an Indy-500 finalist. Apparently, no one else was concerned about this. So I leaned back in my seat and said to myself, lighting another cigarette, "If we careen off of the road and fly down the mountain, at least I have the best view from my window seat. Similarly, if you want to kill yourself by jumping off the Brooklyn Bridge, look left to see the glorious Manhattan skyline as you fall. Looking right, you only see the slums of Red Hook and the dilapidated Brooklyn waterfront."

Every two hours or so, we'd stop at a roadside store; everyone flew out of the bus to grab food and drinks. I got my usual: a warm San Miguel beer and local fresh fruit (the breakfast of champions). The bus would resume once the driver returned. He usually came back after about 20 minutes smiling: either he had had a couple of beers or knew a girl in the neighborhood. Anyhow, I was used to this; in the army, the prevailing philosophy is: "hurry up and wait." After about an hour of being jarred and mixing unwashed fruit with warm beer, I felt a bout of imminent diarrhea coming on soon. I approached the driver, who understood my predicament and stopped the bus. There was no foliage cover, so I had to squat in full view of all of the passengers. After losing about 5 pounds in a single uncontrollable spasm, I cleaned up and returned to my seat. Everyone on the bus was smiling, and one or two even clapped their hands at my performance.

As we rode into the high mountain area, I saw more of the original inhabitants of the country: the native Indians called "Bontocs." They were short and stocky, with broad faces, flat noses, and a darker complexion than the native Malays. I found out later that these people built the original Banaue rice fields thousands of years ago. The Bontoc, for the most part, keep to their original lifestyle, not speaking Spanish or English and living the traditional hunter/gatherer existence with a little subsistence farming.

The countryside is lushly green, and the houses are a combination of patchwork wood, rusty zinc roofs, and cinderblocks; most are surrounded by palms and tropical vegetation and gorgeous flowering shrubs and vines. As we got further out from Manilla, the basic services were non-existent. There was no electricity. Only well water and outhouses were the standards. I couldn't believe that America owned this country for fifty years, and we did nothing outside of Manilla. We rebuilt West Germany and Japan, giving them millions of dollars through the Marshall Plan and other aid programs. What have we done for our former colony? We give the corrupt government of Marcos millions of dollars so that we can retain Clark Air Base, used by our long-range bombers to destroy Vietnam. Marcos stole and squandered these millions, giving nothing to the people. Communism only succeeds if you have nothing to lose. South Korea is slowly rebuilding its economy, and the people are sharing in the rebuilding. The Philippines is like Cuba and ripe for a communist takeover.

The countryside was dotted by small, peeling white wooden churches stuck in rice fields or on the main dirt road. When I drove through North Dakota on the way to California, I took the back roads and passed dozens of white weather-beaten, boarded-up clapboard churches, looking forlorn in a flat, desolate moonscape. The people, sturdy Norwegians, and Germans had moved out during the 1930s dustbowl exodus, heading west for a better life. The land was too dry to support them; they left their churches as relics of a faith that seemingly deserted them in their time of need. The feeling of despair and hopelessness remained a century later.

Here in the Philippines, the churches were still active: the people had nowhere to go.

The bus arrived at a small town, and the farmers and merchants got off. Then the driver announced that this was the final stop until the morning when there would be more customers for Banaue. This was a classic one-horse town, and even that horse had long since died. There was no hotel, restaurant, and only a small general store. Everyone sat around the store, smoking, and drinking. There was the pot-bellied owner/politician, a genteel but shabbily dressed businessman, and a few farmers. The scene was complete with runny-nosed kids, a town drunk, and a mangey, flea-bitten dog lying by the entrance. Of course, everyone had a bottle of warm San Miguel, and it reminded me of a George Caleb Bingham painting of an American country election in the 1850s, with a similar cast of characters.

George Caleb Bingham: Rural Country Elections 1852

There were benches outside, so I ordered a warm San Miguel and listened to the conversations. The owner, Daniel, turned out to be the "unofficial Mayor" of this berg and, more importantly to me, the bus dispatcher and ticket seller. We started talking, and when he found out I was an American, he proudly told me that his eldest son was a US marine stationed in San Diego. "I love America; we should never have declared our independence. All we have now are corrupt politicians that care only about Manilla and don't do anything for the rest of the country. We have no electricity, horrible schools, and no paved roads. Our local representatives do nothing for us until election time when they throw huge parades and feasts to ensure their reelection. My son writes that life in America is beautiful, and my wife and I will visit him one day."

Typical house in the rural countryside

We continued talking and drinking, and I brought up my predicament that I had no place to stay this night. He immediately stopped me and insisted that I stay with his family for dinner and that I spend the night at his house. I thanked him, and after about an hour, he closed the store, and we walked to his house on the outskirts of the village. The house was a single-story wood structure with a zinc metal roof and stood on stilts, with stairs to a porch that ran the length of the house. The porch was covered with bougainvillea vines with red flowers and looked extremely pretty. In the yard were a few stray chickens, and I caught a glimpse of the side of the house, where there was a huge vegetable garden.

His wife, Maitre, was a good-sized woman with a smiling face and welcoming expression. I also met his kid Damen, who was about eight years old and with whom I would share a bed, and his daughter Larisa, who was about ten years old. We had a delicious dinner of chicken, rice, and black beans, served with bottles of warm San Miguel. After dinner, we talked by candlelight since they also didn't have electricity about life in America. His son had written glowing reports, but he had lots of questions about life there, which he kept me answering for over an hour. When it came time for bed, Damen showed me his room, where we would share the same bed, and proceeded to take up where his father left off, asking me question after question about life in America, especially about kids his age. I managed to get a few questions about his life and found that he attended a government school and wanted to follow in his brother's footsteps, joining the US Marines.

In the morning, Damen woke up early and got dressed for school, while Maitre prepared a rice porridge for us before we went our separate ways. I thanked them both for their gracious hospitality and offered to pay them for my room and board, but Daniel refused, saying that I was his guest. I had met a warm, loving couple that had made me feel like I was a part of their family, even if it was for just one night.

We got back to the bus waiting area, and the bus departed only a half-hour behind schedule.

I finally arrived at Banaue in the late afternoon. I could see the terraces in the distance, but now I was looking for a hotel. I walked until I came to a ramshackle farmhouse, set in rice fields, and approached the farmer who was harvesting his field. I tried to ask about a hotel, but he said, "No hotel here."

He must have seen my chagrin since it was getting dark, and I had nowhere to go. He motioned that I come with him. He took me into his home and introduced me to his son. The boy was about eighteen years old and spoke a little English. "My father says you eat, sleep here. No hotel here."

The teenager's name was Carlos, and he was very curious about me as an American. "Why was I here? Do you have wife? Do you have car in America?" I answered as best as I could, and then I was served dinner with the family. For dinner, we had homegrown rice and beans, and he gave me some fermented beer that I believe the family brewed. When it became dark, we had a kerosine lamp. The family also didn't have a spare bedroom, so I shared Carlos' bed. In the morning, we had a rice porridge, and Carlos told me where to go to see the best views of the terraces.

Banaue Rice Terraces

(Author photo)

I was at the bottom of one huge terrace, and the horizon was filled with mountains dug out for the terraces. I found out later that there was a small village on top of the terraces, but for now, I was just walking through the field. There were farmers at different locations and levels of the rice terraces. I started climbing, zigzagging to reach the top of this particular mountain. I walked along skinny earthen paths, and everywhere were green shoots of grass-like rice sprouting out of ponds of irrigated water.

I finally reached the top, and the view was awe-inspiring. Every mountain was carved out with terraces, and in the far distance, I saw a waterfall cascading down the mountain. These terraces are supposed to be two thousand years old and are fed by streams from the plateau mountain tops. On some of the terraces, there were small houses where the farmers kept their work tools. I was lucky: there was no fog or rain that day, and the terraces stood out like huge emeralds glistening in the sun.

Back in New York City, I used to visit avant-garde galleries, where abstract art, consisting of lines, curves, and splashes of color, was displayed on huge canvases in Grecian-columned former factory lofts. Here the rice terraces were shimmering examples of abstract art. I spent hours photographing this living canvas. The terraces that were filled with water seemed to drop off at eye level into nothingness. From certain vantage points, the terraces were curved, and the mountains looked like stream-lined Art Deco skyscrapers that you saw in the canyons of Manhattan. On the terrace tops were small stores and even a small hotel. I bought warm San Miguel beer and bananas, found a perfect lookout, and drank in the scenery along with my beer. As I came back to the farmhouse, the setting sun turned the emerald rice terraces into burnished copper.

I met Carlos, who was talking to a friend. Together they escorted me to his friend's field. His name was Juan, and he also spoke a little English and made it known to me that he was immensely proud of his field. What I saw was a mini forest of tall marijuana plants. He raised this crop and sold it to Filipino businessmen, who brought it back to Manilla. This gave him a good income, much better than rice growing. Soon he motioned with his hands, and I understood that he would be buying a motorcycle with his profits. I also understood him to say that he wanted to expand his operation, and I think Carlos would soon be part of this growing empire. I guess America must have instilled some capitalist initiative in the Philippines; this was an excellent, albeit illegal, way to make money and get out of poverty. They started to roll a joint and offered me a smoke, but I declined. I saw myself as on a mission from God (you are a photojournalist, keep that upper lip stiff); besides, I had become accustomed to warm San Miguel beer, which gave me a comfortable buzz.

The next day I walked along the canyon floor of tropical underbrush and finally reached the waterfall. There was no one around the lake at the bottom of the falls, so I stripped and had a freezing swim. I was alone in paradise, surrounded by a tropical rain forest, the waterfall spray a rainbow of colors in the prism of the sun. This was primeval Eden, and I was Lucy, barely standing erect and gazing out in awe at the wonder around me.

I spent another night at the house, Carlos and I had become fast friends, and I gave him my parent's address, if he ever made it to America, to look me up. In the morning, I left a donation for my stay and caught a bus to Bontoc.

Chapter 74: Hokey Pokey

I set out from Banane to go to the village of Bontoc, where there were more rice fields and a village that produced beautiful weaving. The trip took about seven hours, and the trip took me further North into the mountains. The higher and further I went, the poorer were the people. Filipinos are Malay and a combination of other races that are hard to distinguish; in the mountains, however, the pure Indian (aborigine) is clearly defined by their flat noses, big lips, and short, squat bodies. The little children are dressed in rags, laughing and shouting at me on the bus, saying "Merlicano" (American). Many of the elders of the aborigine speak good American English, from working with the city Filipinos, and are very friendly.

Bontoc is another small, one-horse town, and it is surprising to meet a doctor, Jose Ruiz, who graduated from the London School of Dermatology, as he drunkenly emphasized several times in our conversations. He showed me around the burg (the "Don't blink or you'll miss it all" tour), from there we went to the weaver's village of Samokey, where hand-loom weavers make a beautiful, cotton, finely-woven cloth for scarfs and sweaters. He knew where all of the General Stores were because we stopped at every one where he bought me beers, and he drank a whole quart of gin at every stop. He had what seemed to be an odd personal life, but after learning the customs in the mountains, it wasn't all that strange. He isn't church married, but his "wife" came from one of the houses in the village where all single women of marriageable age live together. These women are courted by the village men who take them as wives on a trial basis: if a woman bears the man a son, the marriage ceremony is performed officially. Dr. Ruiz's wife, a very pretty Filipino girl, was pregnant, and I wished them both the best for a happy future as long as she delivered a son. He then passed me off to another doctor, a Chinese-Filipino, Dr. Lee, who also drank gin continuously. Dr. Lee was another character who wanted to quit his practice in the mountains and join the US Marines. He had made many applications to work in the United States and was waiting to hear if he would be accepted on a work visa. Because of the low pay, many doctors and nurses all wanted to get out of the Philippines and work in America. In the early 70s, many inter-city hospitals in the US had trouble getting American doctors and nurses to fill these hard-working and dangerous positions. Because of our prior relationship with the Philippines (ownership), there were numerous Philippine doctors and nurses in many of the inter-city hospitals.

As I stated before, the national past-time in the mountains is drinking, especially the native gin, and one wasn't considered part of the crowd" unless you kept up with them. Dr. Ruiz had drunk so much that he'd developed cirrhosis of the liver and was being treated for that. The scene in Bontoc is like places in Kentucky or West Virginia with downcast, dispirited men, overworked women, dirty children, and older people sitting on their porches (sans the rocking chairs) watching the world go by. The people led very primitive lives, and there was a strange admixture of loincloths, Western dungarees, and greased hair; cigarettes dangled from the men's mouths, and each carried a machete.

I got a room at the "Wonder Lodge" for two pesos (33 cents a night). At dusk, I promptly wandered off into the Melacon rice fields, which were older than the Benane terraces and built of stone instead of packed earth, but not as extensive. Darkness fell almost immediately, and since there was no electricity in the village, I was stuck in these awesome terraces. After trying to find my way in this maze of rice-field paths, I stepped off the path, got stuck in the clay, and slipped into the rice water. By the time I reached the hotel, I was thoroughly wet and mud-soaked. The owner of the hotel was a very congenial man who saw my predicament and gave me a hot meal. So, I went to bed by candlelight, since there was no electricity, very early. The following day, I returned to Samokey where I purchased a beautifully made scarf and an original tribal spear (which was confiscated by Filipino customs when I left the country). The village was extremely poor, the men wandered around listlessly, and the children were all naked. In the afternoon, I made another short trip to the Melacon rice fields to take photographs, and this time made sure I got home as soon as it started to get dark.

I'd befriended the local town lawyer (bought a bottle of gin and shared it with him), and he supplied me with two native guides, his nephews, and they took me to a native Bontoc village, where they were holding a festival celebrating the planting of new rice. The village young men were all dressed in jeans, cotton shirts, and Japanese tongs, and they lit a big fire in the middle of the village. There they formed a circle, men only, and started a rhythmic dance that changed direction around the fire. The women in the background outside of the circle extended their hands over their breasts and did the same steps that the men were doing. Afterward, they did another dance, this time with the women, called "The Wedding Dance." This dance, with men and women wildly clasping and shaking each other, celebrating all of the newly married couples in the village.

I bought the dancers a bottle of the local gin, which they all drank heartily and quickly, pulling me into the dancing melee and giving me a partner, a young girl who could dance all the modern dances. It was great fun, drinking, and dancing, and everyone felt a part of the group celebration. I didn't get back to the hotel until late in the night, fully drunk and sweated through my clothes from dancing. In the morning, I saw the lawyer, thanked him and his nephews, and got on the bus to Manilla, nursing a terrible hangover (I made a mental note to myself: no more "bathtub" gin, stick with warm San Miguel beer).

Chapter 75: Last Day In Manilla

My last day in Manila was spent walking the streets of Quiapo, observing the poverty: the listless young men, the women hanging laundry from ornate balconies, and the smiling students in their blue and white uniforms. This was a society of have and have-nots. But the most troubling thing that I encountered here is the feeling that the Filipino people did not have a firm identity of who they are in the world. I did not find this in Korea, Japan, or any of the Chinese countries that I visited. The Philippines was ruled by Spain, America, Japanese, and then they became independent, and yet the culture they have is American culture: sex drugs and rock n' roll. The people of Quiapo and most of the Philippines live on the streets. I have encountered this in New York in places like Harlem and Bedford-Stuyvesant, where everyone hangs out on the stoop, and everything goes on at street level. In New York City, the underclass, whether it's poor black or Puerto Rican, can't find jobs, and many young people turn to a life of drugs or crime. Here in the Philippines, what I observed was basically marijuana use and not the hard drugs that we have in New York. With thousands of American soldiers, sailors, airmen, and contractors, the American style of living is a glaring reminder to the Filipino people that they don't have the jobs to support this alluring lifestyle.

Slums of Quiapo (author photo)

I sat in a Chinese restaurant in the middle of Quiapo eating arroz con pollo and looked around me: the Chinese were always busy: cooking, serving cleaning. This was the same culture that I observed in Chinatown in New York City, where the Chinese were always working and had a purpose in their lives. They may not have been rich, but hard work and long hours paid off for many with the golden carrot of success. Here in the Philippines, especially in Quiapo, religion is a cementing bond for the people, but the wealth gap is so enormous that I believe this country is ripe for a communist revolution. Although it is ostensibly a democracy, it does not provide for the mass of the people. The Marcos government tried to distract the people by focusing on making everything Filipino: businesses, language, and culture, Blaming the Chinese for their poverty and making them the scapegoat in the same way as Hitler made a scapegoat of the Jews in pre-World War Two Germany. The society here is very similar to the ghettos in New York and Newark in that the ambitious leave to find jobs and a place in the world. As I mentioned before, nearly 10% of Filipinos work abroad, and everyone I met wants to leave the country, either to emigrate to America or Europe.

I had seen the urban Filipinos and the rural Filipinos, and everywhere there is a lack of opportunity to fulfill the dreams that we had taught them to believe in when we took them over 75 years ago. I do have hope for the Filipino people because as I sit and watch them, I feel an energy that could be tapped to make this a truly free and equalitarian society. The people are open to new ideas, and the brightest and most ambitious will succeed, whether it's at growing marijuana in the countryside or making it in the urban jungle of Quiapo. I will feel sorry for leaving the Philippines because I will miss the openness and the friendliness of the people that I met there.

I spent my last night wandering around Rizal Park, the Central Park of Manila. Everyone was friendly there, greeting me as Filipinos greet all foreigners: "Hello, Joe." There were small crowds everywhere in the park: polite homosexuals with their abortive, furtive advances, "Hey Joe, can I suck your cock?" Young couples, arm in arm, heading to the heavily wooded area for some quality time alone. As I wandered around the Park, I caught an impromptu concert by a guitar-playing DJ who could yodel like Hank Williams.

Around 10 PM, I went back to my hotel room in Quiapo. The Old City was just as alive at night as it was during the day. People were everywhere, and the blaring of jeepney horns kept me awake well past midnight.

Burma: A Buddhist Paradise

Two Burmese Women smoking cigars 1905. "If you got 'em, smoke 'em."- John Wayne

Chapter 76: Burma

The Military Regime had isolated the country and left the economy in shambles. What I knew about Burma was solely from the movies: "The Bridge on the River Kwai" and "The Flying Tigers". As a kid, I had even assembled a model P40 and glued the distinctive red shark jaws decal on the front fuselage. Also, I'm pretty sure that "Burma Shave" doesn't count. I pictured endless jungles, swollen rivers, and a muggy, humid climate. I was traveling alone and arrived in Rangoon in the early morning.

Shwedagon Pagoda print from the early 19th century

No man is an *Island*, intire of it selfe; any mans *death* diminishes *me*, because I am involved in *Mankinde*; And therefore never send to know for whom the *bell* tolls; It tolls for *thee*.
Meditation XVII from "Devotions Upon Emergent Occasions", John Donne (1624)

Rangoon Center is dominated by the imposing Shwedagon Pagoda, which is surrounded by beautifully carved stone gates and stone lions leading up to the 2000-year-old Pagoda (the oldest Buddhist monument in the world). Among other treasures, it supposedly had eight strands of the

Buddha's hair (I always thought he was bald, but what do I know!). This venerable relic didn't stop the British from vandalizing it; in fact, one daft British officer wanted to use the Pagoda as a munitions dump. It has now been restored and features a life-size green jade Buddha and a 42-ton bell. This bell has an interesting history: it is always being stollen by invading armies, but every time the invading army tries to take it out of the country, it somehow falls into the Irrawaddy River, which is then recovered and brought back to the Pagoda.

The old city is best described as shabby colonial: stately buildings, peeling and crumbling in the tropical humidity. There are long-rooted banyan trees and tall gracious Buddhas everywhere. The Burmese Buddha is different from the Chinese one with its fat belly and rounded, well-fed face. Here Buddha is the slim young saint, the Siddhartha. You can sort of think of him as Elvis. The Burmese got the rocking, hip-gyrating, young Elvis and the Chinese, the bloated, white pants-suit, rhinestone-encrusted Las Vegas lounge singer.

Everyone in Burma wears a sarong and spends their time lounging around and drinking tea. The people are extremely friendly, especially for a large city. In countenance, the people are very much like the Thais and Malays but seem to be much more volatile. Everywhere I turned, people were approaching me, almost demanding to talk to me.

A funny, odd professor-type Burmese accompanied by a young boy wanted to show me around the city and took 10 minutes to find his tourist card to prove to me that he was an official tourist representative. I spent the day seeing the sights of the city with this comical "Mutt and Jeff" combo and also learned where the best places to eat were located. The food is similar to Malaysian food, with meat and vegetable-filled roti (wraps). I stayed two days in Rangoon and left for Mandalay by third-class train. This was an adventure. The third-class train was the most crowded I'd ever taken. People climbing in and out of the train windows. Mothers let their babies shit in the aisles, and farmers carried sacks of lentils and rice, which they deposited in the aisles, making through traffic impossible. I arrived in Mandalay, where the atmosphere is totally different from Rangoon. It is very dusty and picturesque except when it rains; then it's very muddy and picturesque. The pace of life in Mandalay is much slower than in Rangoon, which means that life has almost stopped here. The colonial town is built around the market, which is the lifeblood of the city. While sitting in cafes, the people approach you, starting conversations with you. They seem to have all of the time in the world. I found out here that a foreigner hardly pays for anything. The Burmese bought me chais and snacks every time I stopped to sit down.

The cheap hotels were all filled up, and I sat in a cafe wondering what to do. There I was befriended by a young Indian Burmese, who took me to his house. The family was polite and generous. They had a daughter who married an Indian national, and both were now living in the U.K. He said that there was no opportunity here, and everyone wanted to emigrate to the U.K. or America.

While lying in bed in the Indian's daughter's room, I thought of Mandalay's past and WWII. The road to Mandalay continued into China, and the Japanese used it to conquer Burma. Again, movies came to mind: The Flying Tigers singularly defeating the Japanese with their fierce shark-mouthed airplanes. The real-life tale was even more fascinating than the Hollywood pastiche version.

Chapter 77: Flying Tigers

The Flying Tigers was the brainchild of General Claire Lee Chennault and Chiang Kai-Shek and his "Dragon-lady" English-speaking wife. Together they convinced President Roosevelt to support a voluntary air group to defend Burma and attack the Japanese in China. China was being quickly overrun by the Japanese, and they were moving into Southeast Asia. Chang Kai-Shek and his National Chinese Army were the only force preventing a total Japanese conquest. General Chennault was given 100 fighter planes, the Curtis P-40 Warhawk, in 1940. He solicited volunteers: the majority coming from the Army Air Corps, navy, and Marines and a few experienced crop-dusters. They were given a leave of absence from their military duties and trained by the US military in air fighter tactics. They were the first American Volunteer Group (AVG) of the Republic of China, their planes marked with Chinese Nationalist colors but directly under the control of General Chennault.

The Flying Tigers on a mission over China in 1942

When the planes finally arrived in Burma in the fall of 1941, the AVG was organized into three squadrons of 30 planes each, 10 Chinese mechanics, and about 100 pilots. The three squadrons had colorful names: "Adam and Eve", "Panda Bears", and "Hells Angels." The P-40s were painted with a red shark mouth on the front of the fuselage, and General Chennault christened them "The Flying Tigers". They flew their first mission on December 20, 1941, thirteen days after the Pearl Harbor attack.

This was a time of low morale for American forces in the Pacific Theater. Our naval fleet was severely damaged. Japan was conquering one Asian country after another, and they appeared to be invincible. Here comes The Flying Tigers to the rescue. By January 1942, they had shot down 73 Japanese fighters and bombers, destroyed Japanese convoys on the Burma Road, and flew protection missions for the Nationalist Chinese ground troops. They proved that the Japanese military was not invincible and brought a ray of hope to all US forces: we could win this war. They continued downing Japanese aircraft even though they had to move their operational headquarters due to the eventual Japanese conquest of Burma. The Flying Tigers' final airfield was near Kunming, China, where they stopped the Japanese assault on that city.

The Flying Tigers were officially disbanded on the Fourth of July 1942 and incorporated into the US Army 23rd Fighter Group under General Chennault. Their achievements were impressive: shooting down 297 Japanese aircraft, mostly fighting as underdogs to the superior numbers of Japanese aircraft, and losing only 14 pilots and planes. They had slowed the Japanese advance, giving the Americans and their allies time to regroup and prepare for future battles. The experience they brought to the newly created 23rd Fighter Group made them a formidable enemy as the war progressed. Two former "Tigers": James Howard and Pappy Boyington, were awarded the Congressional Medal of Honor for their heroic actions in the war. The Flying Tigers were successful because they were experienced pilots, were trained in tactical air combat, believed in their mission, and demonstrated an enthusiastic esprit-de-corps.

Chapter 78: Pagan

"And I saw the holy city, new Jerusalem, coming down out of heaven from God, prepared as a bride adorned for her husband".

"Revelations", chapter 21, verse 2, King James Bible

"New Jerusalem" from Book of Revelations, Armenian Julfa Bible, 1645

I got up at 4 A.M. and, in the drizzling rain, left Mandalay on an all-day boat to Pagan, the ancient Temple City of Burma. On the boat, we were packed as tight as sardines, so I had to sit with the crew, and they treated me to everything. We passed memorable river scenes: a small landing with seven or eight bullock carts bringing out the produce; women washing clothes and bathing in the mud-colored, rain-swollen Irrawaddy river. Monasteries lined the riverbanks, with monks going to and fro, praying and dispensing alms; meanwhile, on board the vessel, everyone from the teenagers to old grandmothers had a cigar stuck in their mouths. It's a very contagious habit: I smoked about four or five stogies a day.

Some places are magical; they appear like a surreal vision: a galaxy far, far away, totally alien yet enveloped in a spiritual aurora of shapes, smells, and sounds. The visage from the boat was of rust-colored earth, great shadowy green trees, and dazzling white and gold temples and pagodas as far as the eyes could see. Surely this was some make-believe kingdom, run by shaven-head fairies in saffron yellow robes. I got off the boat and started wandering around in a daze. I heard monks chanting, saw huge reclining golden buddhas, and climbed fortress-like temples. I passed dozens of peeling plaster stupas that would soon be swallowed by pipal vines. I imagined the psychic energy and religious fever of thousands of monks and common worshippers invoking their prayers and chants in a consecrated effort to bring heaven to earth. There are about 2600 temples, pagodas, and stupas of all different colors, sizes, shapes, and physical conditions. These were all built over a three-hundred-year period. Throughout the years, earthquakes, wars, and general neglect have destroyed many of the temples, but the main ones like Ananda Temple and Bupaya Pagoda are well-maintained, with schools of monks to perform the Buddhist rituals. I climbed one temple, and the view was a scene of huge trees forming a green canopy with only the white and gold tops of all of the temples protruding through. Laughing to myself, it seemed like a huge "knock-a-mole" (game board) where a heavenly hammer would hit one white dome, and another would pop up through the greenery. I climbed one beautiful white temple, getting all the way to the parapet lookout; when laying in my way was a huge spotted black Burmese pit viper, very deadly and poisonous. For a brief moment, I thought I was Sabu from the movie "The Jungle Book". Sabu talks to the king cobra, who answers back and is a harbinger of destruction. However, as the viper started to move toward me, I quickly realized that discretion is the better part of cowardness and beat a hasty retreat down the stairs, leaving the viper sole guardian of this temple. I found a high, golden temple and sat on the overlook, watching the sun set on this vast sea of spires. The last rays of the setting sun burnished the gold roofs and changed the brilliant white temples into a muted grey as the darkness took possession of the land. In the distance, a farmer, a silhouette in black, was plowing his fields among the ruined and crumbling temples. I had an epiphany of absolute calm. I felt one with nature and God, and quoting Joan Baez: "I could have died then and there." ("Diamonds and Rust")

We see the temple city as a beautiful work of art, a Disneyland to walk through and behold the wonders, not to actively worship in them. I tried to digest what I had seen that day. I thought about the devotion that had inspired Pagan: kings added grandiose temples; rich noblemen donated individual stupas; monks built great pagodas, and craftsmen created innumerable Buddhas, all working together to build the city of God on earth. We in the West visit great shrines as tourist stops. I visited Notre Dame in Paris. The stained glass and gargoyles are impressive, but my first reaction to the cathedral was, "Where did Quasimodo live?" then picturing him ringing the huge bell by swinging back and forth on the gong in the tower.

Yet when I walked through the ruins of Pagan, I felt like I was seeing a living organism: parts die off, and they are replaced with others. The temple city is a living example of the Buddhist concept of "Maya" (illusion). The trees, earthquakes, conquerers, and time show us the ephemeral nature of the world around us. The spiritual presence is everywhere: the monotonous chanting of monks praying, the looming Buddhist statues, and the smell of incense in the air. You need to walk in the red-brown earth, climb the temple stairs and observe how the landscape changes with the movement of the sun. While other ruined cities evoke feelings of death or destruction, this place is alive. To the Buddhist monks, Pagan offers the peace and solitude to find the Buddha through yoga and devotional works of charity.

Chapter 79: Rangoon or Bust

"Wagon Wheel": Old Crow Medicine Show

This song is about the hardships and joys of hitch-hiking in trying to get to a loved one

I had stayed too long in Pagan, and I ran to the train station, but I missed the evening train by fifteen minutes, so I had to get a guest lodging. I found one for a very low price, and I got up at 3 A.M., so I could get back to Rangoon within two days to not overstay my seven-day visa and risk jail. I went to a local cafe for some chai, hoping to hitch a ride back to Rangoon.

I met a middle-aged Burmese man who asked me where I was going and then tried to get me a ride on a truck. One driver was very unwilling to take me; I guess he didn't like freaks, but another offered to take me all the way to Rangoon. He was extremely nice and treated me to all my meals and snacks. I climbed onto the back, sitting on a bamboo mesh with gunny sacks of burlap rice all around me. As I climbed in, I found two men and one woman with a child; all of us being bounced around on a very bad system of pot-holed roads and getting dust all over ourselves.

The day passed on the truck: the green fields, the astonished children pointing, and the men laughing. We stopped for food, drank whiskey, and then got back on the truck again. We drove through some of the most beautiful countrysides that I had ever seen, except that I was getting slightly paranoid (why is this man holding my thigh for so long?). The sun was setting, leaving the sky with a light blue luminescence. We stopped near a temple, and fifteen men piled into the truck. Everyone was smoking a cigar, yet even they were quiet, perhaps silent like so many country people are. It became night, but it was still clear; the moon was full, and everything was visible in the pale light. My paranoia was getting worse, but I wasn't afraid, just not interested. About 10:30 at night, we are barreling along when we see three trucks parked along this lonely tree stretch of road, and I hear women's voices. The women are standing in the middle of nowhere, and these huge trucks are stopping to pick them up.

We pick one up and ride until we find a shady grove and stop the truck. I found out then that my erstwhile homosexual friend turns out to be bi-sexual. He charges off into the bush with this fair young Burmese lass. After he returns, the driver of the truck walks off in the same direction. When he comes back, he motions to me if I want to partake. I stagger off the truck and follow the trail where everyone else went. I found this girl lying naked on a blanket in the underbrush. I tear off my clothes and go to her. She massages my penis until it gets hard, and I finally consummate the act without a rubber on. All the while being watched from above by my overly curious bi-sexual companion. When I returned to the truck, my bi-sexual companion ran off for a second screwing. Finally, everyone is satisfied and gets back on the truck, and we head off again. Now there are only three of us, and we are all sharing my blanket because it has now started to rain. So, he lies over me, and we finally get to bed. He is on top of me but too tired to try anything. I awaken with a start around 7:15 A.M. in the morning and find that we weren't moving; we've broken down. The driver fixed the truck by 10 A.M., and thirty-five miles later, it broke down again at 1:30 P.M. I asked them to drop me at a train station, and I caught the train to Rangoon, arriving at 8 o'clock at night. On the train, I'm wined and dined, given cigars and sugar cane, and escorted to a cheap hotel room by a friendly betel-chewing Burmese man. I got up at 5 A.M. and caught a taxi to the airport.

Chapter 80: The Crack-Up

"Breaking News"

"We are just hearing from our ABC television affiliate station in Mason City, Iowa, that a small engine airplane carrying the popular music singers Buddy Holly, Ritchie Valens, and "The Big Bopper" J.P. Richardson crashed in severe wintry weather conditions near Clearwater Lake, Iowa. The pilot and all three passengers were killed instantly when the plane crashed into a cornfield.

Our station switchboard was jammed with young callers expressing disbelief and then breaking into crying when they found out the tragedy was true. We send our sincere condolences to the singers' families and friends. The outpouring of grief and sorrow is overwhelming. Popular music has lost three bright stars at the height of their careers, beloved by millions of fans throughout the country.

ABC News, reporting live from Mason City, Iowa."

Wreckage of the plane that crashed on 3 February 1959, killing pop singers Buddy Holly, Ritchie Valens, and "The Big Bopper"

My seven-day visa was up, and the military regime wouldn't permit an extension. To make money, the Burmese government mandated that you had to fly Air Burma on leaving the country. So about twenty of us travelers bought our Johnny Walker Black label at the duty-free shop (to sell on the black market) and boarded a medium-sized prop jet. This is the same type of regional aircraft you would use to fly to Sioux City, Iowa, from Fargo, North Dakota. The flight should have taken about an hour and a half, but we were delayed due to heavy monsoon rain.

Finally, we took off, and everything seemed fine. We were in high spirits, relating our experiences, some deciding to drink the Johnny Walker instead of selling it, and we passed the bottle around. After about an hour and a half, everyone was getting dizzy; we seemed to be flying in circles. Looking out of the window, the rain seemed to be coming in unrelenting heavy sheets. Suddenly, we were unexpectedly told that we were going to have to make an emergency landing. I thought we were over the Bay of Bengal and started to panic. The instructions were: drop your head to your knees, so you could kiss your ass goodbye, and I prepared for the worst. The plane hit what looked like a runway at a good speed, and suddenly, we were splattered with water and mud. It felt like the plane was splitting down the middle, as we were still moving, spraying us with more mud and water. When the plane finally stopped, the water was up to our seats, which I guess had stopped us from burning up on impact. We all gasped when we saw that the plane had split down the middle but somehow had held together. I grabbed my camera and the whiskey and made for the exit. We were able to get the door open and rushed out to find ourselves ankle-deep in water and mud. I looked back at the plane, half-submerged, thankful that the water level had saved us. A fellow traveler, a Welsh businessman, told us that he had been a pilot in the Royal Air Force and didn't know how we survived. He kept muttering this refrain, between gulps of Johnny Walker. Most of us were in a state of shock, and yet I still felt totally alive. I tried to come to some sense of why we weren't killed, and I half-jokingly said, "Now we'll probably be arrested for overstaying our visas."

We had crashed on the Burmese island of Akkad, which used to be a pirate's haven two hundred years ago. They flew us back to Rangoon and put us up for the night at the Strand, the grand dame of British Colonial Hotels in Asia. The room was spacious: chandeliers and detailed plaster moldings on the ceiling. We had air conditioning, a large bathroom with a sit-down toilet (not the standard hole in the floor), a bathtub, and a shower. There was a lady's vanity and a large mahogany desk, assorted plush chairs, and two large-sized beds. However, everything from the rugs to the bedsheets and furniture was fraying, soiled, and moth-eaten.

They wined and dined us like royalty, and we were taken to the airport in the morning to fly out again. We later found out that this was the second plane crash within one month. The other wreck had serious injuries, including one Norwegian traveler, who was very badly burned. We never really found out why we crashed. It could have been poor aircraft maintenance, monsoon rains, or pilot error, but we were alive. I am not superstitious, but I really believe one reason we didn't die was psychic energy. My whole purpose for going on this trip was to get to India, and it had something to do with this immense psychic desire of mine to see and experience India that I didn't die (and if you believe this, I have a bridge in Brooklyn I can sell you for a very cheap price!). We arrived safely in Bangkok and now had a grand story (in three-part harmony) to tell my grandchildren.

Chapter 81: The Continuing Adventures of Flash Gordon

Original Flash Gordon serial poster, 1938

Narrator: Well, kiddies, we have followed Flash Gordon on many adventures, from saving American democracy in an alien country to escaping the clutches of vampish femme fatales. He survived a spacecraft crash, a deadly disease (VD), and a knife attack by a crazed Amazon. He survived the "runs" from eating strange exotic eastern foods (where was a McDonald's when he really needed one), discovered strange exotic eastern religions (where was that "Old Time Religion" when he really needed it), and explored ancient exotic eastern ruins (like visiting "Disneyland" without the rides). "He discovered strange new worlds, gone where no man has gone before"… Wait! I can't use these lines; they are stolen from "Star Trek"!

However, his greatest challenge stands before him. He is about to enter the forbidden land of the POD People (Thailand). The body-snatching pods take over your entire body – replacing it with a zombie-like replicant. You may talk and act like your normal self, but aliens have taken over your mind and stifled all emotions and feelings. These cunning aliens are not satisfied with just eating your Buick or destroying Tokyo. Will Captain America (aka Flash Gordon) save the American way of life: God, Mom, and apple pie? Only by reading Volume II, "Sojourner to Stoner" can you find out. Remember this is not available to see at your local movie theater (unfortunately, no one has bought the movie rights), so you must buy the book. Flash Gordon's adventures continue, but don't forget the immortal words of the mad scientist, Dr. Emilo Lizardo, in "The Adventures of Buckaroo Banzai", "Laugh a while you can, Monkey Boy."

Flash Gordon: This is an unabashed, shameless promotion of my book, and I approved this message.

Acknowledgments

I would like to thank the Academy for recognizing a true masterpiece of cinema by adapting my written journal, "From Soldier to Sojourner", for the big screen. Wait, this is the wrong speech! There are two individuals that greatly helped me to make this book a reality. Fanny Lee was a "tough love" critic that gave me a well-deserved wake-up call: to rewrite and organize my journal from a jumble of incoherent ramblings (so much for Joyce's "Stream of Consciousness") into a structured chronological account of my (mis)adventures. She was my first editor, and I can never thank her enough for her efforts.

Arden Gallagher was an insightful muse, tireless Girl Friday and enthusiastic cheerleader for this project. I would bounce my hair-brain ideas to her, and she would bounce them back (love, set, match) with "What you really meant to say was…" I could not have completed this book without her love, patience, understanding, and infallible support. Here's looking at you, kid.

Bibliography & Notes

A Quirky, opinionated, annotated, and asymmetrical Bibliography

"And now you know the rest of the story," Paul Harvey, American radio political commentator.

Paul Harvey

For a great introduction to the Far East and particularly Chinese history and culture, my "Bible" is John King Fairbank's two-volume set: "East Asia: The Great Tradition" and "East Asia: The Modern Transformation".

I am a great believer in travel guides and heartily recommend "The Lonely Planet "guides in each of the countries I traveled to. These are "meat and potatoes" (hold the potatoes) main course books, chock full of historical, political, and social references, as well as describing all the must-see (and the not-so-must-see) attractions, usually with a wry sense of humor. The best cultural guides are the "Blue Guides" series which go into excruciating detail on the monuments and ancient cities, with detailed maps and planned itineraries. The last two series of travel books, "Insight" and "DK" Guides give you a photograph, drawing, or old print of the temple or shrine they are describing in words (somehow, I thought the Statue of Liberty would be bigger). I will also recommend select guidebooks that capture the particular "Zeitgeist" of a country and its people. For in-depth history and culture of a country, I have a cherished eleventh edition of the Encyclopedia Britannica (1911) (Frederick Jackson Turner did the part on American history, John Muir on the scenic beauty of the American wilderness, and Bertrand Russell and T. H. Huxley did articles on philosophy). I must also mention my constant, faithful companion that I carried throughout my wanderings (like Alexander the Great with his well-worn copy of the "Iliad"): "Golden's Guide to Asia". This little red book was my perennial inspiration (and many times my pillow) on my journey and still has an enduring influence on me and occupies first place on my bookshelf.

As far as the songs I cite at the beginning of many of my chapters; they can all be listened to on "YouTube". I implore you also to listen to a Peking and Revolutionary Chinese opera, traditional Korean and Japanese music, and Asian popular music on this resourceful venue.

As for the photographs, drawings, prints, and cultural artifacts that I have embedded in my journal, the majority were found on Wikimedia Commons, which gives legal justification for Creative Commons Share-Alike and public domain for usage. For the other images, I have done my best to get "creative common" fair usage, citing the author or organization that holds the copyright and proper licensing agreements. If I missed any attribution, I sincerely apologize to the owner of the image that I used. There is a complete picture index below with all licensing approvals. I have not included any cookbooks or recipes on the food I have described because any exotic dish preparation can be found in easy-to-follow steps on food channels or "YouTube" videos. I can describe kimchi in so many ways, but you can only understand what I'm talking about if you try it for yourself. DISCLAIMER: I am not responsible for your being kicked out of your apartment for leaving an open jar of kimchi on your kitchen table overnight.

I have annotated with my two-cent comments on many of the books, magazines, newspapers, and videos that I have read on a particular topic or important issue that merits further investigation. I further divided the bibliography by country, giving general books on individual countries and then in-depth studies on my select issues. Enough of this: "The Show Must Go On".

Korea

The best general history of Korea that I have found is Michael Seth's "A Concise History of Korea". This is excellent for discovering topics that the reader can then research further.

Korean Courtesans

Prostitution centers sprung up around military bases, particularly in Asia. (This did not happen in Iraq or Afghanistan because there are no bars {alcohol is forbidden} and the Moslem women are kept at home, secluded, and excluded from any dealings with all men until they are married). In Korea, these centers were called "Camptowns". Surrounding the large military bases, whole towns sprung up like Sinchon, outside of ASCOM Depot. These Camptowns and the Korean prostitutes living there were studied by mostly feminine writers in the 1980s and 90s.

Cynthia Enloe wrote "Bananas, Beaches, and Bases: Making Feminist Sense of International Politics". Her basic premise is that the prostitutes were forced "Comfort Women" for American GIs, actively promoted and coerced by the Korean government to keep the American military in Korea. These poor girls were tricked into prostitution and then subject to harsh rules of the American military to keep them in servitude. This is falsifying facts. Yes, there were some that were promised factory jobs and then brought to the prostitution home of the mamasan. However, they were not held captive and could have chosen to leave, but there were no jobs in the Korean economy in the 1950s through the 1970s for uneducated girls that paid as much as these girls made in prostitution. Many others wanted the "glamorous" lifestyle that prostitution offered to naïve farm girls. Also, the tradition of prostitution was not started by Americans: the prostitution system was set up by Koreans to service Korean men, and this was in existence for hundreds of years. As far as the Americans subjecting these girls to harsh servitude rules, that is a blatant lie. The US Army did interfere with the club managers to ensure that black servicemen would not be discriminated against by Korean prostitutes. If this discrimination continued, the clubs would be declared off-limits to all GIs. When the club owners realized they would have no business, they quickly saw the light and told their girls to service any color GI, or they would lose their jobs and lifestyle. Also, the US military worked with the Korean authorities to ensure prostitute registration and monthly VD checkups, which was beneficial to both the Korean courtesans and their customers, whether they were Americans or Koreans.

"Let the Good Times Roll" by Sandra Pollack Sturdevant and Brenda Stoltzfus. Here prostitution is examined around US military bases in the Philippines, Okinawa, and Korea. Stoltzfus was a Tagalog (Filipino language) speaking Mennonite working with the Filipino prostitutes, and Sturdevant was the photographer. The book contains over 200 black and white photographs of the girls, prostitution clubs, owners, and extensive interviews with the prostitutes themselves. In Korea, the authors describe an organization called: "My Sister's Place," where prostitutes can get help and counseling, especially for young Korean American brides.

I will also mention Katherine Moon's "Sex Among Allies: Military Prostitution in US Military Relations." This book is a retread of the other books mentioned above, which see prostitutes as pawns used by the South Korean government to kowtow to the US military. Prostitutes are performing a "patriotic" act by keeping Americans happy (Fuck for the Fatherland). The books that I've mentioned seem very distorted to me, but the reader should judge for himself.

The best book on this subject I found was "Beyond the Shadow of Camptown" by JIyeon Yuh, which deals with in-depth interviews in America of Korean women in Korean American marriages. From 1954 through 1990, there were approximately 75,000 Korean American marriages. Miss Yuh interviewed a dozen Korean American military wives through Korean American Protestant church groups. Although none of the women interviewed admitted to being prostitutes, they described their struggles to adapt to America and the American way of life. Many were illiterate in basic English, had no marketable job skills, and most of the women were stuck in abusive and/or adulterous relationships. Here the dream of "Streets paved with gold" met the reality of poverty, loneliness, and "Americanization." For the GI husband, he expected a wife who would be submissive and docile. Yet, she must also become an American. She must give up her heritage, language, and food and raise her children as typical "Americans." Most husbands didn't want their children to learn Korean, and wives that couldn't learn English lost control of their own children. "We are in America, now" was the litany that she heard from her children. Most Korean women worked as manual labor factory workers, fruit pickers, or waitresses in Korean-run restaurants.

The Protestant-Korean churches were a haven where they could meet other "internationally-married" Koreans, but even here, there was the prejudice of immigrant Koreans who saw these women as "dirty, bad, Koreans", still prostitutes who were looking to steal their own Korean husbands. This book concentrates on Korean women and how they adjusted (or couldn't adjust) to the American way of life.

Most of the women joined Korean American marriage groups to network for jobs and preserved their Korean heritage. Many lost children who became "Americanized" and went off to live with their divorced fathers. They see their children as Americans, but they see themselves are neither fully Korean, rejected by their families back home for being a prostitute and by fellow Koreans as people of low moral character nor are they accepted by the Americans, who see them as evil "femme fatales" that stole red-blooded Americans from "good old American girls".

The real question is: "Is it not right that they should become American?" I am a first-generation American, and my parents definitely wanted me to be American. Today, we have the "Dreamers", who were brought here as children and are more American than Latin American. In our multi-cultural society, it may seem easier to keep your heritage and still be American, but for Korean married women, the choices depend on their economic status and their willingness to adapt to the dominant American culture.

The draw-down of American troops and the Korean "economic" miracle have greatly brought an end to the "Camptown Prostitution." As of 2021, there are only 28,000 US Army and military members in Korea, all in Tague, about one hundred miles from Seoul. If there are any large "Camptowns" in the future, they will not have a many Korean prostitutes but women from the Philippines, Vietnam, and even Russia. There's still money to be made outside of the one remaining base in Korea and inevitably there will be a foreign "Camptown" that services the US Military forces.

Comfort Women

I have described the life story of Kim Bok- Dong in my chapter on Comfort Women. You can also see her on a YouTube video recorded October 27, 2018. This video goes into painful details of her experience, but the braveness and humility of Miss Dong will stay with you forever. The video is "Life as a Comfort Woman: The story of Kim Bok-Dong" and appears on the Asian blog "Stay Curious, number 9, Asian Boss". I'll now list three other books that feature in-depth interviews with "Comfort Women" that have come forward to tell their individual horrific stories.

"Silence Broken: Korean Comfort Women," (1999 by Dai Sil Kim-Gibson),

"The Comfort Women," (2009 by Chunghee Sarah Son).

"True Stories of the Korean Comfort Women: Testimonies," (1995 by Keith Howard)

North Korean Gulags

While I was in Korea in the early 1970s, there were a few isolated incidents when a North Korean prison guard would defect and tell his story to the South Korean Press of the hardships and degradations that the prisoners at these camps endured.

The first real, in-depth eyewitness accounts of these atrocities would come from a young man, Kang Chol-Hwan, who had been imprisoned in Yodok Camp for ten years. Chol was raised in Pyongyang, North Korea, living a comfortable life with his sister, parents, and grandparents. His grandfather had been sent to Japan during WWII as slave labor but never renounced his Korean citizenship. When the war ended, he returned to North Korea and soon became a high-ranking minister in Kim-il-Sung's Communist Government. In 1997, he was accused of being a Japanese spy, and three generations of his family were sent to Yodok Prison. The author was only ten years old when he was imprisoned. His horrific experiences were described in his book: "The Aquariums of Pyongyang." His family was finally released after ten years, and he was now twenty and engaged in anti-government activities. He felt he was being watched and feared being returned to prison, so he defected with another political prisoner, An Hyuk. Together they made their way to China and from there to South Korea. In 2000, he published his book and received international acclaim. In 2005, he met with President George Bush and discussed his ordeals with the President. Unfortunately, his story doesn't have a happy ending. When he escaped, he told no one in his family he was leaving for fear of reprisals. He didn't hear anything about his family until 2011; when he found out that his sister and her eleven-year-old son were put in a political prison in 2000 because he published his book, which caused international criticism of the North Korean government.

Lee Soon-ok was a woman prisoner in North Korea, and her account of prison rapes, forced abortions, and biological experiments on fellow prisoners were detailed in a book she wrote after being released and having defected to South Korea. The book "Eyes of the Tailless Animals: Prison Memoirs of a North Korean Woman". She has since become a Christian and speaks at churches, and has testified before the US Senate about North Korean human rights abuses. She received a National Endowment for Democracy Award along with fellow recipients Chol and An Hyuk.

The Korean War

As a soldier, I think that the Korean War tested our resolve to stop an aggressive industrialized communist country, backed by China, from taking over a fledgling democratic country of poor subsistence farmers. Hey, wait a minute, are we talking about Korea or South Vietnam? The main difference was the resolve of the people. In South Vietnam, the South Army did not want to fight for a corrupt, greedy government that did nothing for its people. In Korea, the South Korean Army fought desperately to defend their country. It is estimated that four million Korean lives, in both North and South, were lost in this bitter conflict. The South Koreans did not want another country like North Korea dictating to them as the Japanese had done in their attempt to eradicate Korean identity.

However, to understand the hardships of the troops and civilians, you must approach the war on a micro and macro level. The micro-level is most appealing to me because it shows us the war from a grunt perspective: the heroic, cowardly, brutal, and arrogant actions and attitudes on both sides of the conflict. Here I can recommend two books that tell of the suffering and humanity of the common foot soldier. "Last Stand of Fox Company" by Bob Duray and Thomas Clavin and "Give Me Tomorrow "by Patrick O'Donnell. Both books focus on the retreat from Chosin Reservoir when the army and Marines were surrounded by vast numbers of Chinese troops and had to fight their way out to get to the port and safety. Their steadfastness and heroism are truly epic in the same way that the Greek Xenophon recorded the tactical retreat of the Greek mercenary soldiers stuck thousands of miles from home in hostile Persian territory in his "Anabasis". If you enjoy "You Are There" history, then these books put you there in the bitter cold-shooting gallery. A third book I especially recommend is the war photography book: "This is War!" by David Douglass Duncan, excerpts of which first appeared in Life Magazine. Duncan, a Marine himself from WW II, portrayed the struggles of the common foot soldier. The image of a young bone-tired, freezing Marine with sunken hollow eyes staring through the viewer is forever stamped on my mind as a horror of war. This was a time when America only had war correspondent photographs depicting the grisly struggle. Later, Americans watched nightly on the television the ghastly carnage of Vietnam. At first, they were horrified, then disgusted, and finally numb to the killings and destruction.

Now comes the hard part, the macro level, all about the generals and politicians and their conflicting ideologies, pettiness, and shortsightedness. The first book to consider is a "military" history: "This Kind of War: A Study in Unpreparedness" by T.R. Fehrenbach. Fehrenbach was an army officer in the conflict; his book is very thorough on tactics, the "Big Picture". He is a 'military man, "and like many officers I knew, he has an "Us versus Them" mentality". The Us is the military, and the Them are the politicians. He idolizes MacArthur and blames President Truman for letting the army be reduced and unprepared for conflict. I understand and empathize with him because he was leading and losing soldiers that did not have adequate training or equipment.

The second book is a disappointment: "The Coldest Winter: America and the Korean War" by David Halberstam. This is a "political" book, and the actual fighting takes a distant second place to bash MacArthur and even President Truman. To get a more nuanced picture of MacArthur, read "American Caesar "by William Manchester. This book still admires the man but does bring out his arrogance and misjudgments.

My own opinion of MacArthur is that he is a vain and arrogant general and a mediocre tactician. His capture of Inchon was daring and brilliant, but the rest of his conduct of the war was lackluster (but what do I know, I'm only a grunt).

The last book, "The Korean War: A History" by Bruce Cummings, is not recommended (which means the average reader will definitely run out and read this one) because of its anti-American basis. His distorted left-wing view that America is stepping directly into the same repressive colonial rule that Japan forced on Korea is blatantly unsubstantiated.

Amerasians from Vietnam

The chapter on Amerasians from Vietnam was sourced from a Smithsonian Magazine article of June 2009 by David Lamb. Since then, I have discovered two books on this vital subject. The first, "Surviving Twice" by Trin Yarborough, tells the real-life stories of five Viet Amerasians. The second is the "Dust of Life", recorded and edited by Robert McKelvy, which is made up of oral histories of Viet Amerasians telling their tragic stories. Unfortunately, the "Dust" book does not tell us what happened to these desperate children, "Surviving Twice" follows these five children and at least gives some sense of closure about their destinies.

The Homecoming Act, which admitted 26,000 Viet children, might be thought of as a happy conclusion to our efforts "to leave no soldier behind". However, the "Global Post "newspaper article of 2 September 2011 tells of Amerasians still stuck in Vietnam. The article tells of a discriminated group of Amerasians that speak no English and have no documentation to prove their identity. There is also a Dane, Brian Hjorth, based originally in Vietnam, that is using the internet to locate missing American fathers. He is collaborating with a Vietnamese interpreter, Hung Phan, to help him locate Amerasian people, most of whom are now in their middle 40s. He has had some success and personally reunited one American father with his missing son in Vietnam.

As I stated in my journal, the Amerasians in America are the last of a special distinctive race: they will be absorbed by the larger white, black, and Asian ethnic groups, and we Americans can conveniently forget that this national tragedy ever happened.

Korean Christianity

The best book on Korean Christianity is "A History of Korean Christianity "by Sebastian Kim and Kersten Kim. This is an important book that details how and why Christianity is so popular in South Korea. As of 2020, there are more Christians than Buddhists in South Korea, with the Protestant denominations the most numerous of the Christian sects. In America, the Korean American Protestant churches are both a religious and social gathering place for Korean immigrants.

Korean Ceramics

I love Korean vases and have collected them in South Korea and later in the States. If you, too, have an interest in buying or learning more about this unique art, I can recommend two venues to broaden your background so you know what you should be looking for in a celadon vase. The first is a beautifully illustrated art book of a catalog of a Korean Exhibition. "Earth, Fire, Soul" is produced by the National Museum of Korea: here, you find beautiful representations of Korean ceramic masterpieces. The second venue is a YouTube lecture by Robert Mowry: "Korean Ceramics" (Portland Art Museum presentation). This is a good introduction to the importance of Korean ceramics as a world treasure.

Korean Notes

The Gene Cotton Band, the country gospel group that I escorted all over Korea as a USO show, went on to have a successful performance career from 1970-1982 in country music. Gene Cotton had four Billboard Top 40 Country hits; his most famous singles were "Rhymes and Reasons" and "You Got Me Running". He lived near Nashville and started a program for underprivileged children called "Kids on Stage" (KOS). This was a summer camp program for kids to learn how to play musical instruments and perform their talents on stage. Gene got veteran Nashville musicians to come in to teach and perform for the children. Michael McDonald of the Doobie Brothers Band was a frequent performer and a mentor of the KOS children.

Lieutenant William Calley, Jr., the subject of many conversations among the officers at ASCOM Depot, was convicted of killing 22 unarmed civilians in the Vietnamese village of Mai Lai. At his murder trial in November 1970, it was recorded that he ordered his platoon to kill everyone (men, women, and children) even though his platoon was not under enemy fire at the time of that order.

Calley was the only officer of 26 officers charged (all higher up in the chain of command) that was convicted of murder and was given a life sentence. President Nixon changed the sentence to house arrest. At the time, 69% of Americans thought LT. Calley had been made a "scapegoat" for the "guilty" higher-ups in the military command.

LT. Calley appealed his sentence, stating crucial mitigating circumstances had been left out at the original trial. The Military Court agreed and reduced his sentence to 10 years (eligible for parole in 3 years). He was released in 3 years and started a new life. He married, had a child, and became a gemologist. He also spoke at different venues around the country about his actions, publicly stating that he felt remorseful and apologized to the people of Vietnam and to the soldiers involved in the massacre.

Japan

The economic model that General MacArthur encouraged and helped to set up is detailed in the two books below. The first, "The East Asian Miracle," by Oxford University Press, a World Bank Book, gives the reader a primer on how to revitalize one's economy. It might be called "Economic Miracle for Dummies", since if you follow all of the points that they raise, you too can experience an economic miracle. You start with sound development projects, public transportation enhancements, clean water, and electrification. Then you have income sharing where you pay your workers a fair wage which in turn, allows them to accumulate personal savings. You improve the educational facilities for skilled workers in your new industries. You steal, beg, or borrow new technologies in industrial and farm production. You have low taxes both on the individual and on the developing industries. You attract foreign investments by giving tax breaks, and very importantly, you have the cooperation of the government to set low taxation rates, "encouraging" banks to give low-interest loans and industry to create jobs for these skilled workers. You take all these ingredients, put them in an oven of high tariffs on foreign goods (to avoid competition), bake for a set time, and Wallah! You have made your "Economic Miracle" (here you can have your cake and eat it too!).

The second book deals with the human side of the story; that is "The Reckoning" by David Halberstam. This book is an eye-opener, exposing the flaws of our capitalist greed. The Japanese stole our production method but made the worker and not the machine responsible for a great, finished product. It will be interesting to see if the robotic technology of the twenty-first century will surpass the Japanese production model.

The Swiss Who Came Down from the Mountain

There's a book of essays by eminent Japanese monks, scholars, and social critics called "The Japanese Mind," edited by Roger Davis. This book goes into greater detail than my personal, sake-infused conversations with the Swiss pharmaceutical executive. This book is a must for businessmen as well as travelers. It details the "apartness" of Japanese culture and why it's so hard for foreigners to be a part of that culture.

"Japan: A Travel Survival Kit" by Ian McQueen (1994) is excellent in its in-depth descriptions, detailed maps, and thoughtful insights into the Japanese mind. This book sets the standard for travel in Japan and McQueen has a distinctive opinion on many Japanese foibles.

I'm proud to say that I met Ian McQueen (see my chapter "Motorcyclist as Metaphor" in the Nationalist China section) in the early 1970s in Taipei when he planned an around-the-world motorcycle journey. He told me after Nationalist China; he was going on to Japan. It seemed the Land of the Rising Sun captivated him so much that he stayed, married a Japanese woman, and has been a Japan expert for over two decades. Kudos to you, Ian!

Zen Buddhism

The best standard description of Zen Buddhism (still valid, now over 60 years old) is: "The Way of Zen," by Alan Watts (If you can define it, then it isn't Zen).

Another book about Zen is: "The Zen Source Book," a collection of Zen articles, paintings, and poems from monks, scholars, and artists. This book is edited by Stephen Addiss. For Japan and Nationalist China, it would behoove you to read "The Analects of Confucius" and "Tao te Ching" (the Way) by Lao Tzu. These are standard "bibles" to give you a foundation for all Chinese religion, philosophical, and ethical systems.

Japanese Art and Theater

Newsweek has published a series called "Great Museums of the World" and has a full-color coffee table book called "National Museum Tokyo". This is a great introduction to all aspects of Japanese art.

Concerning classical theater such as Noh and Kabuki, I strongly advise the reader to become a listener and viewer. Noh and Kabuki can be seen on YouTube: you may love or hate these performances but watch them for the "Gipper".

Modern Geishas

The groups of Japanese hippies and street people that I encountered in the Ginza have been documented by Japanese fashion photographer Shoichi Aoki in a colorful and highly amusing way in his book "Fruits". For teenagers and young women, the lesson here is that you can dress exclusively off thrift store finds and don't need to buy expensive, designer brand new clothing and apparel.

A Japan Travel Journal

I would be amiss if I did not mention two books that I found fascinating. The first is a photographic essay on the country: "Japan" by Werner Bischof, a Swiss photographer who captured the old changeless Japan while he was in the Orient covering the Korean War. Some of the photographs seem dated (aren't we all getting dated?), but the majority stand out like a traditional woodblock print; only his images are in black and white. The second book is "Walking in Circles: Finding Happiness in Lost Japan" by Todd Wassel. This young American traveler walks from temple to temple and meets a whole array of fascinating characters that enliven his pilgrimage.

Nationalist China

Chiang Kai-Shek

Ruthless Warlord, inept military tactician, Confucian traditionalist, power-grabbing dictator, skilled diplomat, patriot, opportunist, etc. Who was the real Chiang? The one book that digs deeply into all aspects of the man, as well as selections from his personal diaries, is "The Generalissimo: Chiang Kai-Shek and the Struggle for Modern China" by Jay Taylor. Chiang's vision for China seems very prescient, especially for what is happening in mainland China today.

The "Economic Miracle"

Shelly Rigger's "Why Taiwan Matters: Small Island, Global Powerhouse" goes into more detail than I mentioned on how they achieved their "Economic Miracle". It also discusses how Taiwan needs to deal with future developments and relations with their "Big Brother" only 75 miles away.

Stolen Art

If you can't see the masterpieces in real life (don't fret about needing a life, save that for later, just buy this book), the next best thing is the beautiful color representations of classic Chinese art in the "Emperor's Treasures: Chinese Art from the National Museum Taipei" by Jay Xu and Li He. This book also gives a brief history of the emperors' aesthetic preferences and how the art of a period reflected this vision.

Hong Kong And Macau

For history buffs, "A Modern History of Hong Kong 1841-1997 (the latter date is when Hong Kong transferred back to China's control) by Steven Tsang is very detailed and informative, especially on how the Hong Kong Chinese developed their own form of democratic rule and political freedom.

For photography buffs, "The Trope Photographic Series on Hong Kong" gives great images of the island's architecture but is short on people images (I had this problem also, so I sympathize with the 17 photographers that complied this book).

For the sights of Hong Kong and Macau, Lonely Planet Guide is just fine.

High and Low Opera

Again, I implore the reader to find performance excerpts of Peking Opera (high, the emperor's choice) and Revolutionary Opera (low, the people's choice) on YouTube (if you can sit through 16 hours of Wagner's "The Ring", you can endure these operas).

Macau

Macau's sights can be seen in a day, but you should stay an extra day to soak up the ambiance of the old Portuguese city; read the epitaphs on the fading stone graves of the Protestant cemetery. Go now before there is a glitzy casino on every corner (My God, they are growing like Starbucks' mushrooms). If you can't go, read "Macau: The Imaginary City" by Jonathan Potter. This is fascinating cultural commentary, not history.

Philippines

America acquired its overseas empire in late middle age (it is like having a kid when you are 45; you would think that you would be wiser to handle this experience, but now you don't have the stamina or patience to deal with no sleep and constant nerve-wracking crying) and we really screwed this one up. The best "political" book on the Philippines is "In Our Image" by Stanley Karnow. It goes into our sorry handling of this problem child and especially our relationship with President Marcos in the present times. It also gives a "different" view of MacArthur as the military governor and later liberator of the country from the Japanese.

For the comic book fans, "The Illustrated History of the Philippines" is great (lots of photographs and very little history writing).

The natural beauty and sights of the 7000 islands that make up the country are nicely described in the Lonely Planet Guide.

Sacred Images

Esperanza Gatbonton has written two books about Filipino religious sculpture: "A Heritage of Saints", which deals with wooden carved statues, and "Philippine Religious Carving in Ivory". "A Heritage of Saints" goes into great detail, espousing the theory that the majority of wood saints (santos) were carved by indigencies natives, especially in the countryside, for local churches and family shrines. Here we see the native folk art: crude, fatalistic, bloodied Indios (Indians) as the suffering Christ on the cross. The second book illustrates the exquisite skill of the Filipino Chinese ivory carvers, with their rounded Chinese faces, almond eyes, and oriental court costumes. This hybrid art was so popular that many of these sculptures were exported to Europe and Latin America. In Mexico and Peru, these statues influenced native Indian carving and painting.

Japanese Atrocities in the Philippines in WW II

"A Reckoning: Philippine Trials of Japanese War Criminals" by Sharon Chamberlain (2019) is an important book about a story that needs to be told. This book reviews the court documents of hundreds of cases, which were mostly trials of low-level Japanese soldiers that raped, murdered, and mutilated the local Filipinos. Surviving victims identified the actual soldiers who committed these crimes. These soldiers were tried in an Asian court by Filipinos for crimes against civilians and not soldiers. This is very different from the Tokyo War Trials, where high-ranking Japanese officers and government officials were tried by Western judges. The Supreme Japanese Commander of the Philippines, General Yamashita, was convicted of war crimes and hung in 1946.

This book was very disturbing to me as an army officer. As an officer, you are responsible for the actions of the men under your command. If your men go rogue and kill innocent civilians, you are still responsible, but should not the individual rogue soldiers also be put on trial? The court records prove that many of these Japanese soldiers acted on their own (and were not just following orders) when they murdered defenseless men, women, and children. The individual soldier must be held responsible for the crimes that he commits.

That is why this book is so important for our understanding of individual responsibility and guilt in warfare. Thank you, Miss Chamberlain, for documenting and discussing this issue.

Burma

While other ruined cities evoke feelings of death or destruction, Pagan is alive.

If you cannot visit Pagan, the book I would recommend is "Snapshot Pagan, Burma: A Photographic Exploration" by Scott Shaw. Here he captures the varied temple architecture and evokes a sense of grandeur and decay of this fascinating temple city.

Burma is a fascinating country, a mosaic of races, languages, and religions; however, due to time travel restrictions and whole sections of the country being off-limits to foreigners, it is difficult to visit. There are YouTube videos, which give a feel for the country, but they concentrate on the repressive measures of the military. Myanmar (Burma) is in the news because of the pro-democracy vs. the military controversy, but a new book about the people has just been published: "Our Time in Myanmar: Four Years in Yangoon (Rangoon)" by Jessica Mudditt. She is an

Australian news correspondent that worked for the only English language newspaper in Myanmar, and these are her experiences during her stay.

A Note on my Alter Ego

"Flash Gordon" and "Flash Gordon Conquers the Universe" are free to watch on YouTube. Each movie serial has 12 episodes and lasts about three and ½ hours. I remember seeing a few serial episodes at my local theater but was never able to watch an entire movie until I found an old VHS tape of the entire "Flash Gordon" movie in a local thrift store. Flash Gordon is a true "American" hero, not a comic book superhero with supernatural powers.

A word of advice: don't buy the German television production of "Flash Gordon" made in the 1960s (Scheisse!) and avoid like the plague the 1970s American movie "Flash Gordon". Stand up for your rights as a red-blooded American: you want the authentic cheesecake acting, the wire-operated spaceships, the paper Mache monsters, and the cliff-hanging episodes. I could find no better hero to emulate (well, maybe Groucho Marx), and don't forget the stirring musical theme from Franz Liszt's "Preludes" every time Ming the Merciless enters the scene.

ILLUSTRATION CREDITS

Illustration Credits

FRONT COVER OF "SOLDIER TO SOJOURNER": I WOULD LIKE TO THANK THE THREE PHOTOGRAPHERS FOR THE USE OF THEIR IMAGES FROM UNSPLASH, THE FREE PHOTO SERVICE THAT, THROUGH AN ERROR, I DID NOT GIVE CREDIT TO ON MY PHOTOGRAPHY BOOK OF THE SAME TITLE. I AM USING THE SAME PHOTOGRAPHS ON MY JOURNAL TEXTBOOK, AND NOW I WILL FULLY GIVE CREDIT: THE IMAGE OF THE SOLDIER ON THE FRONT COVER IS BY JACOB OWENS, WHICH WAS PHOTOGRAPHED IN 2020 AND THE PHOTOGRAPH OF THE TRAVELER LOOKING AT MOUNTAINS IN THE OCEAN IS BY DANIEL JENSEN I ALSO WANT TO CREDIT THE ENGLISH RED TELEPHONE BOOTH BY TS AT TESSA 22. I FIND YOUR WORK BEAUTIFUL, AND I THANK YOU FOR THE USE OF YOUR PHOTOGRAPHS.

INTRODUCTION: "JAN DAVISZ DE HEEM": THIS IS A FAITHFUL REPRODUCTION OF A TWO-DIMENSIONAL PUBLIC DOMAIN WORK OF ART. PUBLIC DOMAIN IN COUNTRY OF ORIGIN WHERE THE COPYRIGHT TERM IS AUTHOR'S LIFE PLUS 100 YEARS OR FEWER. THIS IS ALSO IN THE PUBLIC DOMAIN OF THE U.S. BECAUSE THE COPYRIGHT WAS TAKEN OUT BEFORE 1927 AND NOT RENEWED. THIS PHOTOGRAPHIC REPRODUCTION IS THEREFORE ALSO CONSIDERED IN THE PUBLIC DOMAIN OF THE UNITED STATES/SOURCE: HTTPS://WWW.PUBHIST.COM

INTRODUCTION: "KOREAN FAMILY": PUBLIC DOMAIN LIBRARY OF CONGRESS (LOC) FRANK AND FRANCIS CARPENTER COLLECTION LOC-USZ62-79999

CHAPTER 1: "QUONSET": AUTHOR PHOTOGRAPH

CHAPTER 3: "GEISHAS" PUBLIC DOMAIN FRANK AND FRANCIS CARPENTER COLLECTION LOC-USZ62-80001

CHAPTER 6: "KOREAN STORE OWNER" PUBLIC DOMAIN CARPENTER COLLECTION LOC USZ62-99491

CHAPTER 7: "GIRL IN LITTER" PUBLIC DOMAIN CARPENTER COLLECTION LOC USZ62-35119

CHAPTER 11: "ASSEMBLY PLANT" PUBLIC DOMAIN IN THE U.S. FIRST PUBLISHED PRIOR TO 1927 COPYRIGHT EXPIRED AND WAS NOT RENEWED/ SOURCE: FORD MOTOR COMPANY

CHAPTER 12: "SONG OF ROLAND" PUBLIC DOMAIN LICENSED UNDER CREATIVE COMMONS ATTRIBUTION 3.0 UNPORTED LICENSE AVAILABLE FOR DOWNLOAD AT THE "GUTTENBURG PROJECT" PUBLIC DOMAIN WORKS OF LITERATURE

"STEPHEN CRANE" PUBLIC DOMAIN IN THE U.S. FIRST PUBLISHED PRIOR TO 1927, COPYRIGHT EXPIRED AND WAS NOT RENEWED

"LTC DON FAITH, JR." PUBLIC DOMAIN, THIS FILE IS OF A U.S. OFFICER TAKEN BY A FEDERAL EMPLOYEE AS PART OF HIS OFFICIAL DUTIES. AS A WORK OF THE U. S. FEDERAL GOVERNMENT, IT IS IN THE PUBLIC DOMAIN

CHAPTER 12: RIVERA PAINTING PUBLIC DOMAIN IN COUNTRY OF ORIGIN 100 YEARS AFTER AUTHOR'S DEATH PUBLIC DOMAIN IN US: 100 YEARS AFTER

AUTHOR'S DEATH/FAITHFUL REPRODUCTION OF A PD ARTWORK IS ALSO CONSIDERED IN THE PD. US LICENSE: CREATIVE COMMONS ATTRIBUTION: SHARE-ALIKE 3.0

CHAPTER 13: "KIM-IL-SUNG" FILE IS LICENSED UNDER CREATIVE COMMONS ATTRIBUTION 2.0 GENERIC LICENSE AUTHOR: YEOWATZUP/SOURCE: HTTPS://WWW.FLICKR.COM/PHOTOS/YEOWATZUP 292 19827778

"CEMETARY" PUBLIC DOMAIN NATIONAL ARCHIVES:530634 DEPARTMENT OF DEFENSE 4/9/1951 FILE IS OF A U.S. SOLDIER TAKEN BY A FEDERAL EMPLOYEE AS PART OF HIS OFFICIAL DUTIES. AS A WORK OF THE U. S. FEDERAL GOVERNMENT, IT IS IN THE PUBLIC DOMAIN

CHAPTER 14: "RICKSHAW" PUBLIC DOMAIN CARPENTER COLLECTION LOC 56-A046443DF78

CHAPTER 17: "RHAPSODY" AUTHOR PHOTOGRAPH

CHAPTER 18: "COMFORT WOMEN" FILE IS OF A U.S. SOLDIER TAKEN BY A FEDERAL EMPLOYEE AS PART OF HIS OFFICIAL DUTIES. AS A WORK OF THE U. S. FEDERAL GOVERNMENT, IT IS IN THE PUBLIC DOMAIN

CHAPTER 19:" CELEDON" GNU FREE DOCUMENTATION LICENSE, VERSION 1.2 BY FREE SOFTWARE FOUNDATION IN THE U. S. IT IS LICENSED UNDER CREATIVE COMMONS ATTRIBUTION 3.0 UNPORTED LICENSE AUTHOR: KOREAN HISTORY AT ENGLISH WIKIMEDIA

"MAITREYA" IS LICENSED UNDER THE KOREAN OPEN GOVERNMENT LICENSE TYPE 1 ATTRIBUTION LICENSED IN THE U.S. AS PUBLIC DOMAIN PUBLISHED PRIOR TO 1927 COPYRIGHT EXPIRED AND WAS NOT RENEWED IN THE U.S.

CHAPTER 20: "MARKET" LOC PRINTS AND PHOTOGRAPHS COLLECTION: C. H. GRAVES PUBLIC DOMAIN

"FAMILY" AUTHOR PHOTOGRAPH

CHAPTER 22: "FANNY EATON" IS A FAITHFUL REPRODUCTION OF A TWO-DIMENSIONAL PUBLIC DOMAIN WORK OF ART. PUBLIC DOMAIN IN COUNTRY OF ORIGIN WHERE THE COPYRIGHT TERM IS AUTHOR'S LIFE PLUS 100 YEARS OR FEWER. THIS IS ALSO IN THE PUBLIC DOMAIN OF THE U.S. BECAUSE THE

COPYRIGHT WAS TAKEN OUT BEFORE 1927 AND NOT RENEWED. THIS PHOTOGRAPHIC REPRODUCTION IS THEREFORE ALSO CONSIDERED IN THE PUBLIC DOMAIN OF THE UNITED STATES/SOURCE PRINCETON UNIVERSITY CREATIVE COMMONS 2.0 SHARE-ALIKE

CHAPTER 23: PAINTING OF COLERIDGE BY PETER VAN DYKE, 1795 SOURCE: THE NATIONAL GALLERY LONDON/ PUBLIC DOMAIN IN COUNTRY OF ORIGIN: AUTHOR'S LIFE PLUS 100 YEARS/ PUBLIC DOMAIN IN US: AUTHOR'S LIFE PLUS 100 YEARS. PHOTOGRAPH OF PAINTING IN THE PD IS ALSO CONSIDERED TO BE IN PD. US LICENSE: CREATIVE COMMONS: ATTRIBUTION- SHARE-ALIKE 3.0

CHAPTER 24: "GATE": AUTHOR PHOTOGRAPH

CHAPTER 26: "TINA MODOTTI" PUBLIC DOMAIN IN THE U.S. BECAUSE COPYRIGHT HAS EXPIRED, FIRST PUBLICATION BEFORE 1927, AND COPYRIGHT WAS NOT RENEWED IN THE U.S.

CHAPTER 28: "ADMIRAL Yi" AUTHOR PHOTOGRAPH

CHAPTER 31: "NUN" PUBLIC DOMAIN LOC GEORGE GRANTHAM BAIN COLLECTION

CHAPTER 32: "KIERKEGAARD" IS A FAITHFUL REPRODUCTION OF A TWO-DIMENSIONAL PUBLIC DOMAIN WORK OF ART. PUBLIC DOMAIN IN COUNTRY OF ORIGIN WHERE THE COPYRIGHT TERM IS AUTHOR'S LIFE PLUS 100 YEARS OR FEWER. THIS IS ALSO IN THE PUBLIC DOMAIN OF THE U.S. BECAUSE THE COPYRIGHT WAS TAKEN OUT BEFORE 1927 AND NOT RENEWED. THIS PHOTOGRAPHIC REPRODUCTION IS THEREFORE ALSO CONSIDERED IN THE PUBLIC DOMAIN OF THE UNITED STATES/ SOURCE LA BIBLIOTECA REAL DE DINAMARCA

CHAPTER 34: "LITTER' LOC CARPENTER COLLECTION PUBLIC DOMAIN

CHAPTER 35: "WOMEN W/STICKS" LOC-USZ62-29309 PUBLIC DOMAIN

CHAPTER 35: "JAPAN DIVIDER" PUBLIC DOMAIN LC- USZ62-87733 (BLACK AND WHITE FILM COPY NEGATIVE)

CHAPTER 36: 'CASTLE" AUTHOR PHOTOGRAPH

"GARDEN" THE COPYRIGHT OWNER CQUEST RELEASED PHOTOGRAPH TO CREATIVE COMMONS ATTRIBUTION SHARE-ALIKE 2.5 GENERIC LICENSE, FREE TO COPY, DISTRIBUTE AND TRANSMIT THE WORK WITHOUT RESTRICTIONS

"TEA CEREMONY": THIS IS A FAITHFUL REPRODUCTION OF A TWO-DIMENSIONAL PUBLIC DOMAIN WORK OF ART. PUBLIC DOMAIN IN COUNTRY OF ORIGIN WHERE THE COPYRIGHT TERM IS AUTHOR'S LIFE PLUS 100 YEARS OR FEWER. THIS IS ALSO IN THE PUBLIC DOMAIN OF THE U.S. BECAUSE THE COPYRIGHT WAS TAKEN OUT BEFORE 1927 AND NOT RENEWED. THIS PHOTOGRAPHIC REPRODUCTION IS THEREFORE ALSO CONSIDERED IN THE PUBLIC DOMAIN OF UNITED STATES LICENSE: CREATIVE COMMONS 2.0 SHARE-ALIKE

CHAPTER 37: "SHIP SCREEN" PUBLIC DOMAIN GNU IN JAPAN. THIS IS A FAITHFUL REPRODUCTION OF A TWO-DIMENSIONAL PUBLIC DOMAIN WORK OF ART. PUBLIC DOMAIN IN COUNTRY OF ORIGIN WHERE THE COPYRIGHT TERM IS AUTHOR'S LIFE PLUS 100 YEARS OR FEWER. THIS IS ALSO IN THE PUBLIC DOMAIN OF THE U.S. BECAUSE THE COPYRIGHT WAS TAKEN OUT OR PUBLISHED BEFORE 1927 AND NOT RENEWED. THIS PHOTOGRAPHIC REPRODUCTION IS THEREFORE ALSO CONSIDERED IN THE PUBLIC DOMAIN OF THE UNITED STATES. LICENSE: CREATIVE COMMONS 2.0 SHARE-ALIKE

"JAPANESE VIRGIN" IS A FAITHFUL REPRODUCTION OF A TWO-DIMENSIONAL PUBLIC DOMAIN WORK OF ART. PUBLIC DOMAIN IN COUNTRY OF ORIGIN WHERE THE COPYRIGHT TERM IS AUTHOR'S LIFE PLUS 100 YEARS OR FEWER. THIS IS ALSO IN THE PUBLIC DOMAIN OF THE U.S. BECAUSE THE COPYRIGHT WAS TAKEN OUT BEFORE 1927 AND NOT RENEWED. THIS PHOTOGRAPHIC REPRODUCTION IS THEREFORE ALSO CONSIDERED IN THE PUBLIC DOMAIN OF THE UNITED STATES. LICENSE: CREATIVE COMMONS 2.0 SHARE-ALIKE

CHAPTER 38: "SAMURAI" THIS IS A FAITHFUL REPRODUCTION OF A TWO-DIMENSIONAL PUBLIC DOMAIN WORK OF ART. PUBLIC DOMAIN IN COUNTRY OF ORIGIN WHERE THE COPYRIGHT TERM IS AUTHOR'S LIFE PLUS 100 YEARS OR FEWER. THIS IS ALSO IN THE PUBLIC DOMAIN OF THE U.S. BECAUSE THE COPYRIGHT WAS TAKEN OUT BEFORE 1927 AND NOT RENEWED. THIS

PHOTOGRAPHIC REPRODUCTION IS THEREFORE ALSO CONSIDERED IN THE PUBLIC DOMAIN OF THE UNITED STATES. LICENSE: CREATIVE COMMONS 2.0 SHARE-ALIKE. PHOTOGRAPH BY FELICE BEATO (1832-1909) SOURCE: TERRY BENNETT "EARLY JAPANESE IMAGES" RUTLAND VERMONT, CHARLES TUTTLE CO. 1975

CHAPTER 39: "NOH" IS A FAITHFUL REPRODUCTION OF A TWO-DIMENSIONAL PUBLIC DOMAIN WORK OF ART. PUBLIC DOMAIN IN COUNTRY OF ORIGIN WHERE THE COPYRIGHT TERM IS AUTHOR'S LIFE PLUS 100 YEARS OR FEWER. THIS IS ALSO IN THE PUBLIC DOMAIN OF THE U.S. BECAUSE THE COPYRIGHT WAS TAKEN OUT BEFORE 1927 AND NOT RENEWED. THIS PHOTOGRAPHIC REPRODUCTION IS THEREFORE ALSO CONSIDERED IN THE PUBLIC DOMAIN OF THE UNITED STATES. LICENSE: CREATIVE COMMONS 2.0 SHARE-ALIKE.

CHAPTER 40: "MACARTHUR" PUBLIC DOMAIN FILE IS OF A U.S. SOLDIER TAKEN BY A FEDERAL EMPLOYEE AS PART OF HIS OFFICIAL DUTIES. AS A WORK OF THE U. S. FEDERAL GOVERNMENT, IT IS IN THE PUBLIC DOMAIN. SOURCE; NATIONAL ARCHIVES/NAVAL HISTORICAL CENTER USA-C-2413

CHAPTER 41: "MISHIMA" COPYRIGHT EXPIRED IN JAPAN IN 1970 AND WAS NOT RENEWED. LICENSE IN U.S. CREATIVE COMMONS 2.0 SHARE-ALIKE. PHOTOGRAPH BYSHIROU AOYAMA. SOURCE: HTTPS://COMMONS.WIKIMEDIA ORG/WIKIFILE YUKIO MISHAMA.JPG

CHAPTER 42: "KABUKI" IS A FAITHFUL REPRODUCTION OF A TWO-DIMENSIONAL PUBLIC DOMAIN WORK OF ART. PUBLIC DOMAIN IN COUNTRY OF ORIGIN WHERE THE COPYRIGHT TERM IS AUTHOR'S LIFE PLUS 100 YEARS OR FEWER. THIS IS ALSO IN THE PUBLIC DOMAIN OF THE U.S. BECAUSE THE COPYRIGHT WAS TAKEN OUT BEFORE 1927 AND NOT RENEWED. THIS PHOTOGRAPHIC REPRODUCTION IS THEREFORE ALSO CONSIDERED IN THE PUBLIC DOMAIN OF UNITED STATES LICENSE: CREATIVE COMMONS 2.0 SHARE-ALIKE. SOURCE: HTTP//WWW.ZENPAKU.WASEDA .JPG. PHOTOGRAPHER: TOYOKUNI

CHAPTER 44: "PROSTITUTES" PUBLIC DOMAIN IN JAPAN THIS IS A FAITHFUL REPRODUCTION OF A TWO-DIMENSIONAL PUBLIC DOMAIN WORK OF ART. PUBLIC

DOMAIN IN COUNTRY OF ORIGIN WHERE THE COPYRIGHT TERM IS AUTHOR'S LIFE PLUS 100 YEARS OR FEWER. THIS IS ALSO IN THE PUBLIC DOMAIN OF THE U.S. BECAUSE THE COPYRIGHT WAS TAKEN OUT BEFORE 1927 AND NOT RENEWED. THIS PHOTOGRAPHIC REPRODUCTION IS THEREFORE ALSO CONSIDERED IN THE PUBLIC DOMAIN OF UNITED STATES LICENSE: CREATIVE COMMONS 2.0 SHARE-ALIKE, PHOTOGRAPHER: POSSIBLY KUSAKABE KIMBEI (1841-1934)

CHAPTER 45: "STORYVILLE" PHOTOGRAPH IN THE PUBLIC DOMAIN/ U.S. COPYRIGHT HAS EXPIRED/ FIRST PUBLICATION OCCURRED BEFORE 1927AND THEN A LACK OF RENEWAL IT BECAME PUBLIC DOMAIN AUTHOR: E. BELLOCQ, SOURCE: "EROTISCHE FOTOGRAFIE 1890-1920"

CHAPTER 46: "JAPANESE WOMAN" PUBLIC DOMAIN IN JAPAN THIS IS A FAITHFUL REPRODUCTION OF A TWO-DIMENSIONAL PUBLIC DOMAIN WORK OF ART. PUBLIC DOMAIN IN COUNTRY OF ORIGIN WHERE THE COPYRIGHT TERM IS AUTHOR'S LIFE PLUS 100 YEARS OR FEWER. THIS IS ALSO IN THE PUBLIC DOMAIN OF THE U.S. BECAUSE PUBLICATION AND OR COPYRIGHT WAS TAKEN OUT BEFORE 1927. THIS PHOTOGRAPHIC REPRODUCTION IS THEREFORE ALSO CONSIDERED IN THE PUBLIC DOMAIN OF UNITED STATES LICENSE: CREATIVE COMMONS 2.0 SHARE-ALIKE

"ACTOR" PUBLIC DOMAIN IN JAPAN IS A FAITHFUL REPRODUCTION OF A TWO-DIMENSIONAL PUBLIC DOMAIN WORK OF ART. PUBLIC DOMAIN IN COUNTRY OF ORIGIN WHERE THE COPYRIGHT TERM IS AUTHOR'S LIFE PLUS 100 YEARS OR FEWER. THIS IS ALSO IN THE PUBLIC DOMAIN OF THE U.S. BECAUSE THE COPYRIGHT WAS TAKEN OUT BEFORE 1927 AND NOT RENEWED. THIS PHOTOGRAPHIC REPRODUCTION IS THEREFORE ALSO CONSIDERED IN THE PUBLIC DOMAIN OF UNITED STATES LICENSE: CREATIVE COMMONS 2.0 SHARELIKE

"WAVE" PUBLIC DOMAIN IN JAPAN IS A FAITHFUL REPRODUCTION OF A TWO-DIMENSIONAL PUBLIC DOMAIN WORK OF ART. PUBLIC DOMAIN IN COUNTRY OF ORIGIN WHERE THE COPYRIGHT TERM IS AUTHOR'S LIFE PLUS 100 YEARS OR FEWER. THIS IS ALSO IN THE PUBLIC DOMAIN OF THE U.S. BECAUSE THE COPYRIGHT WAS TAKEN OUT BEFORE 1927 AND NOT RENEWED. THIS

PHOTOGRAPHIC REPRODUCTION IS THEREFORE ALSO CONSIDERED IN THE PUBLIC DOMAIN OF UNITED STATES LICENSE: CREATIVE COMMONS 2.0 SHARE-ALIKE. SOURCE LOC 1918

"GHOST" PUBLIC DOMAIN IN JAPAN IS A FAITHFUL REPRODUCTION OF A TWO-DIMENSIONAL PUBLIC DOMAIN WORK OF ART. PUBLIC DOMAIN IN COUNTRY OF ORIGIN WHERE THE COPYRIGHT TERM IS AUTHOR'S LIFE PLUS 100 YEARS OR FEWER. THIS IS ALSO IN THE PUBLIC DOMAIN OF THE U.S. BECAUSE THE COPYRIGHT WAS TAKEN OUT BEFORE 1927 AND NOT RENEWED. THIS PHOTOGRAPHIC REPRODUCTION IS THEREFORE ALSO CONSIDERED IN THE PUBLIC DOMAIN OF UNITED STATES LICENSE: CREATIVE COMMONS 2.0 SHARE-ALIKE

CHAPTER 47: "CYPRESS" PUBLIC DOMAIN IN JAPAN IS A FAITHFUL REPRODUCTION OF A TWO-DIMENSIONAL PUBLIC DOMAIN WORK OF ART. PUBLIC DOMAIN IN COUNTRY OF ORIGIN WHERE THE COPYRIGHT TERM IS AUTHOR'S LIFE PLUS 100 YEARS OR FEWER. THIS IS ALSO IN THE PUBLIC DOMAIN OF THE U.S. BECAUSE THE COPYRIGHT WAS TAKEN OUT BEFORE 1927 AND NOT RENEWED. THIS PHOTOGRAPHIC REPRODUCTION IS THEREFORE ALSO CONSIDERED IN THE PUBLIC DOMAIN OF UNITED STATES LICENSE: CREATIVE COMMONS 2.0 SHARE-ALIKE SOURCE TOKYO NATIONAL MUSEUM PHOTOGRAPHER: EMUSEUM

"SPRING" PUBLIC DOMAIN IN JAPAN IS A FAITHFUL REPRODUCTION OF A TWO-DIMENSIONAL PUBLIC DOMAIN WORK OF ART. PUBLIC DOMAIN IN COUNTRY OF ORIGIN WHERE THE COPYRIGHT TERM IS AUTHOR'S LIFE PLUS 100 YEARS OR FEWER. THIS IS ALSO IN THE PUBLIC DOMAIN OF THE U.S. BECAUSE THE COPYRIGHT WAS TAKEN OUT BEFORE 1927 AND NOT RENEWED. THIS PHOTOGRAPHIC REPRODUCTION IS THEREFORE ALSO CONSIDERED IN THE PUBLIC DOMAIN OF UNITED STATES LICENSE: CREATIVE COMMONS 2.0 SHARE-ALIKE SOURCE MOA MUSEUM OF ART PHOTOGRAPHER: EMUSEUM

"METRO" PUBLIC DOMAIN IN COUNTRY OF ORIGIN WHERE THE COPYRIGHT TERM IS AUTHOR'S LIFE PLUS 100 YEARS OR FEWER. THIS IS ALSO IN THE PUBLIC DOMAIN OF THE U.S. BECAUSE THE COPYRIGHT WAS TAKEN OUT BEFORE 1927 AND NOT RENEWED. THIS PHOTOGRAPHIC REPRODUCTION IS THEREFORE ALSO

CONSIDERED IN THE PUBLIC DOMAIN OF UNITED STATES LICENSE: CREATIVE COMMONS 2.0 SHARE-ALIKE

"PINES" PUBLIC DOMAIN IN JAPAN IS A FAITHFUL REPRODUCTION OF A TWO-DIMENSIONAL PUBLIC DOMAIN WORK OF ART. PUBLIC DOMAIN IN COUNTRY OF ORIGIN WHERE THE COPYRIGHT TERM IS AUTHOR'S LIFE PLUS 100 YEARS OR FEWER. THIS IS ALSO IN THE PUBLIC DOMAIN OF THE U.S. BECAUSE THE COPYRIGHT WAS TAKEN OUT BEFORE 1927 AND NOT RENEWED. THIS PHOTOGRAPHIC REPRODUCTION IS THEREFORE ALSO CONSIDERED IN THE PUBLIC DOMAIN OF UNITED STATES LICENSE: CREATIVE COMMONS 2.0 SHARE-ALIKE SOURCE TOKYO NATIONAL MUSEUM PHOTOGRAPHER: EMUSEUM

CHAPTER 49: "YOKO" IMAGE FROM DUTCH NATIONAL ARCHIVE DONATED TO WIKIMEDIA IN CONTEXT OF PARTNERSHIP PROGRAM AS PUBLIC DOMAIN LICENSE CREATIVE COMMONS CCO 1.0 UNIVERSAL PUBLIC DOMAIN

CHAPTER 50: "GEISHA" PUBLIC DOMAIN IN JAPAN. THIS IS A FAITHFUL REPRODUCTION OF A TWO-DIMENSIONAL PUBLIC DOMAIN WORK OF ART. PUBLIC DOMAIN IN COUNTRY OF ORIGIN WHERE THE COPYRIGHT TERM IS AUTHOR'S LIFE PLUS 100 YEARS OR FEWER. THIS IS ALSO IN THE PUBLIC DOMAIN OF THE U.S. BECAUSE THE COPYRIGHT WAS TAKEN OUT BEFORE 1927 AND NOT RENEWED. THIS PHOTOGRAPHIC REPRODUCTION IS THEREFORE ALSO CONSIDERED IN THE PUBLIC DOMAIN OF UNITED STATES LICENSE: CREATIVE COMMONS 2.0 SHARE-ALIKE. SOURCE METROPOLITAN MUSEUM OF ART

"TOKYO AT NIGHT "PHOTOGRAPH BY ANDRE BENZ @TRAPNATION.COM UNSPLASH FREE USAGE UNDER UNSPLASH LICENSE

"NATIONALIST CHINA DIVIDER" PUBLIC DOMAIN LC-USZ62-97967

CHAPTER 52: "COMMUNISTS" THIS PHOTOGRAPH WAS TAKEN BEFORE 1975 UNDER THE JURISDICTION OF THE GOVERNMENT OF THE REPUBLIC OF CHINA AND IS IN THE PUBLIC DOMAIN OF THE REPUBLIC OF CHINA. THIS IS ALSO IN THE PUBLIC DOMAIN OF THE U.S. BECAUSE THE COPYRIGHT WAS TAKEN OUT BEFORE 1927 AND NOT RENEWED. THIS PHOTOGRAPHIC REPRODUCTION IS THEREFORE ALSO CONSIDERED IN THE PUBLIC DOMAIN OF UNITED STATES LICENSE:

CREATIVE COMMONS 2.0 SHARE-ALIKE. SOURCE: INFORMATIONWAR.ORG/PERMISSION: NO RIGHTS RESERVED

'SHANGHAI" PHOTOGRAPH BY U.S. SIGNAL CORPS." PUBLIC DOMAIN, THIS FILE WAS TAKEN BY A FEDERAL EMPLOYEE AS PART OF HIS OFFICIAL DUTIES. AS A WORK OF THE U. S. FEDERAL GOVERNMENT, IT IS IN THE PUBLIC DOMAIN

CHAPTER 53: "MOUNTAINS" THIS IS A FAITHFUL REPRODUCTION OF A TWO-DIMENSIONAL PUBLIC DOMAIN WORK OF ART. PUBLIC DOMAIN IN COUNTRY OF ORIGIN WHERE THE COPYRIGHT TERM IS AUTHOR'S LIFE PLUS 100 YEARS OR FEWER. THIS IS ALSO IN THE PUBLIC DOMAIN OF THE U.S. BECAUSE THE COPYRIGHT WAS TAKEN OUT BEFORE 1927 AND NOT RENEWED. THIS PHOTOGRAPHIC REPRODUCTION IS THEREFORE ALSO CONSIDERED IN THE PUBLIC DOMAIN OF UNITED STATES LICENSE: CREATIVE COMMONS 2.0 SHARE-ALIKE SOURCE NATIONAL PALACE MUSEUM PHOTOGRAPHER: DANIELLE ELISSEEFF

"FOREST" THIS IS A FAITHFUL REPRODUCTION OF A TWO-DIMENSIONAL PUBLIC DOMAIN WORK OF ART. PUBLIC DOMAIN IN COUNTRY OF ORIGIN WHERE THE COPYRIGHT TERM IS AUTHOR'S LIFE PLUS 100 YEARS OR FEWER. THIS IS ALSO IN THE PUBLIC DOMAIN OF THE U.S. BECAUSE THE COPYRIGHT WAS TAKEN OUT BEFORE 1927 AND NOT RENEWED. THIS PHOTOGRAPHIC REPRODUCTION IS THEREFORE ALSO CONSIDERED IN THE PUBLIC DOMAIN OF UNITED STATES LICENSE: CREATIVE COMMONS 2.0 SHARE-ALIKE SOURCE AND PHOTOGRAPHER: NATIONAL PALACE MUSEUM

CHAPTER 54: "GORGE" PHOTOGRAPHER: RUI AN YANG RELEASED COPYRIGHTS TO CREATIVE COMMONS ATTRIBUTION SHARE-ALIKE 4.0 INTERNATIONAL LICENSE

"HONG KONG DIVIDER" PUBLIC DOMAIN LC-USZ62-118501

CHAPTER 55: "BMW "PHOTOGRAPHER": BADSEED. RELEASED PHOTO TO GNU FREE DOCUMENTATION LICENSE VERSION, 1.2 IN U. S., LICENSED UNDER CREATIVE COMMONS ATTRIBUTION 3.0 UNPORTED LICENSE

"BSA" PHOTOGRAPHER: MFUTCHIAS RELEASED TO CREATIVE COMMONS ATTRIBUTION 3.0 UNPORTED LICENSE IN UK AND U. S. RELEASED TO PUBLIC DOMAIN BY AUTHOR "FOR ANY PURPOSE WORLDWIDE"

CHAPTER 56: "PRINT" THIS IS A FAITHFUL REPRODUCTION OF A TWO-DIMENSIONAL PUBLIC DOMAIN WORK OF ART. PUBLIC DOMAIN IN COUNTRY OF ORIGIN WHERE THE COPYRIGHT TERM IS AUTHOR'S LIFE PLUS 100 YEARS OR FEWER. THIS IS ALSO IN THE PUBLIC DOMAIN OF THE U.S. BECAUSE THE COPYRIGHT WAS TAKEN OUT BEFORE 1927 AND NOT RENEWED. THIS PHOTOGRAPHIC REPRODUCTION IS THEREFORE ALSO CONSIDERED IN THE PUBLIC DOMAIN OF UNITED STATES LICENSE: CREATIVE COMMONS 2.0 SHARE-ALIKE

"PORT STRIKERS" LOC CARPENTER COLLECTION LC-USZ62-120788. PUBLIC DOMAIN

CHAPTER 57: "SCROLL' THIS IS A FAITHFUL REPRODUCTION OF A TWO-DIMENSIONAL PUBLIC DOMAIN WORK OF ART. PUBLIC DOMAIN IN COUNTRY OF ORIGIN WHERE THE COPYRIGHT TERM IS AUTHOR'S LIFE PLUS 100 YEARS OR FEWER. THIS IS ALSO IN THE PUBLIC DOMAIN OF THE U.S. BECAUSE THE COPYRIGHT WAS TAKEN OUT BEFORE 1927 AND NOT RENEWED. THIS PHOTOGRAPHIC REPRODUCTION IS THEREFORE ALSO CONSIDERED IN THE PUBLIC DOMAIN OF UNITED STATES LICENSE: CREATIVE COMMONS 2.0 SHARE-ALIKE, PHOTOGRAPHER: SZILAS

CHAPTER 58: "MA0" PUBLIC DOMAIN IN THE PEOPLE'S REPUBLIC OF CHINA. PHOTOGRAPHS OF NATURAL PERSONS OR ORGANIZATIONS WHOSE COPYRIGHT PERIOD PROTECTION EXPIRES BEFORE JUNE 1, 2021, BELONG TO THE PUBLIC DOMAIN IN THE PEOPLE'S REPUBLIC OF CHINA. PUBLIC DOMAIN IN THE U. S. BECAUSE THE PHOTOGRAPH WAS COPYRIGHTED BETWEEN 1927 AND 1963 AND WAS NOT RENEWED IN THE U. S. LICENSE: CREATIVE COMMONS CCO 2.0 ATTRIBUTION SHARE-ALIKE LICENSE. SOURCE: MAO ZEDONG'S "LITTLE RED BOOK". AUTHOR: THE PEOPLES' REPUBLIC OF CHINA PRINTING OFFICE. PORTRAIT OF MAO ZEDONG

CHAPTER 59: "CHINESE COURTESANS" LOC CARPENTER COLLECTION LOC USZ62-80001. PUBLIC DOMAIN

CHAPTER 60: "FOOT BINDING" LOC CARPENTER COLLECTION LOC LC-USZ62-80206 PUBLIC DOMAIN

"EGGS" FILE LICENSED UNDER THE TERMS OF GNU DOCUMENTATION LICENCE 1.2. LICENSED IN U.S. UNDER CREATIVE COMMONS ATTRIBUTION-SHARE-ALIKE 3.0 UNPORTED. PHOTOGRAPHER/SOURCE: S. BALLARD

"ANDREWS": LOC GEORGE GRANTHAM BAIN COLLECTION LOC 2014719636 PUBLIC DOMAIN

CHAPTER 62: "MARX BROTHERS" OWNER: HERITAGE AUCTION CO. AUTHOR: AL HIRSHFELD RELEASED POSTER TO PUBLIC DOMAIN U.S. LICENSE: CREATIVE COMMONS ATTRIBUTION SHARE-ALIKE 3.0 UNPORTED

"REVOLUTIONARY OPERA": WHITE HOUSE PHOTOGRAPH BY BYRON SCHUMAKER. PUBLIC DOMAIN, THIS FILE WAS TAKEN BY A FEDERAL EMPLOYEE AS PART OF HIS OFFICIAL DUTIES. AS A WORK OF THE U. S. FEDERAL GOVERNMENT, IT IS IN THE PUBLIC DOMAIN

CHAPTER 63: "ST. PAUL'S CHURCH" LIBRARY OF CONGRESS: COUNTRY STUDIES PHOTOGRAPH, PUBLIC DOMAIN: PHOTO TAKEN BY A FEDERAL EMPLOYEE AS PART OF HIS OFFICIAL DUTIES. AS A WORK OF THE U. S. FEDERAL GOVERNMENT, IT IS IN THE PUBLIC DOMAIN

THIS IS A FAITHFUL REPRODUCTION OF A TWO-DIMENSIONAL PUBLIC DOMAIN WORK OF ART. PUBLIC DOMAIN IN COUNTRY OF ORIGIN WHERE THE COPYRIGHT TERM IS AUTHOR'S LIFE PLUS 100 YEARS OR FEWER. THIS IS ALSO IN THE PUBLIC DOMAIN OF THE U.S. BECAUSE THE COPYRIGHT WAS TAKEN OUT BEFORE 1927 AND NOT RENEWED. THIS PHOTOGRAPHIC REPRODUCTION IS THEREFORE ALSO CONSIDERED IN THE PUBLIC DOMAIN OF UNITED STATES LICENSE: CREATIVE COMMONS 2.0 SHARE-ALIKE

"MACAO POSTER" PUBLIC DOMAIN IN U.S. BECAUSE PHOTOGRAPH WAS COPYRIGHT FROM 1927 AND 1963 AND WAS NOT RENEWED IN THE U. S. LICENSE: CREATIVE COMMONS 2.0 ATTRIBUTION SHARE-ALIKE LICENSE.

"TWO JESUITS" PUBLIC DOMAIN IS A FAITHFUL REPRODUCTION OF A TWO-DIMENSIONAL PUBLIC DOMAIN WORK OF ART. PUBLIC DOMAIN IN COUNTRY OF ORIGIN WHERE THE COPYRIGHT TERM IS AUTHOR'S LIFE PLUS 100 YEARS OR FEWER. THIS IS ALSO IN THE PUBLIC DOMAIN OF THE U.S. BECAUSE THE COPYRIGHT WAS TAKEN OUT BEFORE 1927 AND NOT RENEWED. THIS PHOTOGRAPHIC REPRODUCTION IS THEREFORE ALSO CONSIDERED IN THE PUBLIC DOMAIN OF UNITED STATES LICENSE: CREATIVE COMMONS 2.0 SHARE-ALIKE

"GRAVES" PHOTOGRAPH BY GILO AUTHOR RELEASED PHOTOGRAPH TO PUBLIC DOMAIN "TO USE WORK FOR ANY PURPOSE" LICENSE IN U. S. CREATIVE COMMONS ATTRIBUTION-SHARE-ALIKE 3.0 UNPORTED

CHAPTER 64: "HONG KONG 1972" AUTHOR PHOTOGRAPH

"PHILIPPINES DIVIDER" MANILA STREET 1900: PUBLIC DOMAIN IN THE PHILIPPINES AND US WHERE THE IMAGE IS AUTHOR'S LIFE PLUS 100 YEARS OR FEWER. SOURCE: ANIMO/US LICENSE: CREATIVE COMMONS ATTRIBUTION-SHARE-ALIKE 3.0

CHAPTER 65: "FILIPINO FIGHTERS" AUTHOR UNKNOWN PUBLIC DOMAIN IN COUNTRY OF ORIGIN WHERE THE COPYRIGHT TERM IS AUTHOR'S LIFE PLUS 100 YEARS OR FEWER. THIS IS ALSO IN THE PUBLIC DOMAIN OF THE U.S. BECAUSE THE COPYRIGHT WAS TAKEN OUT BEFORE 1927 AND NOT RENEWED. THIS PHOTOGRAPHIC REPRODUCTION IS THEREFORE ALSO CONSIDERED IN THE PUBLIC DOMAIN OF UNITED STATES LICENSE: CREATIVE COMMONS 2.0 SHARE-ALIKE

"TEENAGERS" AUTHOR PHOTOGRAPH

CHAPTER 66: "JEEPNEY" AUTHOR PHOTOGRAPH

CHAPTER 67: "CROSS" AUTHOR PHOTOGRAPH

CHAPTER 68: "MOTHER OF GOD" AUTHOR: INTERAKSYON, WHO RELEASED IT TO CREATIVE COMMONS ATTRIBUTION SHARE-ALIKE 3.0 UNPORTED IN THE U.S. AND WORLDWIDE TO USE WITHOUT RESTRICTIONS

"GUANYIN" OWNER/PHOTOGRAPHER: THE WALTERS ART MUSEUM, IN PARTNERSHIP WITH WIKIMEDIA, RELEASED PHOTOGRAPHIC IMAGE TO CREATIVE COMMONS CCO 2.0 ATTRIBUTION SHARE-ALIKE LICENSE IN THE U.S.

"CHRIST" PHOTOGRAPHER: RAMON F. VELASQUEZ AUTHOR RELEASED PHOTOGRAPH TO CREATIVE COMMONS ATTRIBUTION SHARE-ALIKE 3.0 UNPORTED IN THE U.S.

CHAPTER 69: "GIRL STUDENTS" LOC CARPENTER COLLECTION LOC-USZ62-103377 PUBLIC DOMAIN

CHAPTER 70: "OLD MANILLA" AUTHOR IS UNKNOWN PUBLIC DOMAIN IN THE PHILIPPINES BECAUSE THE COPYRIGHT (1911) HAS EXPIRED AND WAS RENEWED. PUBLIC DOMAIN IN THE U. S. BECAUSE 70 YEARS HAVE PASSED AND THERE WAS NO U. S. COPYRIGHT, AND IT WAS PUBLISHED BEFORE 1927

"TROOPS FIGHTING" LOC 62-6000 FILE IS OF A U.S. SOLDIER TAKEN BY A FEDERAL EMPLOYEE AS PART OF HIS OFFICIAL DUTIES. AS A WORK OF THE U. S. FEDERAL GOVERNMENT, IT IS IN THE PUBLIC DOMAIN

CHAPTER 71: "POEM" IS LICENSED IN THE U. S. UNDER CREATIVE COMMONS ATTRIBUTION-SHARE-ALIKE 3.0 UNPORTED

"RIZAL PHOTOGRAPH" PUBLIC DOMAIN IN COUNTRY OF ORIGIN WHERE THE COPYRIGHT TERM IS AUTHOR'S LIFE PLUS 100 YEARS OR FEWER. THIS IS ALSO IN THE PUBLIC DOMAIN OF THE U.S. BECAUSE THE COPYRIGHT WAS TAKEN OUT BEFORE 1927 AND NOT RENEWED. THIS PHOTOGRAPHIC REPRODUCTION IS THEREFORE ALSO CONSIDERED IN THE PUBLIC DOMAIN OF UNITED STATES LICENSE: CREATIVE COMMONS 2.0 SHARE-ALIKE

"RUINS" AUTHOR PHOTOGRAPH

CHAPTER 72: "CLASSROOM" PUBLIC DOMAIN LIBRARY OF CONGRESS PHOTOGRAPH. THE FILE IS OF A U.S. TEACHER TAKEN BY A FEDERAL EMPLOYEE

AS PART OF HIS OFFICIAL DUTIES. AS A WORK OF THE U. S. FEDERAL GOVERNMENT, IT IS IN THE PUBLIC DOMAIN

"BINGHAM" IS THE PUBLIC DOMAIN OF THE U.S. BECAUSE IT IS THE PUBLIC DOMAIN IN THE COUNTRY OF ORIGIN WHERE THE COPYRIGHT TERM IS THE AUTHOR'S LIFE PLUS 100 YEARS OR FEWER. THIS IS ALSO IN THE PUBLIC DOMAIN OF THE U.S. BECAUSE THE COPYRIGHT WAS TAKEN OUT BEFORE 1927 AND NOT RENEWED. THIS PHOTOGRAPHIC REPRODUCTION IS THEREFORE ALSO CONSIDERED IN THE PUBLIC DOMAIN OF UNITED STATES LICENSE: CREATIVE COMMONS 2.0 SHARE-ALIKE

"RURAL HOUSE" AUTHOR PHOTOGRAPH

"RICE FIELDS" AUTHOR PHOTOGRAPH

CHAPTER 74: "SLUM" AUTHOR PHOTOGRAPH

"BURMA DIVIDER" PUBLIC DOMAIN LC-USZ62-19526

CHAPTER 75: "TEMPLE PRINT" IS PUBLIC DOMAIN BECAUSE IT IS PUBLIC DOMAIN IN THE COUNTRY OF ORIGIN WHERE THE COPYRIGHT TERM IS THE AUTHOR'S LIFE PLUS 100 YEARS OR FEWER. THIS IS ALSO IN THE PUBLIC DOMAIN OF THE U.S. BECAUSE THE COPYRIGHT WAS TAKEN OUT BEFORE 1927 AND NOT RENEWED. THIS PHOTOGRAPHIC REPRODUCTION IS THEREFORE ALSO CONSIDERED IN THE PUBLIC DOMAIN OF UNITED STATES LICENSE: CREATIVE COMMONS 2.0 SHARE-ALIKE

CHAPTER 76: "FLYING TIGERS" SOURCE: SAN DIEGO AIR AND SPACE MUSEUM ARCHIVE CATALOGUE NUMBER 1606. PHOTOGRAPHER: R.T. SMITH. THE PHOTOGRAPH IS COPYRIGHT FREE SINCE IT HAS NOT BEEN RENEWED SINCE PUBLICATION, AND 70 YEARS HAVE PASSED NOW IT'S IN THE PUBLIC DOMAIN. LICENSE: CREATIVE COMMONS 2.0 SHARE-ALIKE

CHAPTER 77: "NEW JERUSALEM" THIS IS A FAITHFUL REPRODUCTION OF A TWO-DIMENSIONAL PUBLIC DOMAIN WORK OF ART. PUBLIC DOMAIN IN COUNTRY OF ORIGIN WHERE THE COPYRIGHT TERM IS AUTHOR'S LIFE PLUS 100 YEARS OR FEWER. THIS IS ALSO IN THE PUBLIC DOMAIN OF THE U.S. BECAUSE THE COPYRIGHT WAS TAKEN OUT BEFORE 1927 AND NOT RENEWED. THIS

PHOTOGRAPHIC REPRODUCTION IS THEREFORE ALSO CONSIDERED IN THE PUBLIC DOMAIN OF UNITED STATES LICENSE: CREATIVE COMMONS 2.0 SHARE-ALIKE.

CHAPTER 79: "CRASH" SOURCE: CIVIL AERONAUTICS BOARD AIRCRAFT ACCIDENT REPORT- FILE NUMBER 2-0001 FILE IS OF A CRASH TAKEN BY A FEDERAL EMPLOYEE AS PART OF HIS OFFICIAL DUTIES. AS A WORK OF THE U. S. FEDERAL GOVERNMENT, IT IS IN THE PUBLIC DOMAIN. CREATIVE COMMONS ATTRIBUTION SHARE-ALIKE 3.0 UNPORTED

CHAPTER 80: "FLASH GORDON" PUBLIC DOMAIN POSTER IS COPYRIGHT FREE SINCE IT HAS NOT BEEN RENEWED SINCE PUBLICATION (1938), AND 70 YEARS HAVE PASSED NOW IT IS THE PUBLIC DOMAIN. LICENSE: CREATIVE COMMONS 2.0 SHARE-ALIKE

BIBLIOGRAPHY: "PAUL HARVEY" PUBLIC DOMAIN FILE IS OF A PRESIDENTIAL MEDAL OF FREEDOM AWARDEE TAKEN BY A FEDERAL EMPLOYEE AS PART OF HIS OFFICIAL DUTIES. AS A WORK OF THE U. S. FEDERAL GOVERNMENT, IT IS IN THE PUBLIC DOMAIN. CREATIVE COMMONS ATTRIBUTION SHARE-ALIKE 3.0 UNPORTED

About the Author

I am a first-generation American, born to immigrant Norwegian and Swiss parents. I was the first in my family to attend college (Lafayette College) on a Reserve Officer Training Corps scholarship and a second-generation soldier (my father served in the U.S. Army during World War II). I served three years in the Army and close to two years traveling in Asia. I grew up in the 1960s, the High Noon of the American Empire, and I see myself as a child of both Woodstock and Vietnam.

The patriotic idealism of the Peace Corps in the Kennedy years dissipated in the societal division and carnage of a senseless war. Yet my generation believed that everything was possible. We could remake America to be that visionary "Shining City on the Hill" our forefathers had envisioned. The peace, love, and music of Woodstock seemed to be a harbinger of a new age, of "swords into ploughshares".

It is this optimism that inspired my book. It is also my "Bildungsroman", a young man trying to understand the world and himself. I have an insatiable sense of curiosity and wonder about the world, and this Zeitgeist is what I strive to convey in my journal.

www.ingramcontent.com/pod-product-compliance
Lightning Source LLC
Chambersburg PA
CBHW081614100526
44590CB00021B/3433